Exploring Guitar For Dummies®

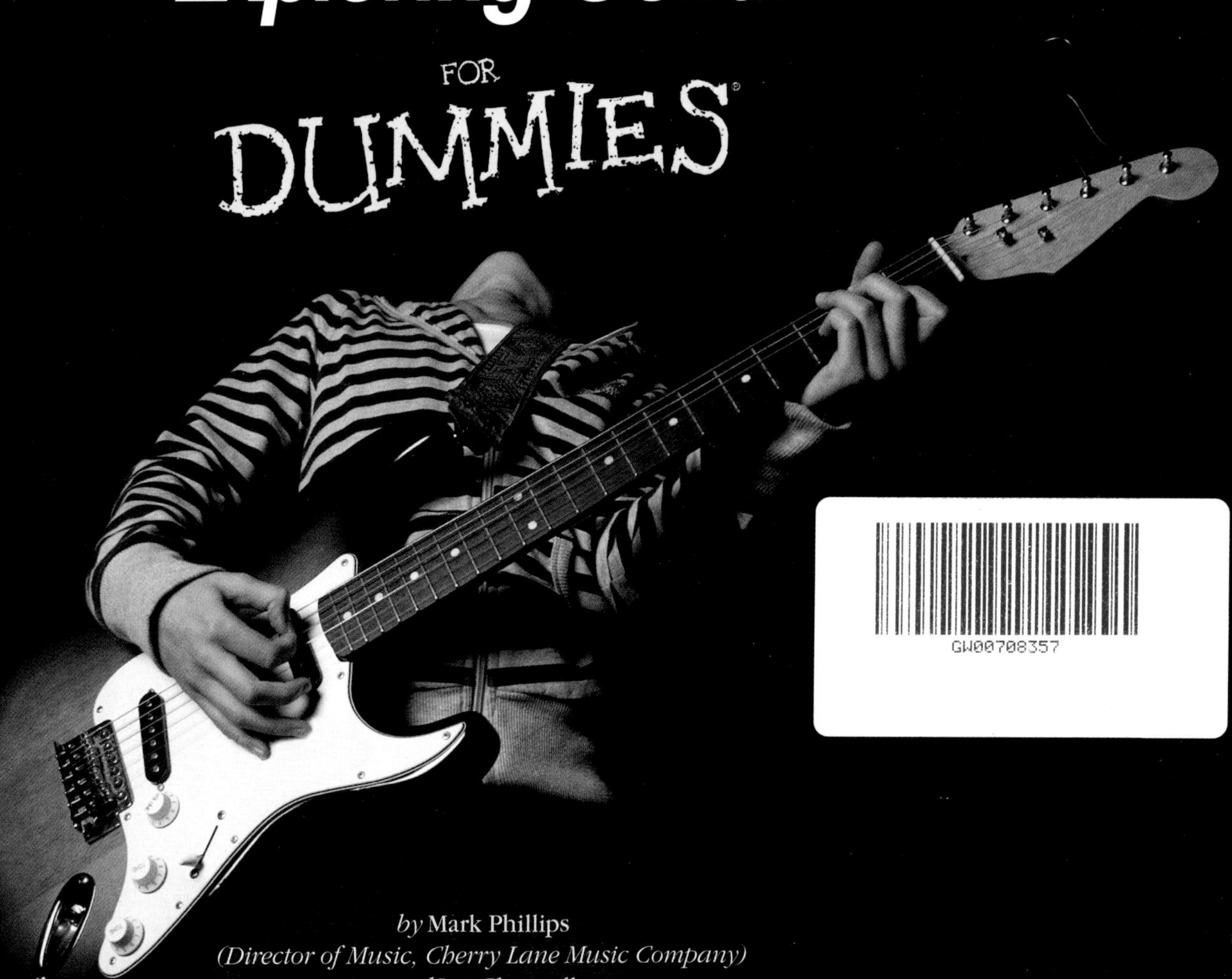

by Mark Phillips
(Director of Music, Cherry Lane Music Company)
and Jon Chappell
(Award-winning guitarist and author)

Exploring Guitar For Dummies®
Published by John Wiley & Sons, Ltd,
The Atrium, Southern Gate,
Chichester, West Sussex,
PO19 8SQ, England
E-mail (for orders and customer service enquires):
cs-books@wiley.co.uk
Visit our Home Page on
www.wiley.com or www.dummies.com

For general information on our other products and services, please contact our Customer Care Department within the U.S. at 800-762-2974, outside the U.S. at 317-572-3993, or fax 317-572-4002.
For technical support, please visit
www.wiley.com/techsupport.
Wiley also publishes its books in a variety of electronic formats. Some content that appears in print may not be available in electronic books.
British Library Cataloguing in Publication Data:
A catalogue record for this book is available from the British Library
ISBN: 978-0-470-97874-0
Printed and bound in Great Britain by Stones the Printers, Banbury
10 9 8 7 6 5 4 3 2 1

FOR DUMMIES®

Publisher's Acknowledgements
We're proud of this bookazine; please send us your comments at http://dummies.custhelp.com. For other comments, please contact our Customer Care Department within the U.S. at 877-762-2974, outside the U.S. at 317-572-3993, or fax 317-572-4002.

Some of the people who helped bring this bookazine to market include the following:

Acquisitions, Editorial, and Media Development
Project Editors:
Simon Bell, Steve Edwards
Commissioning Editors:
Emma Swaisland, Mike Baker
Assistant Editor:
Ben Kemble
Production Manager:
Daniel Mersey
Text Compiler:
Traci Cumbay
Designer:
Keith Jones
Cover design:
Michael Trent
Cover Photos:
©Nigel Osbourne/Redferns/gettyimages
Chord Photos:
©Éditions First, 2008; ©Rebecca Kerr
Stock Art:
©Steve Catlin/Redferns/gettyimages (page 20); ©Nigel Osbourne/Redferns/gettyimages (pages 3, 16, 17, 18, 19, 20, 21, 64, 65, and 87); ©Photolibraryltd; ©Pictorial Press Ltd/Alamy.

Publishing and Editorial for Consumer Dummies
Diane Graves Steele,
Vice President and Publisher, Consumer Dummies
Kristin Ferguson-Wagstaffe,
Product Development Director, Consumer Dummies
Ensley Eikenburg,
Associate Publisher, Travel
Kelly Regan,
Editorial Director, Travel
Publishing for Technology Dummies
Andy Cummings,
Vice President and Publisher, Dummies Technology/General User
Composition Services
Debbie Stailey,
Director of Composition Services

For advertising inquiries, please contact Emma Swaisland at eswaisla@wiley.com

Contents

P28

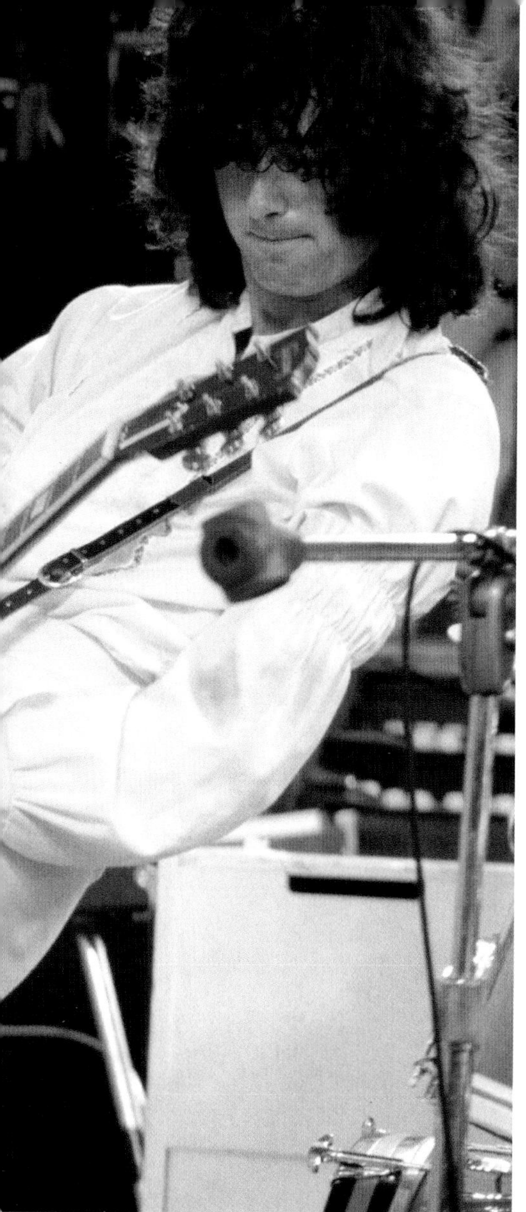

P112

P64

P72

So you

wanna play guitar, huh?

Because you may as well face it: In the music world, guitars set the standard for cool (and we're not just being biased here). Since the 1950s, many of the greatest showmen in rock 'n' roll, blues, jazz, country, metal, pop and countless other musical genres have played the guitar. Think of Chuck Berry doing his one-legged hop across the stage (the "duck walk") while belting out "Johnny B. Goode," Jimi Hendrix wailing on his upside-down, right-handed (and sometimes flaming) Stratocaster, Eric Clapton getting' down with the blues, Bonnie Raitt playing slide guitar, Garth Brooks with his acoustic guitar and flannel shirts, B.B. King's authoritative bending and expressive vibrato on his guitar "Lucille," or George Benson's mellow jazz guitar stylings. (Even Elvis Presley, whose guitar prowess may not have exceeded five chords, still used the guitar effectively onstage as a prop.) The list goes on.

Playing electric guitar can put you out in front of a band, where you're free to roam, sing, and make eye contact with your adoring fans. Playing acoustic guitar can make you the star of the holiday campfire singalong. And playing any kind of guitar can bring out the music in your soul and become a valued lifetime hobby.

Believe it or not, though, many would-be guitarists never really get into playing because they simply have the wrong guitar. Or maybe the strings are too difficult to push down (causing a great deal of pain). So, we give you suggestions and tips to help you match yourself with the guitar and equipment that fit your needs and budget.

When you come to striking the strings of your guitar for the first time, *Exploring Guitar For Dummies* sets you going in the right direction. Whereas most guitar books want you to practise the guitar by learning about where the notes fall on the staff and the length of time that you're supposed to hold the notes, practicing scales and learning song after unrecognisable song that you probably don't care about playing, this bookazine is different.

The truth is that many great guitarists don't know how to read music, and many who can read music learned to do so after they learned to play the guitar. So repeat after us: You don't need to read music to play the guitar. Chant this mantra until you believe it!

One of the coolest things about the guitar is that, even though you can devote your lifetime to perfecting your skills, you can start faking it rather quickly. We assume that, instead of concentrating on what the 3/4 time signature means, you want to play music — real music (or at least recognisable music). We want you to play music, too, because that's what keeps you motivated and practicing. Here are the ways in which this bookazine starts you playing and developing real guitar skills quickly:

- **Look at the photos**. Fingerings that you need to know appear in photos in the book. Just form your hands the way we show you in the photos. Simple.
- **Read guitar tablature, or "tab"**. Guitar tablature is a guitar-specific shorthand for reading music that actually shows you what strings to strike and what frets to hold down on the guitar for creating the sound that's called for. Tab (as it's known to its friends and admirers) goes a long way toward enabling you to play music without reading music. Just don't try this stuff on the piano!
- **Look at the music staff as you improve**. To those who would charge that *Exploring Guitar For Dummies* doesn't give you diddley in terms of reading music, we respond: "Not so, Fret Breath!" The music for all the exercises and songs appears above the shortcut methods. So you get the best of both worlds: You can associate the music notation with the sound you're making after you already know how to make the sound. Pretty cool, huh?

Exploring Guitar For Dummies has been carefully crafted so that you can find what you want or need to know about learning the guitar and no more. It delivers everything you need to get started as a guitarist: From buying a guitar to tuning the guitar, to playing the guitar, to caring for the guitar, this bookazine has it all!

And why wouldn't you?

Guitar 101

IN THIS ARTICLE

- *Identifying the different parts of the guitar*
- *Understanding how the guitar works*
- *Grasping guitar notation*
- *Putting hand to strings*
- *Playing a chord*

All guitars — whether painted purple with airbrushed skulls and lightning bolts or finished in a natural-wood pattern with a fine French lacquer — share certain physical characteristics that make them behave like guitars and not violins or tubas. If you're confused about the difference between a headstock and a pickup or you're wondering which end of the guitar to hold under your chin, you've come to the right place.

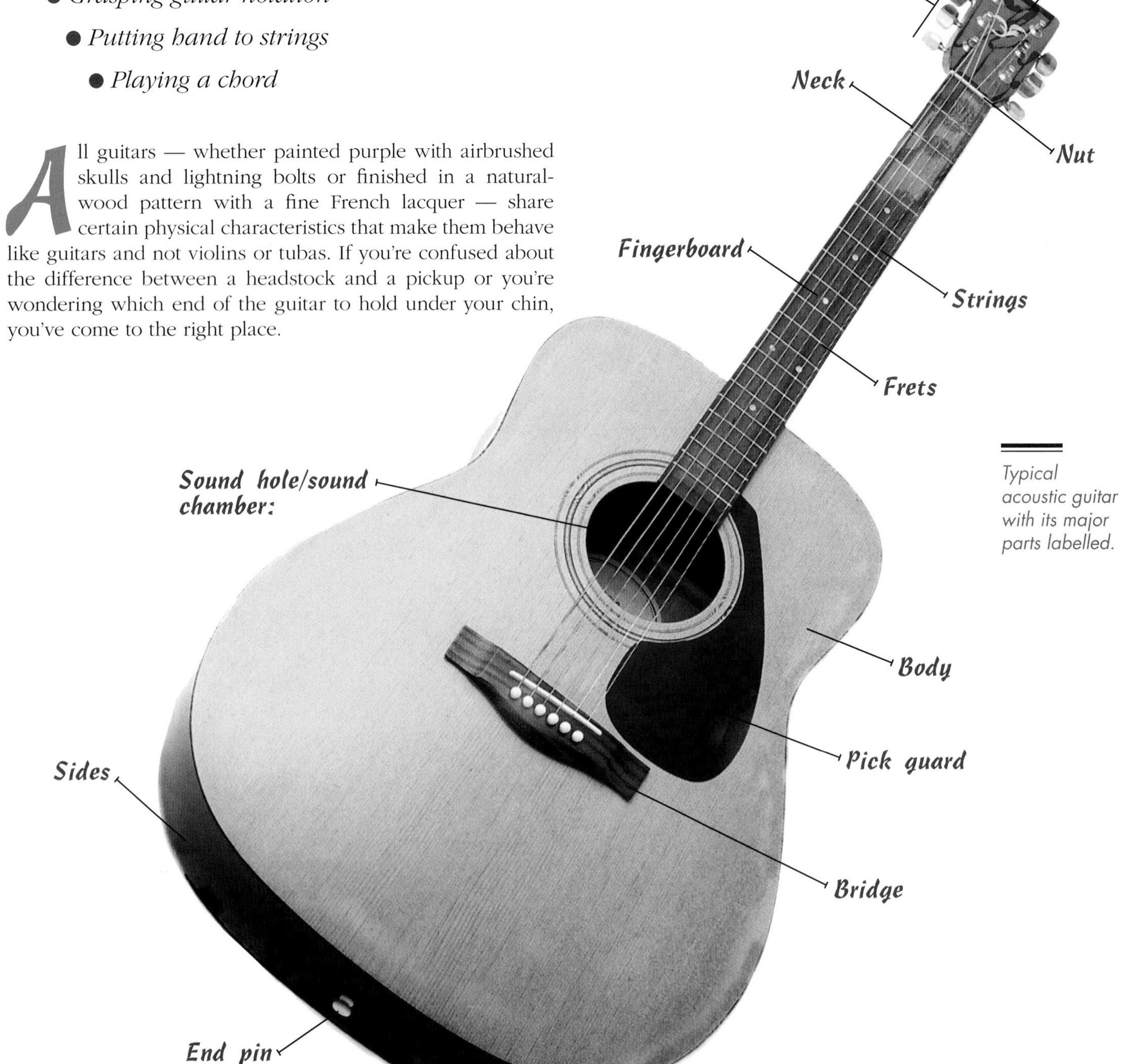

Typical acoustic guitar with its major parts labelled.

Anatomy of a Guitar

Guitars come in two basic flavours: acoustic and electric. From a hardware standpoint, electric guitars have more components and doohickeys than do acoustic guitars. Guitar makers generally agree, however, that making an acoustic guitar is harder than making an electric guitar. That's why, pound for pound, acoustic guitars cost just as much or more than their electric counterparts. But both types follow the same basic approach to such principles as neck construction and string tension.

Acoustic and electric guitars have very similar constructions, despite a sometimes radical difference in tone production (unless, of course, you think that Segovia and Metallica are indistinguishable). The photos show the various parts of an acoustic and electric guitar.

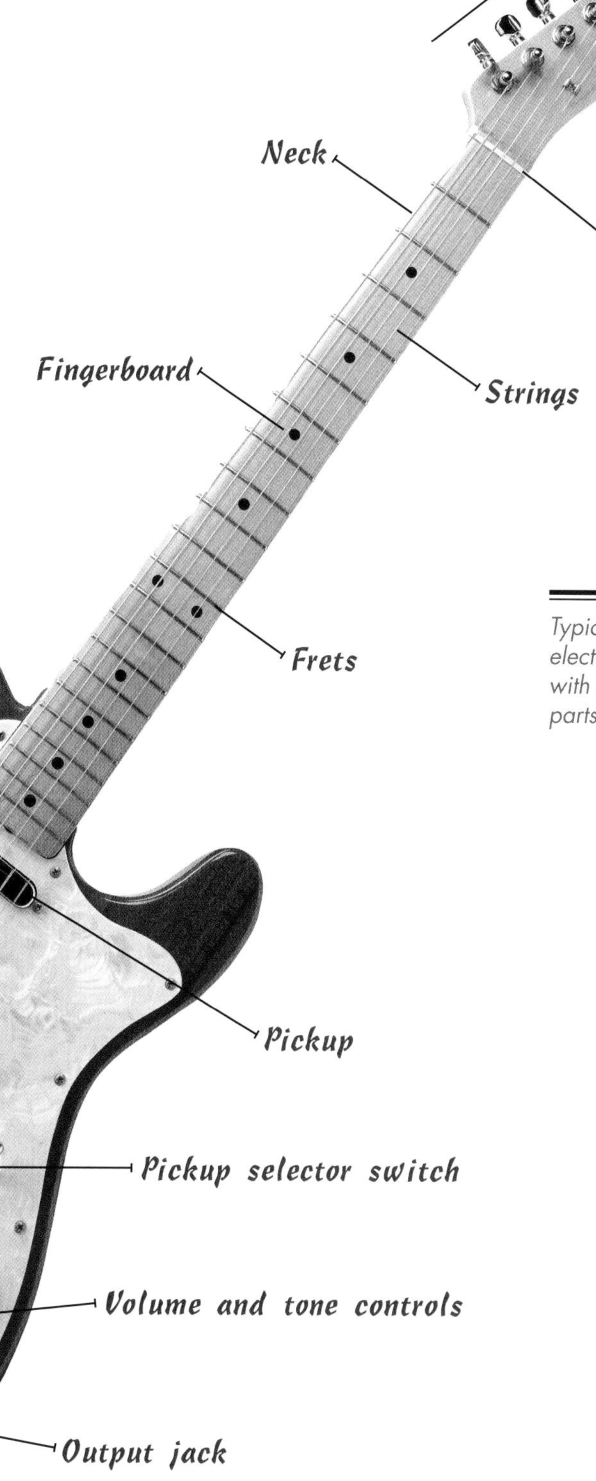

Typical electric guitar with its major parts labelled.

The following list tells you the functions of the various parts of a guitar:

- **Back (acoustic only):** The part of the body that holds the sides in place; made of two or three pieces of wood.
- **Bar (electric only):** A metal rod attached to the bridge that varies the string tension by tilting the bridge back and forth. Also called the tremolo bar, whammy bar, vibrato bar, and wang bar.
- **Body:** The box that provides an anchor for the neck and bridge and creates the playing surface for the right hand. On an acoustic, the body includes the amplifying sound chamber that produces the guitar's tone. On an electric, it consists of the housing for the bridge assembly and electronics (pickups as well as tone and volume controls).
- **Bridge:** The metal (electric) or wooden (acoustic) plate that anchors the strings to the body.
- **End pin:** A metal post where the rear end of the strap connects. On acoustic-electrics (acoustic guitars with built-in pickups and electronics), the pin often doubles as the output jack where you plug in.
- **Fingerboard:** A flat, planklike piece of wood that sits atop the neck, where you place your left-hand fingers to produce notes and chords. The fingerboard is also known as the fretboard, because the frets are embedded in it.
- **Frets: 1**) Thin metal wires or bars running perpendicular to the strings that shorten the effective vibrating length of a string, enabling it to produce different pitches. **2**) A verb describing worry, as in "He frets about how many little parts are on his guitar."
- **Headstock:** The section that holds the tuning machines (hardware assembly) and provides a place for the manufacturer to display its logo.
- **Neck:** The long, clublike wooden piece that connects the headstock to the body.
- **Nut:** A grooved sliver of stiff nylon or other synthetic substance that stops the strings from vibrating beyond the neck. The strings pass through the grooves on their way to the tuners in the headstock. The nut is one of the two points at which the vibrating area of the string ends. (The other is the bridge.)
- **Output jack (electric only):** The insertion point for the cord that connects the guitar to an amplifier or other electronic device.
- **Pickup selector (electric only):** A switch that determines which pickups are currently active.
- **Pickups (electric only):** Barlike magnets that create the electrical current, which the amplifier converts into musical sound.
- **Sides (acoustic only):** Separate curved wooden pieces on the body that join the top to the back.
- **Strap pin:** Metal post where the front, or top, end of the strap connects. (Not all acoustics have a strap pin. If the guitar is missing one, tie the top of the strap around the headstock.)
- **Strings:** The six metal (for electric and steel-string acoustic guitars) or nylon (for classical guitars) wires that, drawn taut, produce the notes of the guitar. Although not strictly part of the actual guitar (you attach and remove them at will on top of the guitar), strings are an integral part of the whole system, and a guitar's entire design and structure revolves around making the strings ring out with a joyful noise.
- **Top:** The face of the guitar. On an acoustic, this piece is also the sounding board, which produces almost all the guitar's acoustic qualities. On an electric, the top is merely a cosmetic or decorative cap that overlays the rest of the body material.
- **Tuning machines:** Geared mechanisms that raise and lower the tension of the strings, drawing them to different pitches. The string wraps tightly around a post that sticks out through the top, or face, of the headstock. The post passes through to the back of the headstock, where gears connect it to a tuning key. Also known as tuners, tuning pegs, tuning keys, and tuning gears.
- **Volume and tone controls (electric only):** Knobs that vary the loudness of the guitar's sound and its bass and treble frequencies.

How Guitars Work

After you can recognize the basic parts of the guitar, you may also want to understand how those parts work together to make sound. We present this information so that you know why your guitar sounds the way it does, instead of like a kazoo or an accordion. The important thing to remember is that a guitar makes the sound, but you make the music.

String vibration and string length

Any instrument must have some part of it moving in a regular, repeated motion to produce musical sound (a sustained tone, or pitch). In a guitar, this part is the vibrating string. A string that you bring to a certain tension and then set in motion (by a plucking action) produces a predictable sound — for example, the note A. If you tune a string of your guitar to different tensions, you get different tones. The greater the tension of a string, the higher the pitch.

You couldn't do very much with a guitar, however, if the only way to change pitches was to frantically adjust the tension on the strings every time you pluck a string. So guitarists resort to the other way to change a string's pitch — by shortening its effective vibrating length. They do so by fretting — pushing the string against the fretboard so that it vibrates only between the fingered fret (metal wire) and the bridge. This way, by moving the left hand up and down the neck (toward the bridge and the nut, respectively), you can change pitches comfortably and easily.

Using both hands to make a sound

The guitar normally requires two hands working together to create music. If you want to play, say, middle C on the piano, all you do is take your index finger, position it above the appropriate white key under the piano's logo, and drop it down: donnnng.

The guitar is somewhat different. To play middle C on the guitar, you must take your left-hand index finger and fret the 2nd string (that is, press it down to the fingerboard) at the first fret. This action, however, doesn't itself produce a sound. You must then strike or pluck that 2nd string with your right hand to actually produce the note middle C audibly. Music readers take note: The guitar sounds an octave lower than its written notes. For example, playing a written, third-space C on the guitar actually produces a middle C.

Frets and half steps

The smallest interval (unit of musical distance in pitch) of the musical scale is the half step. On the piano, the alternating white and black keys represent this interval (except for the places where you find two adjacent white keys with no black key in between). To proceed by half steps on a keyboard instrument, you move your finger up or down to the next available key, white or black.

On the guitar, frets — the horizontal metal wires (or bars) that you see embedded in the fretboard, running perpendicular to the strings — represent these half steps. To go up or down by half steps on a guitar means to move your left hand one fret at a time, higher or lower on the neck.

Pickups

Vibrating strings produce the different tones on a guitar. But you must be able to hear those tones, or you face one of those if-a-tree-falls-in-a-forest questions. For an acoustic guitar, that's no problem, because an acoustic instrument provides its own amplifier in the form of the hollow sound chamber that boosts its sound . . . well, acoustically.

But an electric guitar makes virtually no acoustic sound at all. An electric instrument creates its tones entirely through electronic means. The vibrating string is still the source of the sound, but a hollow wood chamber isn't what makes those vibrations audible. Instead, the vibrations disturb, or modulate, the magnetic field that the pickups — wire-wrapped magnets positioned underneath the strings — produce. As the vibrations of the strings modulate the pickup's magnetic field, the pickup produces a tiny electric current that exactly reflects that modulation.

Guitars make sound either by amplifying string vibrations acoustically (by passing the sound waves through a hollow chamber), or electronically (by amplifying and outputting a current through a speaker). That's the physical process anyway. How a guitar produces different sounds is up to you and how you control the pitches that those strings produce. Left-hand fretting is what changes these pitches. Your right-hand motions not only help produce the sound by setting the string in motion, but they also determine the rhythm (the beat or pulse), tempo (the speed of the music), and feel (interpretation, style, spin, magic, mojo, je ne sais quoi, whatever) of those pitches.

You Don't Have to Read Music to Understand Guitar Notation

Although you don't need to read music to play the guitar, musicians have developed a few simple tricks through the years that aid in communicating such basic ideas as song structure, chord construction, chord progressions, and important rhythmic figures. Pick up on the shorthand devices for chord diagrams, rhythm slashes, and tablature (which we describe in the following sections), and you're sure to start coppin' licks faster than Steve Vai shredding after three cups of coffee.

Getting by with a little help from a chord diagram

Don't worry — reading a chord diagram is not like reading music; it's far simpler. All you need to do is understand where to put your fingers to form a chord. A chord is defined as the simultaneous sounding of three or more notes.

The diagram shows the anatomy of a chord chart, and the following list briefly explains what the different parts of the diagram mean:

- The grid of six vertical lines and five horizontal ones represents the guitar fretboard, as if you stood the guitar up on the floor or chair and looked straight at the upper part of the neck from the front.
- The vertical lines represent the guitar strings. The vertical line at the far left is the low 6th string, and the right-most vertical line is the high 1st string.
- The horizontal lines represent frets. The thick horizontal line at the top is the nut of the guitar, where the fretboard ends. So the first fret is actually the second vertical line from the top.
- The dots that appear on vertical string lines between horizontal fret lines represent notes that you fret.
- The numerals directly below each string line (just below the last fret line) indicate which left-hand finger you use to fret that note. On the left hand, 1 = index finger; 2 = middle finger; 3 = ring finger; and 4 = little finger. You don't use the thumb to fret, except in certain unusual circumstances.
- The X or O symbols directly above some string lines indicate strings that you leave open (unfretted) or that you don't play. An X above a string means that you don't pick or strike that string with your right hand. An O indicates an open string that you do play.

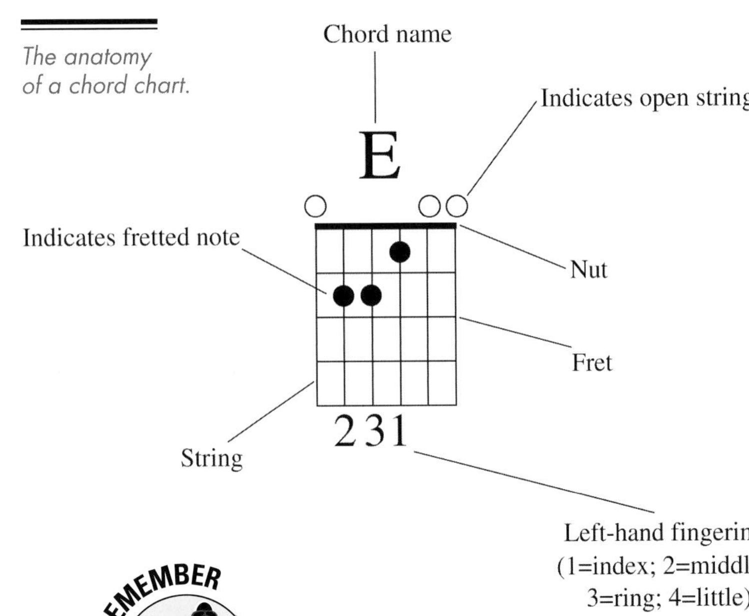

The anatomy of a chord chart.

If a chord starts on a fret other than the first fret, a numeral appears to the right of the diagram, next to the top fret line, to indicate in which fret you actually start. (In such cases, the top line is *not* the nut.) In most cases, however, you deal primarily with chords that fall within only the first four frets of the guitar. Chords that fall within the first four frets typically use open strings, so they're referred to as *open* chords.

Reading rhythm slashes

Musicians use a variety of shorthand tricks to indicate certain musical directions. They use this shorthand because, although a particular musical concept itself is often simple enough, to notate that idea in standard written music form may prove unduly complicated and cumbersome. So they use a "cheat sheet" or a "road map" that gets the point across yet avoids the issue of reading (or writing) music.

Rhythm slashes are slash marks (/) that simply tell you how to play rhythmically but not what to play. The chord in your left hand determines what you play. Say, for example, that you see this diagram.

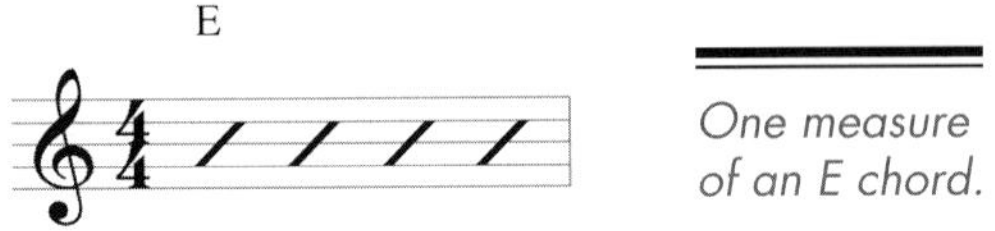

One measure of an E chord.

If you see such a chord symbol with four slashes beneath it, as shown in the figure, you know to finger an E chord and strike it four times.

Taking a look at tablature

Tablature (or just tab, for short) is a notation system that graphically represents the frets and strings of the guitar. Whereas chord diagrams do so in a static way, tablature shows how you play music over a period of time.

For the musical examples that appear in this bookazine, you see a tablature staff (or tab staff, for short) beneath the standard notation staff. This second staff reflects exactly what's going on in the regular musical staff above it — but in guitar language. Tab is guitar-specific — in fact, many call it simply guitar tab. Tab doesn't tell you what note to play. It does, however, tell you what string to fret and where exactly on the fingerboard to fret that string.

Here you see the tab staff and some sample notes and a chord. The top line of the tab staff represents the 1st string of the guitar — high E. The bottom line of the tab corresponds to the 6th string on the guitar, low E. The other lines represent the other four stings in between — the second line from the bottom is the 5th string, and so on. A number appearing on any given line tells you to fret that string in that numbered fret. For example, if you see the numeral 2 on the second line from the top, you need to press down the 2nd string in the second fret above the nut (actually, the space between the first and second metal frets). A 0 on a line means that you play the open string.

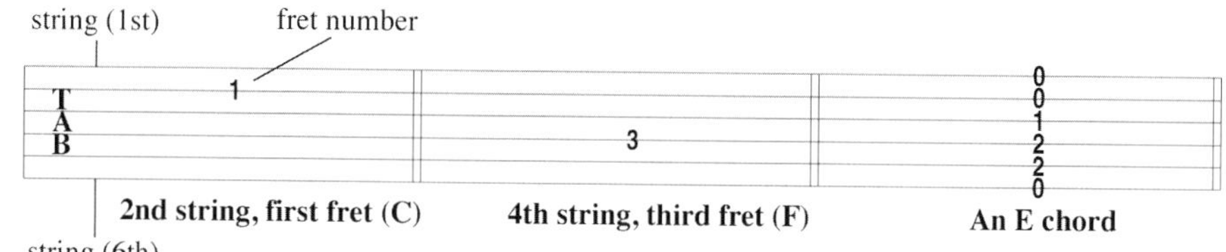

Three examples of tab staff.

And So It Begins: Playing Your First Chord

After you think that you understand (somewhat) the guitar notation that we describe in the preceding sections, your best bet is to just jump right in and play your first chord. We suggest that you start with E major, because it's a particularly guitar-friendly chord and one that you use a lot.

After you get the hang of playing chords, you eventually find that you can move several fingers into position simultaneously. For now, however, just place your fingers one at a time on the frets and strings, as the following instructions indicate:

1. **Place your first (index) finger on the 3rd string, first fret (actually between the nut and first fret wire but closer to the fret wire).**

   Don't press down hard until you have your other fingers in place. Apply just enough pressure to keep your finger from moving off the string.

2. **Place your second (middle) finger on the 5th string (skipping over the 4th string), second fret.**

   Again, apply just enough pressure to keep your fingers in place. You now have two fingers on the guitar, on the 3rd and 5th strings, with an as-yet unfretted string (the 4th) in between.

3. **Place your third (ring) finger on the 4th string, second fret.**

   You may need to wriggle your ring finger a bit to get it to fit in there between the first and second fingers and below the fret wire. Check out the photo of how your E chord should look after all your fingers are positioned correctly.

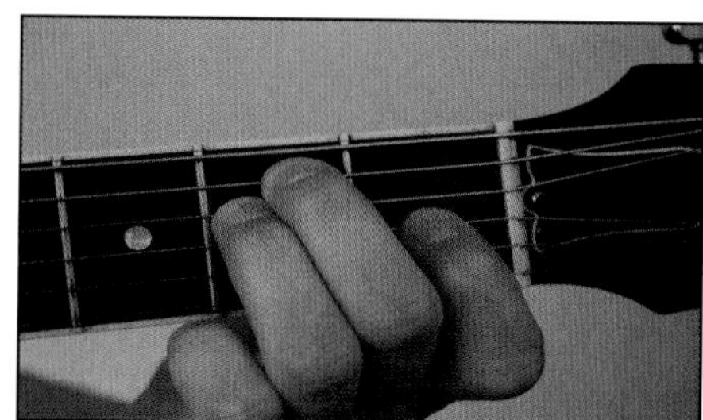

Notice how the fingers curve and the knuckles bend on an E chord.

When your fingers are in position, strike all six strings with your right hand to hear your first chord, E.

One of the hardest things to do in playing chords is to avoid buzzing. Buzzing results if you're not pressing down quite hard enough when you fret. A buzz can also result if a fretting finger accidentally comes in contact with an adjacent string, preventing that string from ringing freely. Without removing your fingers from the frets, try "rocking and rolling" your fingers around on their tips to eliminate any buzzes when you strum the chord.

To Sit or to Stand, and How to Hold your Hands

IN THIS ARTICLE

- *Sitting and standing with the guitar*
- *Positioning your hands*
- *Using a pick*

Guitars are user-friendly instruments. They fit comfortably into the arms of most humans, and the way your two hands fall on the strings naturally is pretty much the position from which you play. Good posture and position, at the very least, prevent strain and fatigue and, at best, help develop good concentration habits and tone.

You can sit or stand while playing the guitar, and the position you choose makes virtually no difference to your tone or technique. Most people prefer to practise while sitting but perform publicly while standing. The one exception to the sit or stand option is the classical guitar, which you normally play in a sitting position. The orthodox practice is to play in a seated position. This practice doesn't mean that you can't play a classical-style guitar or classical music while standing, but the serious pursuit of the classical guitar requires that you sit while playing.

Settling In to a Sitting Position

To hold the guitar in a sitting position

1. Rest the waist of the guitar on your right leg. (The waist is the indented part between the guitar's upper and lower bouts, which are the protruding curved parts that look like shoulders and hips.)

2. Place your feet slightly apart.

3. Balance the guitar by lightly resting your right forearm on the bass bout, as the photo shows. Don't use the left hand to support the neck. You should be able to take your left hand completely off the fretboard without the guitar dipping toward the floor.

Classical guitar technique, on the other hand, requires you to hold the instrument on your left leg, not on your right. This position puts the center of the guitar closer to the center of your body, making the instrument easier to play, especially with the left hand, because you can better execute the difficult fingerings of the classical-guitar music in that position.

You must also elevate the classical guitar, which you can do either by raising the left leg with a specially made guitar foot stool (the traditional way) or by using a support arm, which goes between your left thigh and the guitar's lower side (the modern way). This device enables your left foot to remain on the floor and pushes the guitar up in the air.

Standing While You Play

To stand and play the guitar, you need a strap that is securely fastened to both strap pins on the guitar (or otherwise tied to the guitar). Then you can stand in a normal way and check out how cool you look in the mirror with that guitar slung over your shoulders. You may need to adjust the strap to get the guitar at a comfortable playing height.

Your body makes a natural adjustment in going from a sitting to a standing position. So don't try to overanalyze where your arms fall relative to your sitting position. Just stay relaxed and, above all, look cool, like the guy in the photograph. (You're a guitar player now! Looking cool is just as important as knowing how to play . . . well, almost.)

If your strap slips off a pin while you're playing in a standing position, you have about a fifty-fifty chance of catching your guitar before it hits the floor (and that's if you're quick and experienced with slipping guitars). So don't risk damaging your guitar by using an old or worn strap or one with holes that are too large for the pins to hold securely. Guitars aren't built to bounce, as Pete Townshend has demonstrated so many times.

Left-Hand Position: Fretting Made Easy

To get an idea of correct left-hand positioning on the guitar, extend your left hand, palm up, and make a loose fist, placing your thumb roughly between your first and second fingers. All your knuckles should be bent. Your hand should look about like that after you stick a guitar neck in there. The thumb glides along the back of the neck, straighter than if you were making a fist but not rigid. The finger knuckles stay bent whether they're fretting or relaxed. Again, the left hand should fall in place very naturally on the guitar neck — as if you were picking up a specially made tool that you've been using all your life.

To fret a note, press the tip of your finger down on a string, keeping your knuckles bent. Try to get the fingertip to come down vertically on the string rather than at an angle. This position exerts the greatest pressure on the string and prevents the sides of the finger from touching adjacent strings — which may cause either buzzing or muting (deadening the string, or preventing it from ringing). Use your thumb from its position underneath the neck to help "squeeze" the fingerboard for a tighter grip.

When playing a particular fret, remember that you don't place your finger directly on the metal fret wire, but in between the two frets (or between the nut and first fret wire). For example, if you're playing the fifth fret, place your finger in the square between the fourth and fifth fret wires. Don't place it in the center of the square (midway between the fret wires), but closer to the higher fret wire. This technique gives you the clearest sound and prevents buzzing.

Left-hand fretting requires strength, but don't be tempted to try speeding up the process of strengthening your hands through artificial means. Building up the strength in your left hand takes time. You may see advertisements for hand-strengthening devices and believe that these products may expedite your left-hand endurance. Although we can't declare that these devices never work (and the same goes for the home-grown method of squeezing a racquet ball or tennis ball), one thing's for sure: Nothing helps you build your left-hand fretting strength better or faster than simply playing guitar.

Because of the strength your left hand exerts while fretting, other parts of your body may tense up to compensate. At periodic intervals, make sure that you relax your left shoulder, which has a tendency to rise up as you work on your fretting. Take frequent "drop-shoulder" breaks. Make sure as well that your left elbow doesn't stick out to the side, like that of some rude dinner guest. You want to keep your upper arm and forearm parallel to the side of your body. Relax your elbow so that it stays at your side.

The important thing to remember in maintaining a good left-hand position is that you need to keep it comfortable and natural.

If your hand starts to hurt or ache, stop playing and take a rest. As with any other activity that requires muscular development, resting enables your body to catch up.

Electric endeavours

The electric guitar neck lies comfortably between the thumb and the first finger as the first finger frets a note.

Electric necks are both narrower (from the 1st string to the 6th) and shallower (from the fingerboard to the back of the neck) than acoustics. Electric guitars are, therefore, easier to fret. But the space between each string is smaller, so you're more likely to touch and deaden an adjacent string with your fretting finger. The biggest difference, however, between fretting on an electric and on a nylon or steel-string acoustic is the action.

A guitar's action refers to how high above the frets the strings ride and, to a lesser extent, how easy the strings are to fret. On an electric guitar, fretting strings is like passing a hot knife through butter. The easier action of an electric enables you to use a more relaxed left-hand position than you normally would on an acoustic, with the palm of the left hand facing slightly outward. The photo shows a left hand resting on the fingerboard of an electric guitar, fretting a string.

Classical conditions

Because nylon-string guitars have a wide fingerboard and are the model of choice for classical music, their necks require a slightly more (ahem) formal left-hand approach. Try to get the palm-side of your knuckles (the ones that connect your fingers to your hand) to stay close to and parallel to the side of the neck so that the fingers run perpendicular to the strings and all the fingers are the same distance away from the neck. (If your hand isn't perfectly parallel, the little finger "falls away" or is farther from the neck than your index finger.) Check out the photo to see the correct left-hand position for nylon-string guitars.

Correct left-hand position for a classical guitar.

Getting Your Right Hand in Position

REMEMBER

If you hold a guitar in your lap and drape your right arm over the upper bout, your right hand, held loosely outstretched, crosses the strings at about a 60-degree angle. This position is good for playing with a pick. For fingerstyle playing, you want to turn your right hand more perpendicular to the strings. For classical guitar, you want to keep the right hand as close to a 90-degree angle as possible.

If you're using a pick

You do almost all your electric guitar playing with a pick, whether you're belting out rock 'n' roll, blues, jazz, country, or pop. On acoustic, you can play either with a pick or with your fingers. On both electric and acoustic, you play most rhythm (chord-based accompaniment) and virtually all lead (single-note melodies) by holding the pick, or plectrum (the old-fashioned term), between the thumb and index finger. The photo shows the correct way to hold a pick — with just the tip sticking out, perpendicular to the thumb.

If you're strumming (playing rhythm), you strike the strings with the pick by using wrist and elbow motion. The more vigorous the strum, the more elbow you must put into the mix. For playing lead, you use only the more economical wrist motion. Don't grip the pick too tightly as you play — and plan on dropping it a lot for the first few weeks that you use it.

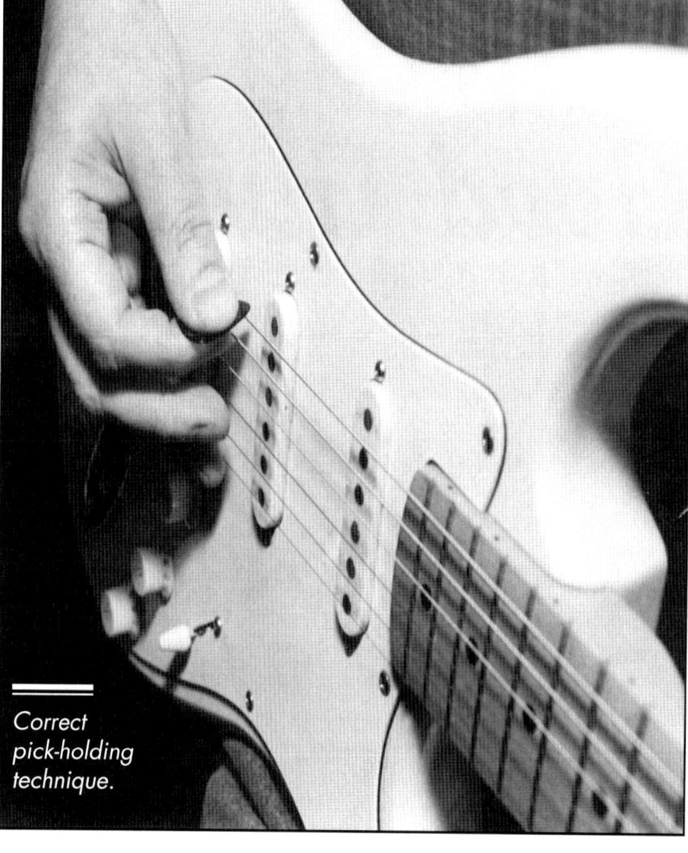

Correct pick-holding technique.

If you're using your fingers

If you eschew such paraphernalia as picks and want to go au naturel with your right hand, you're fingerpicking (although you can fingerpick with special individual, wraparound picks that attach to your fingers — called, confusingly enough, fingerpicks).

Fingerpicking means that you play the guitar by plucking the strings with the individual right-hand fingers. The thumb plays the bass, or low, strings, and the fingers play the treble, or high, strings. In fingerpicking, you use the tips of the fingers to play the strings, positioning the hand over the sound hole (if you're playing acoustic) and keeping the wrist stationary but not rigid. Maintaining a slight arch in the wrist so that the fingers come down more vertically on the strings also helps.

Because of the special right-hand strokes that you use in playing classical guitar (the free stroke and the rest stroke), you must hold your fingers almost perfectly perpendicular to the strings to execute the correct technique. A perpendicular approach enables your fingers to draw against the strings with maximum strength.

REMEMBER

Picks come in various gauges.

A pick's gauge indicates how stiff, or thick, it is.

Thinner picks are easier to manage for the beginner.

Medium picks are the most popular, because they're flexible enough for comfortable rhythm playing, yet stiff enough for leads.

Heavy - gauge picks may seem unwieldy at first, but they're the choice for pros, and eventually all skilled instrumentalists graduate to them (although a few famous holdouts exist - Neil Young being a prime example).

Perfectly Good Guitars

IN THIS ARTICLE

● *Knowing what you want in a guitar* ● *Understanding quality*

● *Matching music styles to guitar models* ● *Developing a buying strategy*

Acoustic blues: National Steel (right), Gibson J-200.

Buying a guitar can be like what happens after you think that you have the basics of a foreign language down pat and then visit the country where it's spoken: You practise your best Berlitz for weeks, but the first time that a native starts speaking to you, you're completely flustered. But don't rush it; hang in there.

Even if you don't have enough experience to recognize the subtle differences between a good guitar and a great guitar, at least expose yourself to them. And don't wait until the day that you decide to buy an instrument to pick one up for the first time. Make several visits to the music store before you're ready to buy and then take the time to absorb your experiences.

Try to visit several different music stores. Some stores may be the exclusive dealer of a specific brand in your region; other retailers may not be able to sell that brand of guitar. Also, you pick up far more knowledge about what makes a good, playable guitar than you may think just by handling several different instruments.

Beginner Guitars

If you're just starting out as a novice guitarist, you may ask the musical question, "What's the minimum I need to spend to avoid winding up with a piece of junk?" That's a good question, because modern manufacturing practices now enable luthiers (the fancy term for guitar makers) to turn out some pretty good stuff for around £150 — and even less sometimes.

If you're an adult (that is, someone older than 14), and you're looking to grow with an instrument, plan to spend between £150 and £250 for an acoustic guitar and a little less for an electric. (Electric guitars are a little easier to build than acoustics are, so they usually cost a bit less than comparable acoustics.) Not bad for something that can provide a lifetime of entertainment and help you develop musical skills, is it?

Heavy metal:
Gibson Explorer,
Flying V (above), and SG;
Fender Stratocaster;
Dean; Ibanez Iceman;
Jackson Soloist.
Bluegrass:
Martin Dreadnought (above),
Taylor Dreadnought,
Collings Dreadnought,
Santa Cruz Dreadnought,
Gallagher Dreadnought.

TIP

In trying to decide on a prospective guitar, consider the following criteria:

- **Appearance:** If you don't like the way a particular guitar looks, you're never really happy with it. So use your eye and your sense of taste (and we're referring here to your sense of aesthetics, so please, don't lick the guitar with your tongue) to select possible candidates.

- **Playability:** Just because a guitar is relatively inexpensive doesn't necessarily mean that it's difficult to play (although this correlation was often the case in the past). You should be able to press the strings down to the fretboard with relative ease. And you shouldn't find the up-the-neck frets unduly difficult either, although they're sometimes harder to play than the lower frets are.

  Here's a way to get some perspective on playability. Go to that Ferrari - er, more expensive guitar-at the other end of the rack and see how a high-quality guitar plays. Then return to the more affordable instrument you're considering. Is the playability wildly different? It shouldn't be. If your prospective instrument doesn't feel comfortable to you, move on.

- **Intonation:** Besides being relatively easy to play, a guitar must play in tune. Test the intonation by playing a twelfth fret harmonic on the first string and match that to the fretted note at the twelfth fret. Although the notes are of a different tonal quality, the pitch should be exactly the same. Apply this test to all six strings. Listen especially to the 3rd and the 6th strings.

  On a guitar that's not set up correctly, these strings are likely to go out of tune first. If you don't trust your ears to tell the difference, enlist the aid of an experienced guitarist on this issue; it's crucial.

- **Solid construction:** If you're checking out an acoustic, rap gently on the top of the instrument (like your doctor does to check your ribs and chest) to make sure that it's rattle free. Peer inside the hole, looking for gobs of glue and other evidence of sloppy workmanship. (Rough-sanded braces are a big tip-off to a hastily constructed instrument.) On an electric, test that the metal hardware is all tightly secured and rattle free.

  Without plugging into an amp, strum the open strings hard and listen for any rattling. Running your hand along the edge of the neck to check that the frets are smooth and filed correctly is another good test. If you're not sure what you should be feeling, consult an experienced guitarist on this "fret check."

Models for a Particular Style

Asking for a type of guitar by musical style is completely legitimate. Ask for a heavy-metal guitar, for example, and the salesperson nods knowingly and leads you to the corner of the store with all the scary-looking stuff. If you request a jazz guitar, you and the salesperson trundle off in a different direction (down toward the guys wearing berets and black turtlenecks sporting "Bird lives!" buttons).

Notice the diversity in shape and style that the collection of popular models shows.

Now, some musical styles do share guitar models. You can play blues and rock, for example, with equal success on a Fender Stratocaster. And a Gibson Les Paul is just as capable of playing a wailing lead as a Strat. (As a rule, however, the tone of a Les Paul is going to be fatter and less jangly than that of a Strat.) Making your own kind of music on the guitar of your choice is part of the fun.

Many people associate the classic guitars pictured in this article with certain musical styles. This article is by no means exhaustive but does include recognized standard bearers of the respective genres:

REMEMBER

Although this article contains guitars that people generally associate with given styles, don't let that limit your creativity. Play the music you want to play on the guitar you want to play it on, no matter what some chart tells you.

Country: Fender Telecaster, Gretsch 6120 (below), Fender Stratocaster.

Classical: Ramirez, Hopf, Khono, Humphrey (above), Hernandez, Alvarez.

Rock: Fender Stratocaster, Gibson Les Paul (above), and SG, Ibanez RG and signature series, Paul Reed Smith, Tom Anderson.

Buying an Axe to Grind

Buying a guitar is similar to buying a car or house in that it's an exciting endeavour and a lot of fun, but you must exercise caution and be a savvy customer, too. Only you know the right guitar for you, what the right price is for your budget and commitment level, and whether a deal feels right or not. Don't deny your natural instincts as a shopper, even if you're new to guitar shopping. Look, listen, consider, go have lunch before the big buy, and talk it over with your sweetie.

Bringing along an expert

A certain saying goes, "An expert is someone who knows more than you do." If you have a friend whose knowledge and experience in guitars exceeds your own, then bring the friend along, by all means. This friend not only knows about guitars, but also knows you. A salesperson doesn't know you, nor does he necessarily have your best interests in mind. But a friend does. And another opinion never hurts, if only to help you articulate your own.

Folk: Dreadnoughts and Grand Concerts by Martin, Taylor, Collings, Larrivée, Lowden, and Guild, Gibson J-200 (above), Ovation Adamas.

Enlist your guitar teacher (if you have one) to help you navigate the guitar buyer's jungle, especially if he's been with you a while and knows your tastes and playing style.

Your teacher may know things about you that you may not even realize about yourself - for example, that you've got sidetracked in the steel-string section although your principal interests lie in nylon-string guitar music.

A good teacher asks questions, listens to your answers, and gently guides you to where you want to go.

The shopping experience is no different with guitars than with any other commodity. Do your research and get differing opinions before you buy. And trust your instincts.

Meeting the salesperson

Dealing with a salesperson doesn't need to be a stressful, adversarial affair, but some people get pretty anxious about the entire situation. If you establish your priorities before you enter the shop, you don't come off as vague and unprepared as he begins his salvo of questions.

A typical first question from a salesperson may be "How much do you want to spend?" In essence, the question means "What price range are you looking at so that I know to which end of the shop to take you?" It's a fair question, and if you can answer directly, you end up saving a lot of time. He may also ask about your playing ability and your style preferences, so be ready to answer those questions, too.

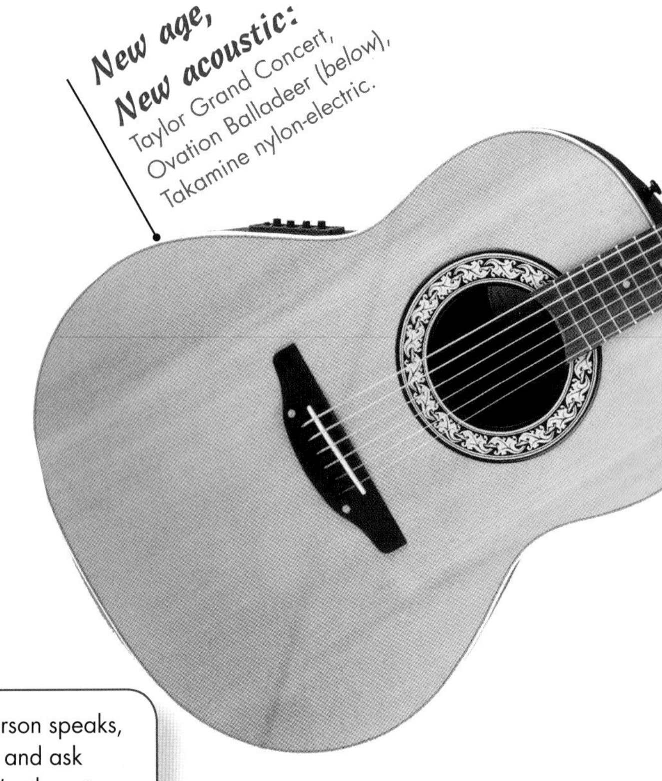

New age, New acoustic: Taylor Grand Concert, Ovation Balladeer (below), Takamine nylon-electric.

Be prepared to answer the salesperson's questions succinctly - for example, "I prefer Strat-style guitars, although not necessarily by Fender, and I'm an intermediate blues player - not a shredder - and I'd like to keep costs at less than £400." Answers such as these make you sound decisive and thoughtful.

The salesperson should have plenty to go on from that kind of information. But if you instead say, "Oh, for the right guitar, price is no object; I like the one that what's-his-name plays on MTV," you're not going to be taken seriously - nor are you likely to end up with the instrument you need.

As the salesperson speaks, listen carefully and ask questions. You're there to observe and absorb, not impress. If you decide you're not ready to buy at this point, tell him that. Thank him for his time and get his card. You're certainly free to go elsewhere and investigate another shop. To do so not only is your option - it's your duty!

Electric blues: Gibson ES-355, Fender Telecaster (above), Fender Stratocaster, Gibson Les Paul.

Jazz:
Gibson ES-175 (above), Super 400 L-5, and Johnny Smith; archtops by D'Angelico, D'Aquisto, and Benedetto; Epiphone Emperor Regent; Ibanez signature models.

The art of the deal

You can find out the retail, or list, price of an instrument before you walk into the store. The manufacturer presets these numbers, and they're public knowledge. Look at the ads in guitar magazines for the company's contact info and call the company or visit its website to determine the manufacturer's suggested retail price on a particular product or to receive literature. As of this writing, a Gibson Les Paul Standard lists for around £2,500, and a Fender American Standard Stratocaster lists for just under £1,000.

Again, the preceding numbers are list prices. Music stores offer discounts, and the range can vary greatly. Big, urban-based stores that buy mass quantities of instruments can usually offer greater discounts than can smaller shops in outlying or remote areas. Mail-order and online outlets can match and sometimes beat big-store prices, because they don't have the overhead of maintaining a retail facility.

R&B:
Fender Stratocaster, Gibson ES-335 (above).

TIP

In deciding where to buy, don't neglect the value of service. Retail stores - unlike online and mailorder houses - are in a better position to devote close, personal service to a new guitar customer. Perhaps as a result of facing stiff competition from the booming online and mail-order biz, many stores are upping their service incentives. Service includes anything from fixing minor problems and making adjustments to providing periodic setups (sort of like a tune-up and oil change for your guitar). A music shop can be a great place to just hang out and talk guitars!

Remember, however, that list prices are public knowledge, and salespeople from all types of vendors must tell you their selling price with no strings attached (uh, by that we mean with no conditions). The vendor can rightfully charge up to list price; you must wrangle the maximum discount yourself.

How you do that is as old as bargaining itself, but a reasonable haggling range is somewhere between the cut-rate quote of a nationally advertising online and mail-order house and 10 per cent off list.

Guitar Goodies You May Want (But Don't Absolutely Need)

You can treat yourself to a number of little contraptions that make guitar playing a lot more painless and convenient. In no particular order, consider some of these gizmos, which are often worth their weight in thumbpicks:

- **Bridge pins:** These little plastic pieces wedge your strings into the bridge of your acoustic guitar. The problem is this: If you lose one (because it goes flying off a dock or into the grass after you yank it out), you can't find anything to substitute for it. Matchsticks are the closest things, but who carries those around these days? The next time you're at the music shop buying strings, pick up a couple of extra bridge pins.
- **Cable tester and volt/ohm meter:** These items cost about £10 and £15, respectively, and earn their keep the first time they diagnose a bad or reverse-wired cable. Learn how to use the volt-ohm meter with respect to your equipment — that is, know what power supplies you have and what the appropriate settings are on the meter. You can impress your friends with your "gearhead-geek" aptitude.
- **Cords and cables:** A crackling cable is no fun for either you or your audience. That nasty sound means that your connections are worn and bad — it happens. Keep extra cables on hand of both the long variety (for connecting your guitar to an effect or an amp) and the short (for interpedal connections).

- **U Cloth:** You should always wipe down your guitar after playing to remove body oils that can corrode strings and muck up the finish. Cotton is good, and chamois is better. At least give your fingerboard a wipe before you put it in the case, and if you're playing with short sleeves, give the top a rubdown, too.
- **Duct tape:** This stuff is the musician's baking soda — an all-purpose utility product that cures a multitude of maladies. You can use duct tape to fix everything from a rattling tailpiece to a broken microphone clip. Even the roll itself is handy: You can use it to tilt your amp up for better monitoring. Use duct tape to fix your car's upholstery or even patch the holes of your jeans, onstage or off. In some circles, it's even considered fashionable.
- **Earplugs:** If you play electric guitar and find yourself in a lot of impromptu jam sessions, carry earplugs. Your ears are your most precious musical commodities — more important than even your fingers. Don't damage them by exposing them to loud noises in close rehearsal quarters. Buy the kind of earplugs made especially for music listening; they attenuate (reduce) frequencies at equal rates across the spectrum. So it's like hearing the original music . . . only softer. Many guitarists are advocates of earplugs, including The Who's Pete Townshend, who claims to have suffered significant hearing loss resulting from long-term exposure to loud music.
- **Fuses:** Any new environment can have unpredictable wiring schemes that could cause havoc with your gear — and especially your amp. Your amp's first line of defense is its fuse. If the house current is weird, the fuse blows, and you must have a replacement to get the amp working again.
- **Peg winder:** This inexpensive crank turns your tuning keys at about 10 times the rate that you can turn them by hand. At no extra charge, these devices include a notched groove that's perfect for removing stuck bridge pins in your acoustic.
- **Pencil and paper:** Always carry something that you can write with and on. That way, you can jot down lyrics, a cool chord that someone shows you, a cheat sheet so that you can pick up a chord progression in a jiffy, or even a surreptitious note to another musician. ("Please tell your bass player to turn it down — I've lost three fillings already!")
- **Reversible screwdriver:** You can fix everything from a rattling pickup to a loose-set screw in a tuning key with such a handy screwdriver. Get one that has both a Phillips and straight-blade tip.
- **Tuning fork/Pitch pipe:** Having one of these low-tech tuning devices as a spare never hurts, in case the battery on your electronic tuner fails or the tuner itself gets stepped on by the gravitationally challenged drummer. Both of these devices are like rowboats in a speedboat and sailboat world: After the gas is gone and the wind stops blowing, you can still function using your own power.
- **Wire cutters/needle-nose pliers:** Strings are, after all, wires. When you change strings, use wire cutters to trim away any excess and use the pliers for digging out the stubborn remnants of a broken string from a tuning post.

Tuning Your Guitar:

Five Methods for Fixing Flats

IN THIS ARTICLE

- *Tuning the guitar relatively (to itself)*
- *Tuning to a fixed source*

Tuning is to guitarists what parallel parking is to city drivers: an everyday and necessary activity that can be vexingly difficult to master. Unlike the piano, which a professional tunes and you never need to adjust until the next time the professional tuner comes to visit, the guitar is normally tuned by its owner — and it needs constant adjusting.

One of the great injustices of life is that, before you can even play music on the guitar, you must endure the painstaking process of getting your instrument in tune. You can use any of several different methods to get your guitar in tune, as this article describes.

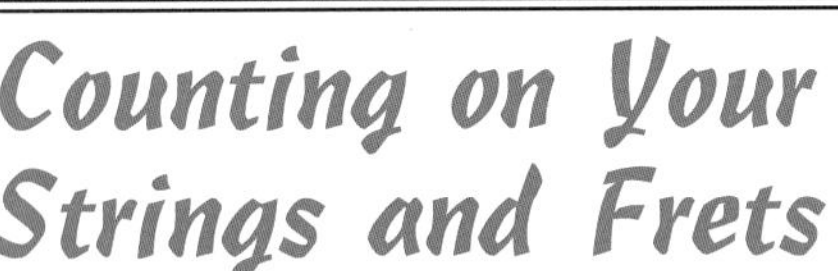

Counting on Your Strings and Frets

To tune your guitar, you need to know how to refer to strings and frets.

- **Strings** are numbered consecutively 1 through to 6. The 1st string is the skinniest, located closest to the floor when you hold the guitar in playing position. Working your way up, the 6th string is the fattest, closest to the ceiling. Memorize the letter names of the open strings (E, A, D, G, B, E, from 6th to 1st) so that you're not limited to referring to them by number. An easy way to memorize the open strings in order is to remember "Eddie Ate Dynamite; Good Bye, Eddie."
- **Fret** can refer to either the space where you put your left-hand finger or to the thin metal bar running across the fingerboard. Whenever you deal with guitar fingering, fret means the space between the metal bars - where you can comfortably fit a left-hand finger. The first fret is the region between the nut (the thin, grooved strip that separates the headstock from the neck) and the first metal bar. The fifth fret, then, is the fifth square up from the nut - technically, the region between the fourth and fifth metal fret bars. (Most guitars have amarker on the fifth fret, either a decor-ative design embedded in the finger-board or a dot on the side of the neck, or both.)

One more point of business to square away. You come across the terms open strings and fretted strings from this point on. Here's what they mean:

- **Open string:** A string that you play without pressing down on it with a left-hand finger.
- **Fretted string:** A string that you play while pressing down on it at a particular fret.

Everything's Relative: Tuning the Guitar to Itself

Relative tuning is so named because you don't need any outside reference to which you tune the instrument. As long as the strings are in tune in a certain relationship with each other, you can create sonorous and harmonious tones. Those same tones may turn into sounds resembling those of a catfight if you try to play along with another instrument, but as long as you tune the strings relative to one another, the guitar is in tune with itself.

To tune a guitar using the relative method, choose one string as the starting point — say, the 6th string. Leave the pitch of that string as is, and then tune all the other strings relative to that 6th string.

The fifth-fret method derives its name from the fact that you almost always play a string at the fifth fret and then compare the sound of that note to that of the next open string. You need to be careful, however, because the fourth fret (the fifth fret's jealous understudy) puts in a cameo appearance toward the end of the process. The diagram shows how you place your fingers to play through the steps.

Here's how to get your guitar in tune by using the fifth-fret method:

1. **Play the fifth fret of the 6th (low E) string (the fattest one, closest to the ceiling) and then play the open 5th (A) string (the one next to it).**

   Let both notes ring together. Their pitches should match exactly. If they don't seem quite right, determine whether the 5th string is higher or lower than the fretted 6th string. If the 5th string seems lower, or flat, turn its tuning key with your left hand to raise the pitch. If the 5th string seems sharp, or higher sounding, use its tuning key to lower the pitch. You may go too far with the tuning key if you're not careful; if so, you need to reverse your motions. In fact, if you can't tell whether the 5th string is higher or lower, tune it flat intentionally (that is, tune it too low) and then come back to the desired pitch.

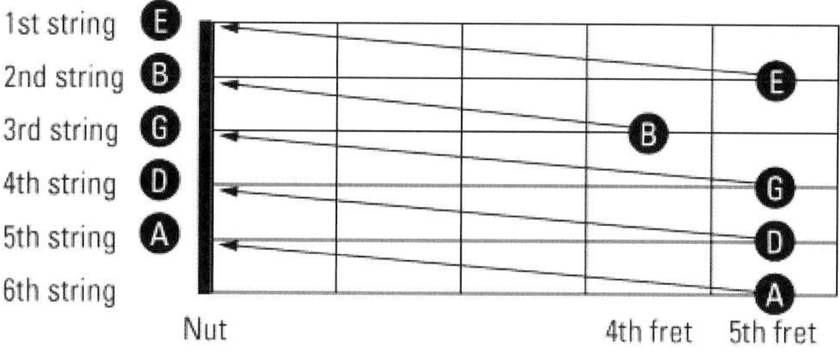

Place your fingers on the frets as shown and match the pitch to the next open string.

2. **Play the fifth fret of the 5th (A) string and then play the open 4th (D) string.**

   Let both of these notes ring together. If the 4th string seems flat or sharp relative to the fretted 5th string, use the tuning key of the 4th string to adjust its pitch accordingly. Again, if you're not sure whether the 4th string is higher or lower, "overtune" it in one direction — flat, or lower, is best — and then come back.

3. **Play the fifth fret of the 4th (D) string and then play the open 3rd (G) string.**

   Let both notes ring together. If the 3rd string seems flat or sharp relative to the fretted 4th string, use the tuning key of the 3rd string to adjust the pitch accordingly.

4. **Play the fourth (not the fifth!) fret of the 3rd (G) string and then play the open 2nd (B) string.**

Let both strings ring together. If the 2nd string seems flat or sharp, use its tuning key to adjust the pitch accordingly.

5. **Play the fifth (yes, back to the fifth for this one) fret of the 2nd (B) string and then play the open1st (high E) string.**

   Let both notes ring together. If the 1st string seems flat or sharp, use its tuning key to adjust the pitch accordingly. If you're satisfied that both strings produce the same pitch, you've now tuned the upper (that is, "upper" as in higher-pitched) five strings of the guitar relative to the fixed (untuned) 6th string. Your guitar's in tune with itself.

You may want to go back and repeat the process, because some strings may have slipped out of tune. When you tune in the normal way, you use your left hand to turn the tuning peg. But after you remove your finger from the string that you're fretting, it stops ringing; therefore, you can no longer hear the string you're trying to tune to (the fretted string) as you adjust the open string. You can actually tune the open string while keeping your left-hand finger on the fretted string. Simply use your right hand! After you strike the two strings in succession (the fretted string and the open string), take your right hand and reach over your left hand (which remains stationary as you fret the string) and turn the tuning peg of the appropriate string until both strings sound exactly the same.

In Deference to a Reference: Tuning to a Fixed Source

Getting the guitar in tune with itself through the relative method is good for your ear but isn't very practical if you need to play with other instruments or voices. If you want to bring your guitar into the world of other people, you need to know how to tune to a fixed source, such as a piano, pitch pipe, tuning fork, or electronic tuner. Using such a source ensures that everyone is playing by the same tuning rules. Besides, your guitar and strings are built for optimal tone production if you tune to standard pitch.

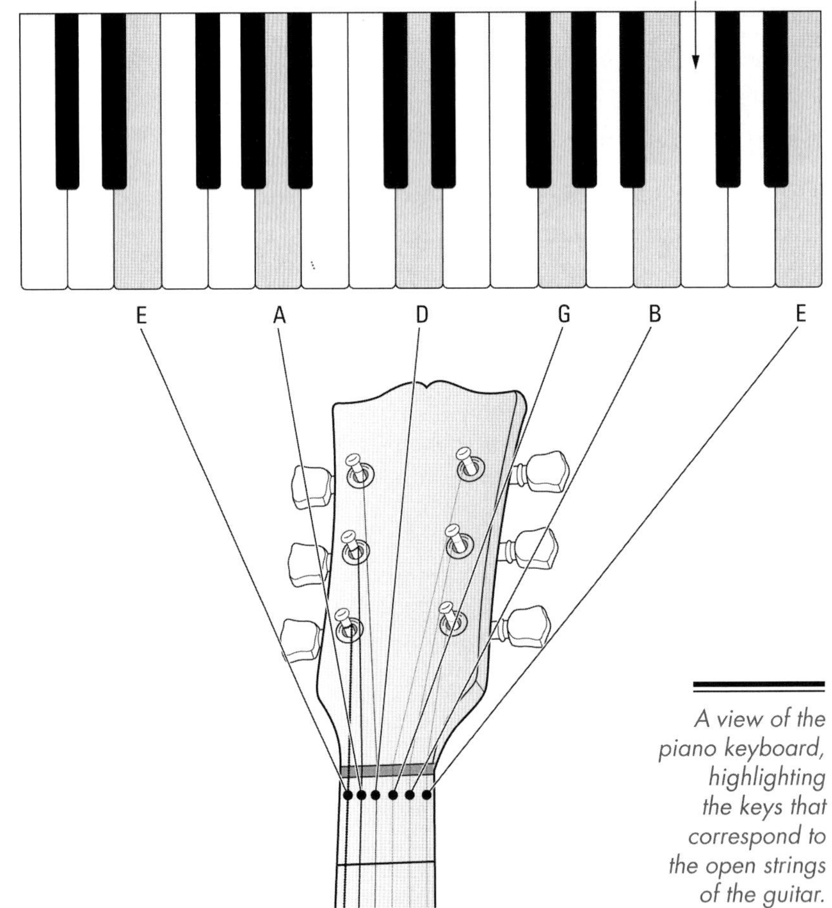

A view of the piano keyboard, highlighting the keys that correspond to the open strings of the guitar.

Taking a turn at the piano

Because it holds its pitch so well (needing only biannual or annual tunings, depending on the conditions), a piano is a great tool that you can use for tuning a guitar. Assuming that you have an electronic keyboard or a well-tuned piano around, all you need to do is match the open strings of the guitar to the appropriate keys on the piano. You get a clear view of the way piano keys and guitar strings align in the image .

Tuning your guitar with a pitch pipe

If you're off to the beach with your guitar, you're not going to want to put a piano in the back of your car, even if you're really fussy about tuning. So you need a smaller and more practical device that supplies standard-tuning reference pitches. Enter the pitch pipe.

For guitarists, special pitch pipes exist consisting of pipes that play only the notes of the open strings of the guitar (but sounding in a higher range) and none of the in-between notes. The advantage of a pitch pipe is that you can hold it firmly in your mouth while blowing, keeping your hands free for tuning. The disadvantage to a pitch pipe is that you sometimes take a while getting used to hearing a wind-produced pitch against a struck-string pitch. But with practice, you can tune with a pitch pipe as easily as you can with a piano. And a pitch pipe fits much more easily into your shirt pocket than a piano does!

Sinking your teeth into the tuning fork

After you get good enough at discerning pitches, you need only one single-pitched tuning reference to get your whole guitar in tune. The tuning fork offers only one pitch, and it usually comes in only one flavour: A. But that note's really all you need. If you tune your open 5th string (A) to the tuning fork's A (although the guitar's A sounds in a lower range), you can tune every other string to that string by using the relative tuning method.

Using a tuning fork requires a little finesse. You must strike the fork against something firm, such as a tabletop or kneecap, and then hold it close to your ear or place the stem (or handle) — and not the tines (or fork prongs) — against something that resonates. This resonator can be the tabletop again or even the top of the guitar. (You can even hold it between your teeth, which leaves your hands free!) At the same time, you must somehow play an A note and tune it to the fork's tone. The process is like pulling your house keys out of your pocket while you're loaded down with an armful of groceries. The task may not be easy, but if you do it enough, you eventually become an expert.

Experiencing the electronic tuner

The quickest and most accurate way to get in tune is to employ an electronic tuner. This handy device seems to possess witchcraftlike powers. Newer electronic tuners made especially for guitars can usually sense what string you're playing, tell you what pitch you're nearest, and indicate whether you're flat (too low) or sharp (too high). About the only thing these devices don't do is turn the tuning keys for you (although we hear they're working on that). Some older, graph-type tuners feature a switch that selects which string you want to tune.

A electronic tuner makes tuning easy.

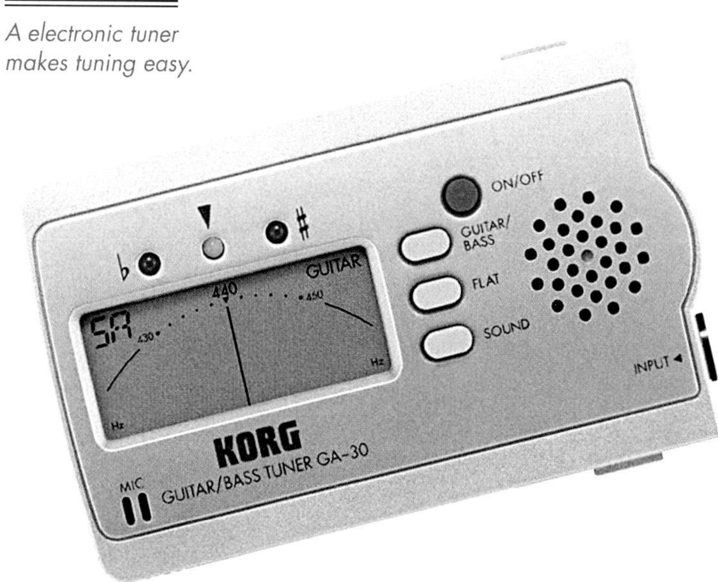

You can either plug your guitar into the tuner (if you're using an electric instrument) or you can use the tuner's built-in microphone to tune an acoustic. In both types of tuners — the ones where you select the strings and the ones that automatically sense the string — the display indicates two things: what note you're closest to (E, A, D, G, B, E) and whether you're flat or sharp of that note.

Electronic tuners are usually powered by 9-volt batteries or two AAs that can last for a year with regular usage (up to two or even three years with only occasional usage). Many electronic tuners are inexpensive (as low as £15 or so) and are well worth the money.

The Easiest Way to Play:

Basic Major and Minor Chords

IN THIS ARTICLE

- *Playing A-, D-, G-, and C-family chords*
- *Playing songs with the oldies progression*

Accompanying yourself as you sing your favourite songs — or as someone else sings them if your voice is less than melodious — is one of the best ways to pick up basic guitar chords. If you know how to play basic chords, you can play a lot of popular songs right away.

In this article, we organize the major and minor chords into families. A family of chords is simply a group of related chords. We say they're related because you often use these chords together to play songs.

Think of a family of chords as a plant. If one of the chords - the one that feels like home base in a song (usually the chord you start and end a song with) - is the plant's root, the other chords in the family are the different shoots rising up from that same root. Together, the root and shoots make up the family. Put 'em all together and you have a lush garden... er, make that a song. By the way, the technical term for a family is key. So you can say something like "This song uses A-family chords" or "This song is in the key of A."

Playing Chords in the A Family

The A family is a popular family for playing songs on the guitar because, like other families we present in this chapter, its chords are easy to play. That's because A-family chords contain open strings (strings that you play without pressing down any notes). Chords that contain open strings are called open chords, or open-position chords. Listen to "Fire and Rain," by James Taylor, to hear the sound of a song that uses A-family chords.

The basic chords in the A family are A, D, and E. Each of these chords is what's known as a major chord. A chord that's named by a letter name alone is always major.

Fingering A-family chords

Remember that when fingering chords, you use the "ball" of your fingertip, placing it just behind the fret (on the side toward the tuning pegs). Arch your fingers so that the fingertips fall perpendicular to the neck. And make sure that your left-hand fingernails are short so that they don't prevent you from pressing the strings all the way down to the fingerboard. The image shows the fingering for the A, D, and E chords — the basic chords in the A family.

Don't play any strings marked with an X (the 6th string on the A chord and the 5th and 6th strings on the D chord). Strike just the top five (5th to 1st) strings in the A chord and the top four (4th to 1st) strings in the D chord. Selectively striking strings may be awkward at first, but keep at it and you get the hang of it.

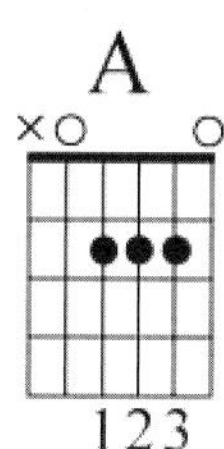

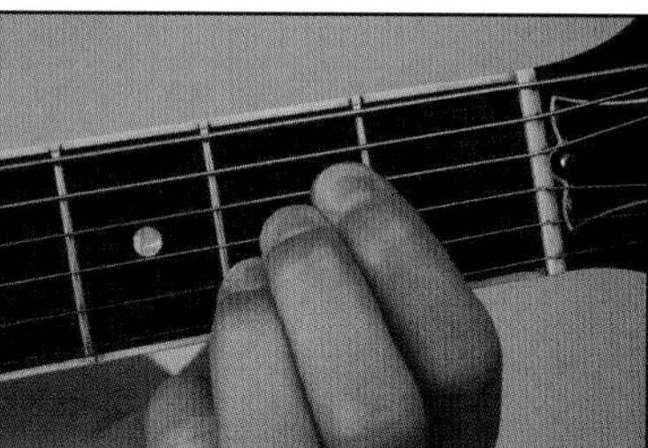

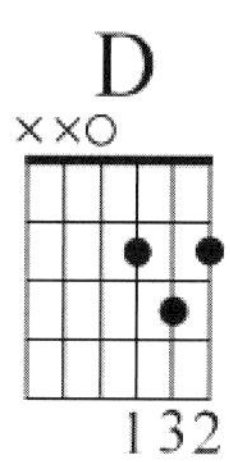

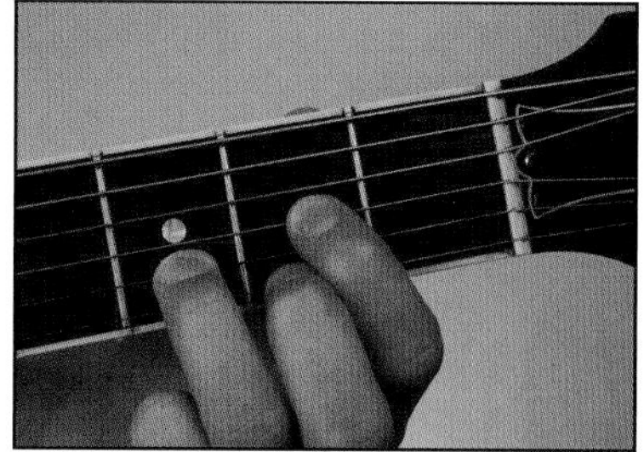

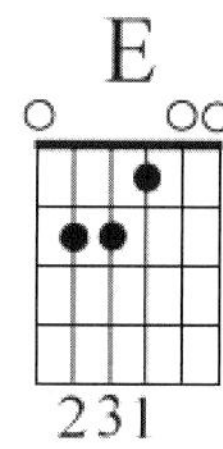

Chord diagrams showing the A, D, and E chords. Notice how the diagrams graphically convey the left-hand positions in the photos.

Strumming A-family chords

Use your right hand to strum these A-family chords with one of the following:

- A pick
- Your thumb
- The back of your fingernails (in a brushing motion toward the floor)

Start strumming from the lowest-pitched string of the chord (the side of the chord toward the ceiling as you hold the guitar) and strum toward the floor.

A progression is simply a series of chords that you play one after the other. You strum each chord of the progression in the image — in the order shown (reading from left to right) — four times. Use all downstrokes (dragging your pick across the strings toward the floor) as you play.

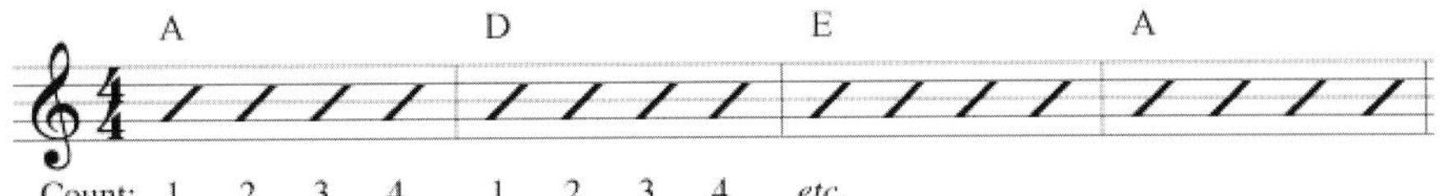

A simple chord progression in the key of A (using only chords in the A family).

After strumming each chord four times, you come to a vertical line in the music that follows the four strum symbols. This line is a bar line. It's not something that you play. Bar lines visually separate the music into smaller sections known as measures, or bars. (You can use these terms interchangeably; they both mean the same thing.) Measures make written music easier to grasp, because they break up the music into little, digestible chunks.

Don't hesitate or stop at the bar line. Keep your strumming speed the same throughout, even as you play "between the measures" — that is, in the imaginary "space" from the end of one measure to the beginning of the next that the bar line represents. Start out playing as slowly as necessary to help you keep the beat steady. You can always speed up as you become more confident and proficient in your chord fingering and switching.

By playing a progression over and over, you start to develop left-hand strength and calluses on your fingertips. Try it (and try it . . . and try it. . .).

Playing Chords in the D Family

The basic chords that make up the D family are D, Em (pronounced "E minor"), G, and A. The D family, therefore, shares two basic open chords with the A family (D and A) and introduces two new ones: Em and G. Because you already know how to play D and A from the preceding section ("Playing Chords in the A Family"), you need to work on only two more chords to add the entire D family to your repertoire: Em and G. Listen to "Here Comes the Sun," by the Beatles, to hear the sound of a song that uses D-family chords.

Minor describes the quality of a type of chord. A minor chord has a sound that's distinctly different from that of a major chord. You may characterize the sound of a minor chord as sad, mournful, scary, or even ominous. Remember that the relationship of the notes that make up the chord determines a chord's quality. A chord that's named by a capital letter followed by a small "m" is always minor.

Fingering D-family chords

The image shows you how to finger the two basic chords in the D family that aren't in the A family. You may notice that none of the strings in either chord diagram displays an X symbol, so you get to strike all the strings whenever you play a G or Em chord. If you feel like it, go ahead and celebrate by dragging your pick or right-hand fingers across the strings in a big keraaaang.

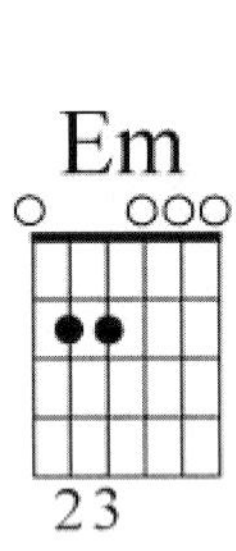

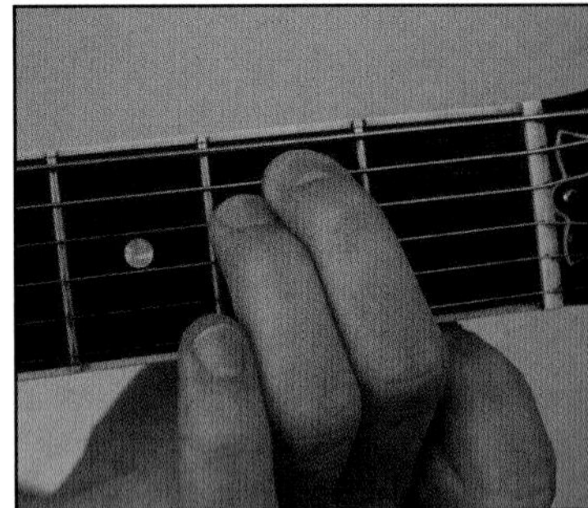

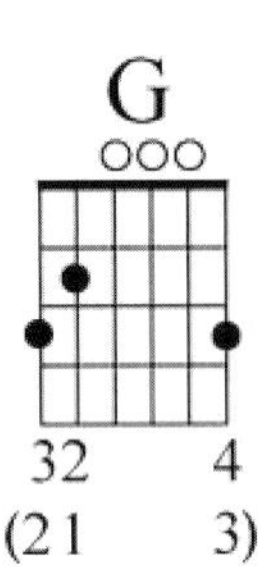

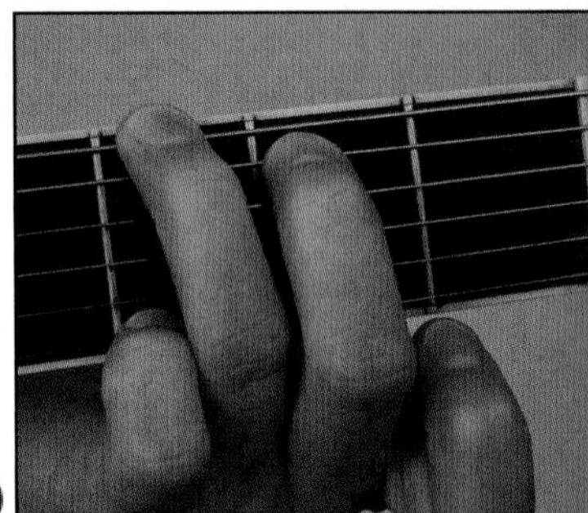

The Em and G chords. Notice that all six strings are available for play in each chord.

Try the following trick to quickly pick up how to play Em and to hear the difference between the major and minor chord qualities: Play E, which is a major chord, and then lift your index finger off the 3rd string. Now you're playing Em, which is the minor-chord version of E. By alternating the two chords, you can easily hear the difference in quality between a major and minor chord. Also, notice the alternative fingering for G (1-2-3 instead of 2-3-4). You may want to start off with the initially easier 1-2-3 fingering before switching to the 2-3-4 fingering you see in the photo as your hand gains strength and becomes more flexible. You can switch to other chords with greater ease and efficiency by using the 2-3-4 fingering for G.

Strumming D-family chords

Here's a simple chord progression using D-family chords. (See image.) Notice the difference in the strum in this figure versus that of the earlier one for the A-family progression. In the earlier progression, you strum each chord four times per measure. Each strum is one pulse, or beat. This new progression divides the second strum of each measure (or the second beat) into two strums — up and down — both of which together take up the time of one beat, meaning that you must play each strum in beat 2 twice as quickly as you do a regular strum.

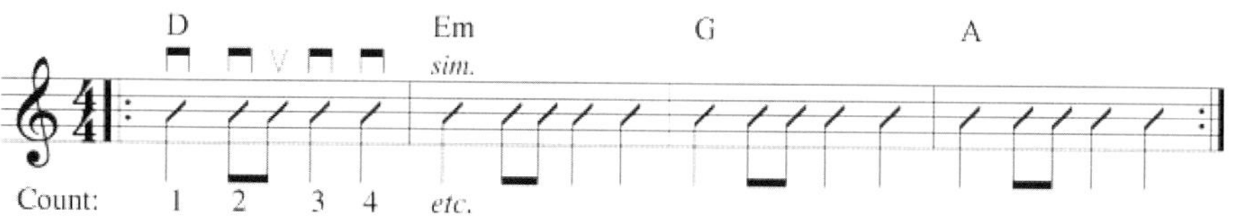

The additional symbol ▬ with the strum symbol means that you strum down toward the floor, and V means that you strum up toward the ceiling. (If you play your guitar while hanging in gravity boots, however, you must reverse these last two instructions.) The term sim. is an abbreviation of the Italian word simile, which instructs you to keep playing in a similar manner — in this case to keep strumming in a down, down-up, down, down pattern.

If you're using only your fingers for strumming, play upstrokes with the back of your thumbnail whenever you see the symbol V.

Playing Chords in the G Family

By tackling related chord families, you carry over your knowledge from family to family in the form of chords that you already know from earlier families. The basic chords that make up the G family are G, Am, C, D, and Em. If you already know G, D, and Em (which we describe in the preceding sections on the A and D families), you can now try Am and C. Listen to "You've Got a Friend," as played by James Taylor, to hear the sound of a song that uses G-family chords.

Fingering G-family chords

The new chords that you need to play in the G family are Am and C. Notice from the image that the fingering of these two chords is similar: Each has finger 1 on the 2nd string, first fret, and finger 2 on the 4th string, second fret. (Only finger 3 must change — adding or removing it — in switching between these two chords.) In moving between these chords, keep these first two fingers in place on the strings. Switching chords is always easier if you don't need to move all your fingers to new positions. The notes that different chords share are known as common tones. Notice the X over the 6th string in each of these chords. Don't play that string while strumming either C or Am. (We mean it!)

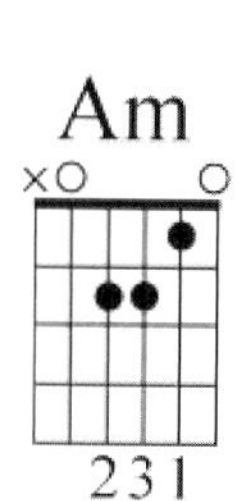

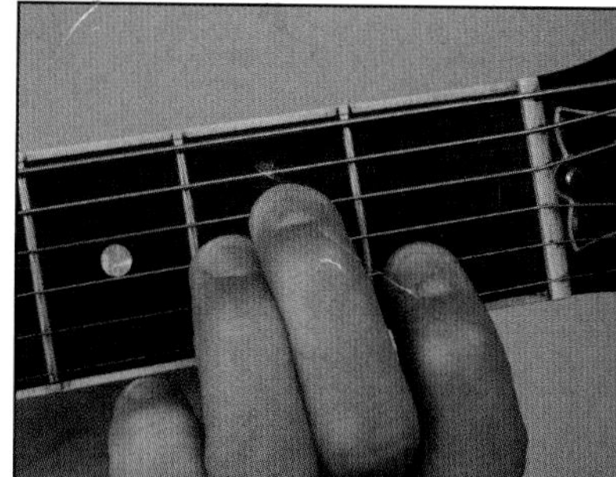

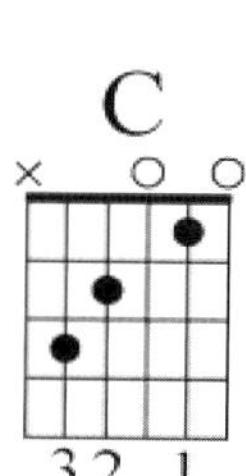

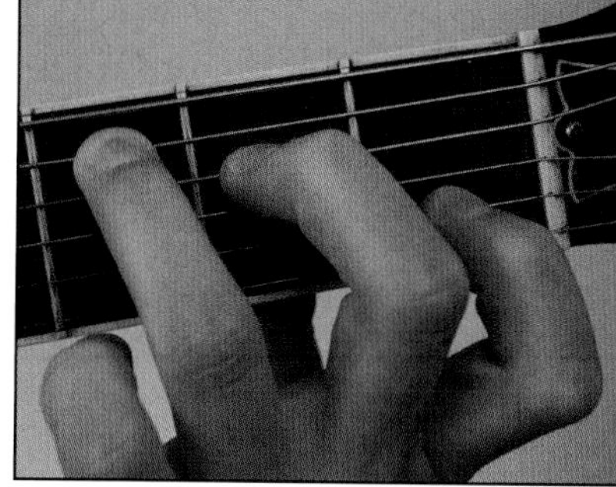

(Above) This progression contains chords commonly found in the key of D. (Right) The fingering for the Am and C chords.

Strumming G-family chords

Here's a simple chord progression that you can play by using G-family chords. Play this progression over and over to accustom yourself to switching chords and to build up those left-hand calluses. It does get easier after a while. We promise!

Notice that, in each measure, you play beats 2 and 3 as "down-up" strums.

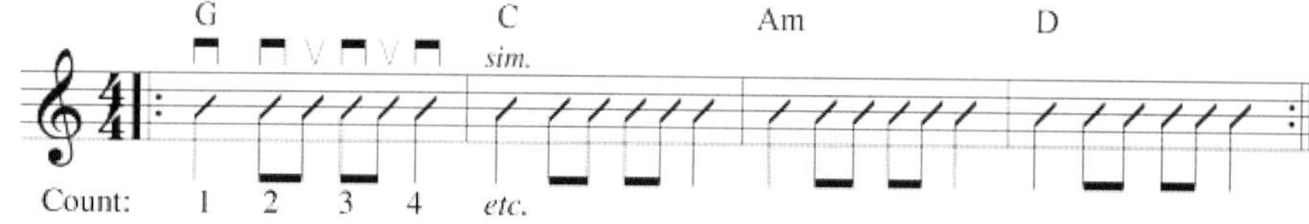

(Above) A chord progression that you can play by using only G- family chords.

Playing Chords in the C Family

Some people say that C is the easiest key to play in. That's because C uses only the white-key notes of the piano in its musical scale and, as such, is sort of the music-theory square one — the point at which everything (and, usually, everyone) begins in music.

The basic chords that make up the C family are C, Dm, Em, F, G, and Am. If you practise the preceding sections on the A-, D-, and G-family chords, you know C, Em, G, and Am. (If not, check them out.) So in this section, you need to pick up only two more chords: Dm and F. After you know these two additional chords, you have all the basic major and minor chords that we describe in this chapter down pat. Listen to "Dust in the Wind," by Kansas or "The Boxer," by Simon and Garfunkel to hear the sound of a song that uses C-family chords

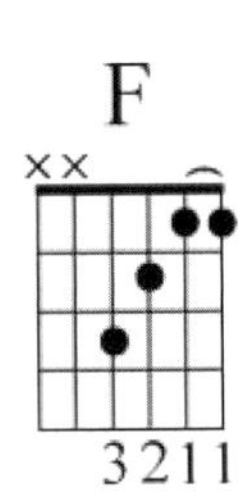

Many people find the F chord the most difficult chord to play of all the basic major and minor chords. That's because F uses no open strings, and it also requires a barre. A barre is what you're playing whenever you press down two or more strings at once with a single left-hand finger. To play the F chord, for example, you use your first finger to press down both the 1st and 2nd strings at the first fret simultaneously.

You must exert extra finger pressure to play a barre. At first, you may find that, as you strum the chord (hitting the top four strings only, as the Xs in the chord diagram indicate), you hear some buzzes or muffled strings. Experiment with various placements of your index finger. Try adjusting the angle of your finger or try rotating your finger slightly on its side. Keep trying until you find a position for the first finger that enables all four strings to ring clearly as you strike them.

Strumming C-family chords

Here's a simple chord progression that you can play by using C-family chords. Play the progression over and over to get used to switching among the chords in this family and, of course, to help build up those nasty little calluses.

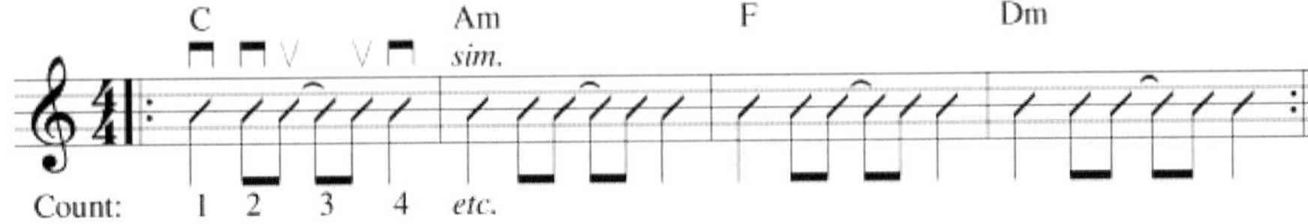

A simple chord progression that you play by using the C-family chords (below).

Fingering C-family chords

The pictures show the new chords that you need to play in the C family. Notice that both the Dm and F chords have the second finger on the 3rd string, second fret. Hold this common tone down as you switch between these two chords.

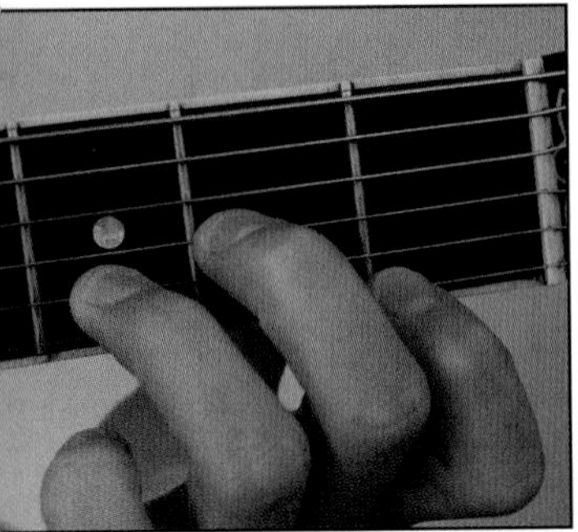

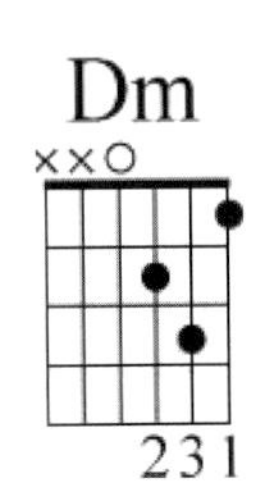

The Dm (right) and F chords (above). Notice the indication in the (⌒) F-chord diagram that tells you to fret (or barre) two strings with one finger.

The small curved line joining the second half of beat 2 to beat 3 is known as a tie. A tie tells you not to strike the second note of the two tied notes (in this case, the one on beat 3). Instead, just keep holding the chord on that beat (letting it ring) without restriking it with your right hand.

This slightly jarring rhythmic effect is an example of syncopation. In syncopation, the musician either strikes a note (or chord) where you don't expect to hear it or fails to strike a note (or chord) where you do expect to hear it. You probably usually expect to strike notes on the beats (1, 2, 3, 4). In this example, however, you strike no chord on beat 3. That variation in the strumming pattern makes the chord on beat 2 ½ feel as if it's accentuated (or, as musicians say, accented). This accentuation interrupts the normal (expected) pulse of the music, resulting in the syncopation of the music.

The balance between expectation and surprise in music is what holds a listener's interest. (Well, that and the promise of free hors d'oeuvres at the intermission.)

Having Fun with Basic Major and Minor Chords: The "Oldies" Progression

As soon as you know the basic major and minor chords, you can play a lot of popular songs. One cool thing that you can do right now is play oldies — songs from the late '50s and early '60s such as "Earth Angel" and "Duke of Earl." These songs are based on what's sometimes called the oldies progression. The oldies progression is a series of four chords; they're repeated over and over to form the accompaniment for a song.

You can play the oldies progression in any key, but the best guitar keys for the oldies progression are C and G. In the key of C, the four chords that make up the progression are C-Am-F-G. And in the key of G, the chords are G-Em-C-D. Try strumming the progression in each key by playing four down-strums per chord. Play the four chords over and over, in the sequence given. If you need help with the fingerings for these chords, check out the sections "Playing Chords in the C Family" and "Playing Chords in the G Family," earlier in this chapter.

For some songs, you play four one-beat strums per chord; for others, you play eight or two. Below, we list some songs you can play with the oldies progression right now. Next to each, we show you how many times you strum each chord. Don't forget to sing. Have fun!

- **All I Have to Do Is Dream. Two strums per chord.**
- **Blue Moon. Two strums per chord.**
- **Breaking Up Is Hard to Do. Two strums per chord.**
- **Come Go with Me. Two strums per chord.**
- **Duke of Earl. Four strums per chord.**
- **Earth Angel. Two strums per chord.**
- **Heart and Soul. Two strums per chord.**
- **Hey Paula. Two strums per chord.**
- **In the Still of the Night. (The one by the Five Satins, not the Cole Porter one.) Four strums per chord.**
- **Little Darlin'. Eight strums per chord.**
- **Poor Little Fool. Four strums per chord.**
- **Runaround Sue. Eight strums per chord.**
- **Sherry. Two strums per chord.**
- **Silhouettes. Two strums per chord.**
- **Stay. Two strums per chord.**
- **Take Good Care of My Baby. Four strums per chord.**
- **Tears on My Pillow. Two strums per chord.**
- **Teenager in Love. Four strums per chord.**
- **What's Your Name. Two strums per chord.**
- **Why Do Fools Fall in Love? Two strums per chord.**
- **You Send Me. Two strums per chord.**

Adding Some Spice with Basic 7th Chords

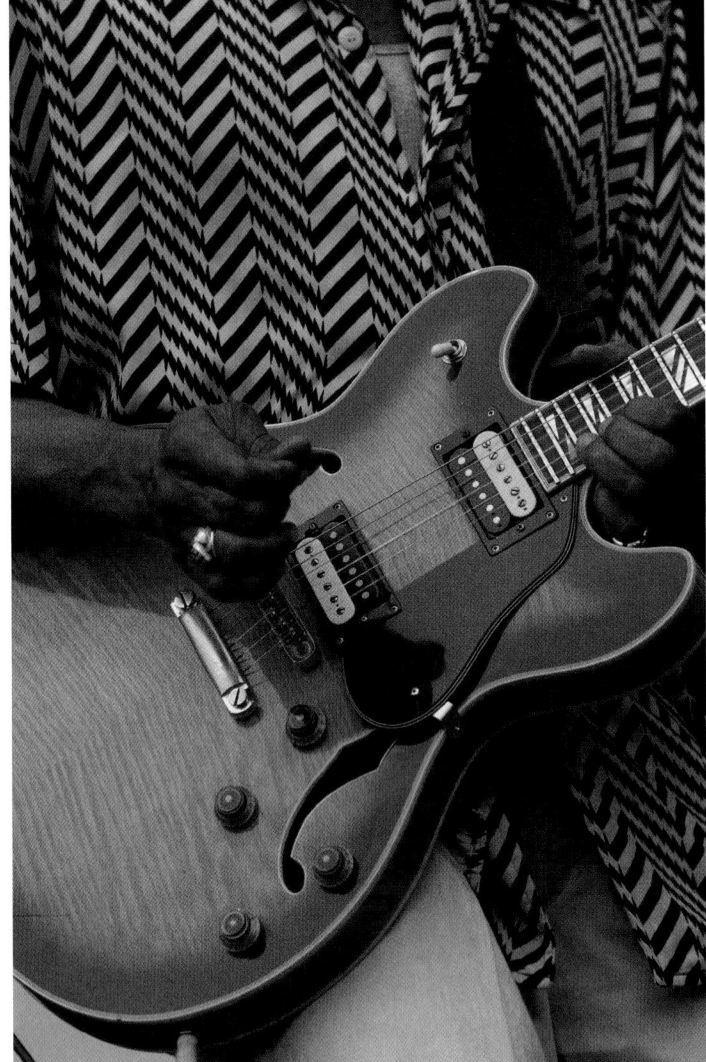

IN THIS ARTICLE

- *Playing dominant, minor, and major 7th chords*
- *Playing songs that use 7th chords*
- *Having some fun with 7th chords*

Here you find out how to play what are known as open-position 7th chords. Seventh chords are no more difficult to play than are the simple major or minor chords, but their sound is more complex than that of major and minor chords (because they're made up of four different notes instead of three), and their usage in music is a little more specialized.

The situation's kind of like that of the knives in your kitchen. Any big, sharp knife can cut a pizza and a pineapple, but if you spend a lot of time doing either, you figure out that you need to use the circular-bladed gizmo for the pizza and a cleaver for the pineapple. These utensils may not be as versatile or as popular as your general-purpose knives, but if you're making Hawaiian-style pizza, nothing beats 'em. The more your culinary skills develop, the more you appreciate specialised cutlery. And the more your ear skills develop, the more you understand where to substitute 7th chords for the more ordinary major and minor chords. The different 7th chords can make the blues sound "bluesy" and jazz sound "jazzy."

Dominant 7th Chords

Dominant seems a funny, technical name for a chord that's called a plain "seven" if you group it with a letter-name chord symbol. If you say just C7 or A7, for example, you're referring to a dominant 7th chord.

Call these chords "dominant 7ths" to distinguish them from other types of 7th chords (minor 7ths and major 7ths). Note, too, that 'dominant' has nothing whatsoever to do with leather and studded collars. You can hear the sound of dominant sevenths in such songs as Sam the Sham and the Pharaohs' "Wooly Bully" and the Beatles' "I Saw Her Standing There."

D7, G7, and C7

The D7, G7, and C7 chords are among the most common of the open dominant 7ths. The diagrams show these three chords, which guitarists often use together to play songs.

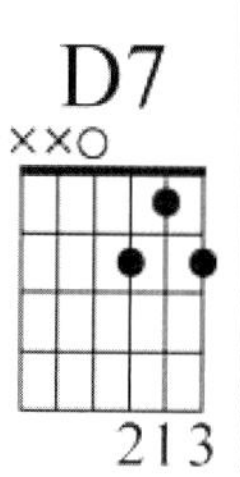

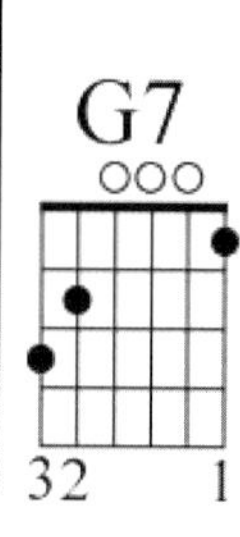

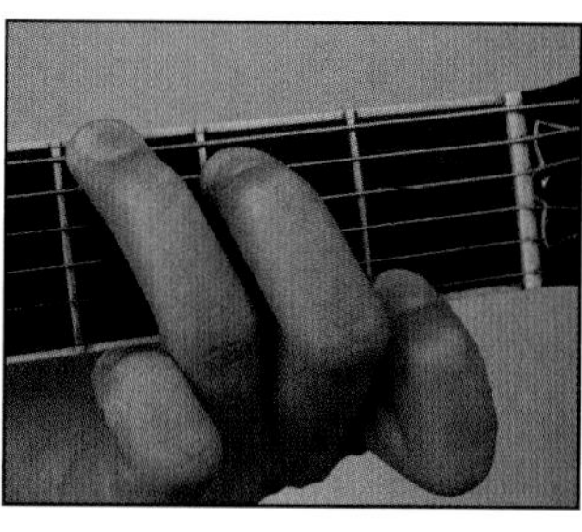

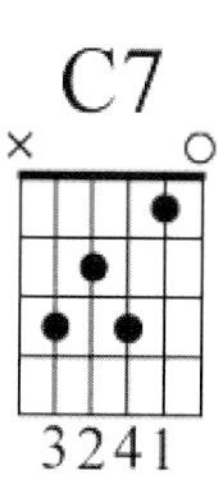

Chord diagrams for D7, G7, and C7.

If you already know how to play C (the previous article shows you how), you can form C7 by simply adding your pinky on the 3rd string (at the third fret).

Notice the Xs above the 5th and 6th strings on the D7 chord. Don't play those strings as you strum. Similarly, for the C7 chord, don't play the 6th string as you strum.

Practise strumming D7, G7, and C7. You don't need written music for this exercise, so you're on the honour system to do it. Try strumming D7 four times, G7 four times, and then C7 four times. You want to accustom your left hand to the feel of the chords themselves and to switching among them.

E7 and A7

Two more 7th chords that you often use together to play songs are the E7 and A7 chords. The diagram shows how you play these two open 7th chords.

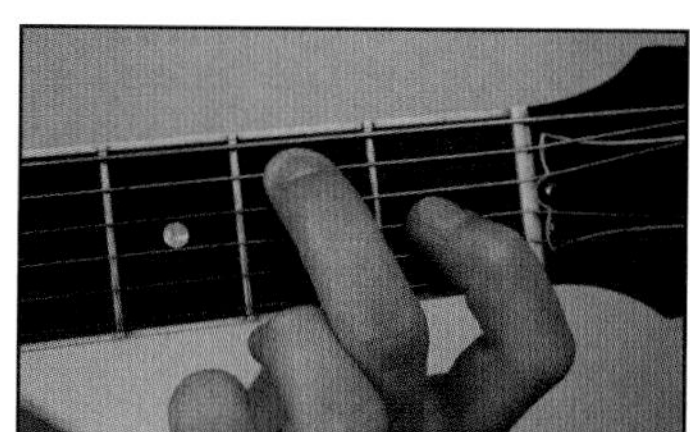

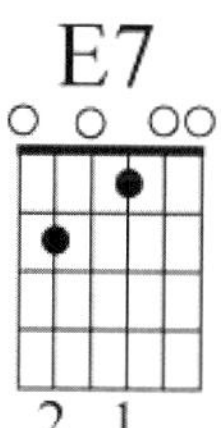

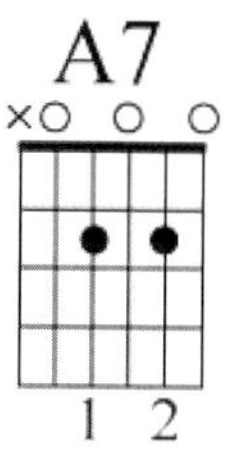

Chord diagrams for E7 and A7.

If you know how to play E (check out the previous article), you can form E7 by simply removing your 3rd finger from the 4th string.

This version of the E7 chord, as the figure shows, uses only two fingers. You can also play an open position E7 chord with four fingers (as we describe in the following section). For now, however, play the two-finger version, because it's easier to fret quickly, especially if you're just starting out.

Practise E7 and A7 by strumming each chord four times, switching back and forth between them. Remember to avoid striking the 6th string on the A7 chord.

E7 (four-finger version) and B7

Two more popular open-position 7th chords are the four-finger version of E7 and the B7 chord. The diagram shows you how to finger the four-finger E7 and the B7 chords. Most people think that this E7 has a better voicing (vertical arrangement of notes) than does the two-finger E7. You often use the B7 chord along with E7 to play certain songs. Remember to avoid striking the 6th string on the B7 chord.

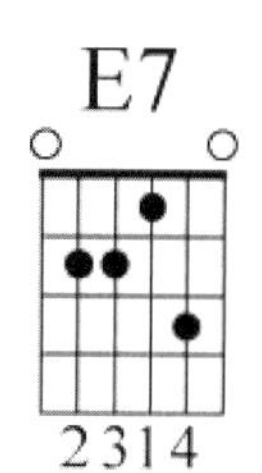

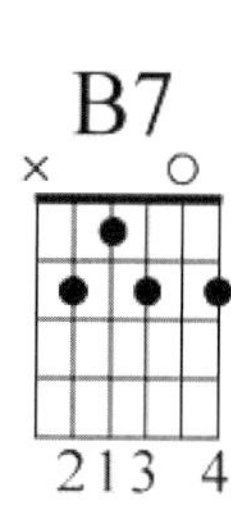

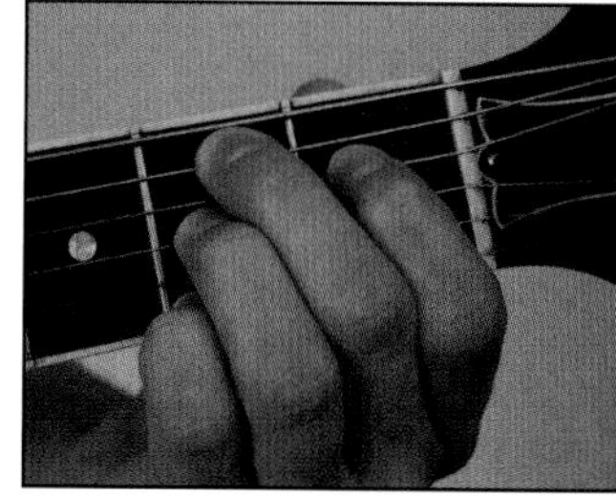

Chord diagrams for E7 (the four-finger version) and B7.

Minor 7th Chords Dm7, Em7, and Am7

Minor 7th chords differ from dominant 7th chords in that their character is a little softer and jazzier. Minor 7th chords are the chords you hear in "Moondance," by Van Morrison, and the verses of "Light My Fire," by the Doors.

The diagrams show the three open-position minor 7th (m7) chords. Notice that the Dm7 uses a two-string barre — that is, you press down two strings with a single finger (the first finger, in this case) at the first fret. Angling your finger slightly or rotating it on its side may help you fret those notes firmly and eliminate any buzzes as you play the chord. The 6th and 5th strings have Xs above them. Don't strike those strings while strumming.

Dm7

××○

211

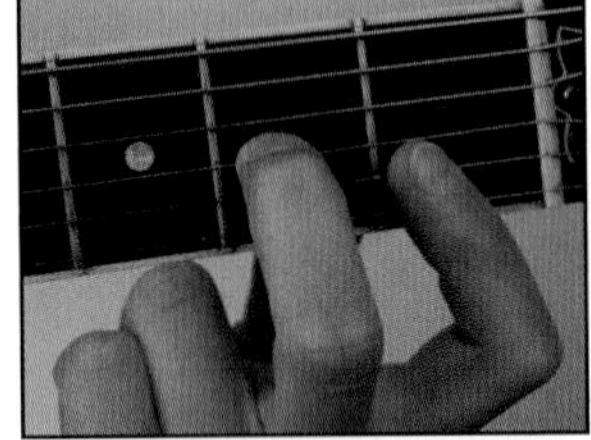

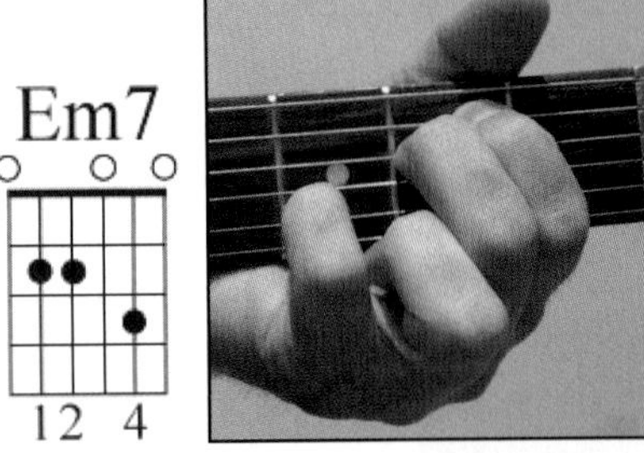

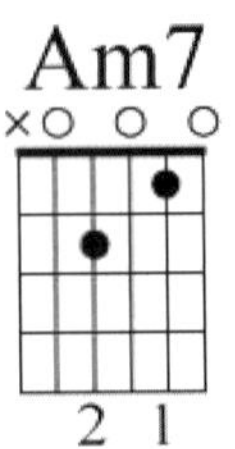

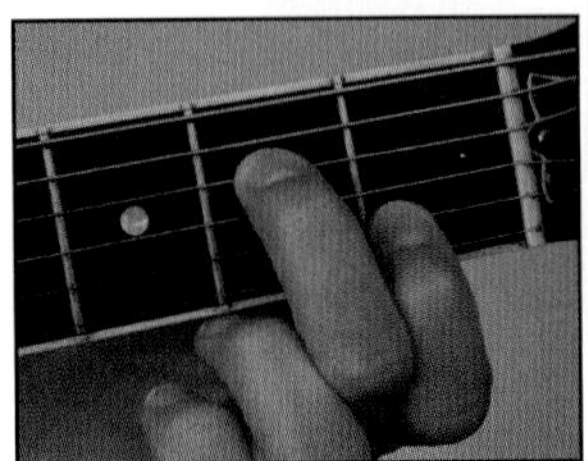

Chord diagrams for Dm7,Em7, and Am7.

You finger the Am7 chord much like you do the C chord that we showed you in the previous article; just lift your third finger off a C chord — and you have Am7. In switching between C and Am7 chords, remember to hold down the two common tones with your first and second fingers. This way, you can switch between the chords much more quickly. And if you know how to play an F chord (see the previous article), you can form Dm7 simply by removing your third finger.

Major 7th Chords Cmaj7, Fmaj7, Amaj7, and Dmaj7

Major 7th chords differ from dominant 7th chords and minor 7th chords in that their character is bright and jazzy. You can hear this kind of chord at the beginning of "Ventura Highway," by America and "Don't Let the Sun Catch You Crying," by Gerry and the Pacemakers.

The diagrams show you four open-position major 7th (maj7) chords. Notice that the Dmaj7 uses a three-string barre with the first finger. Rotating the first finger slightly on its side helps make the chord easier to play. Don't play the 6th or 5th strings as you strike the Dmaj7 or Fmaj7. And don't play the 6th string on the Amaj7 or Cmaj7.

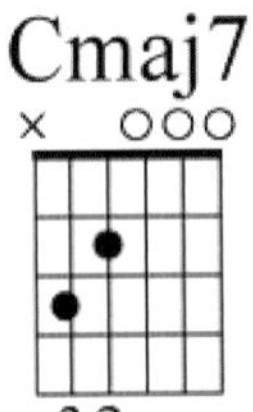

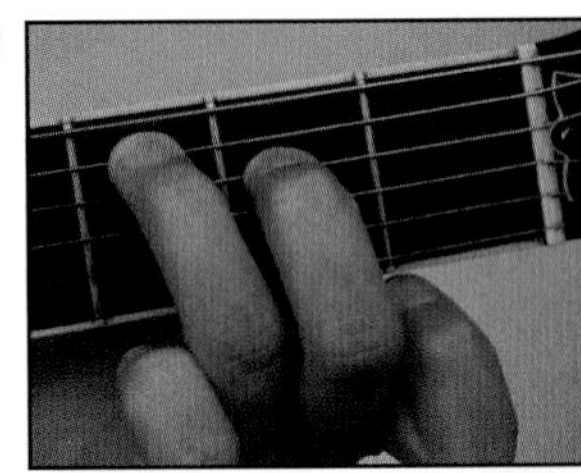

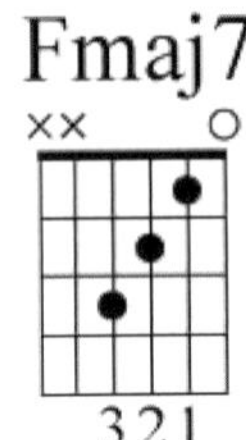

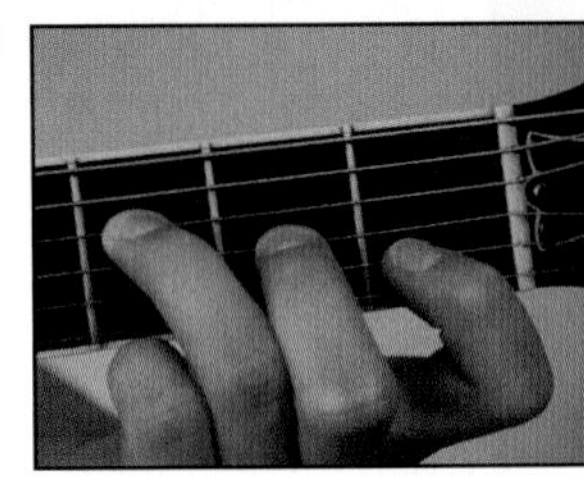

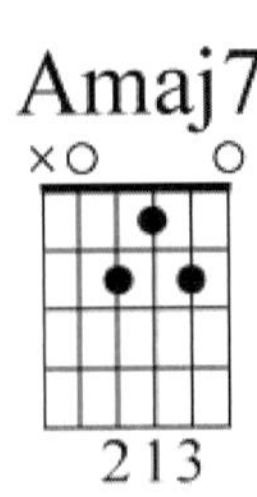

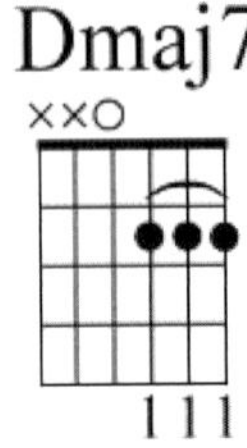

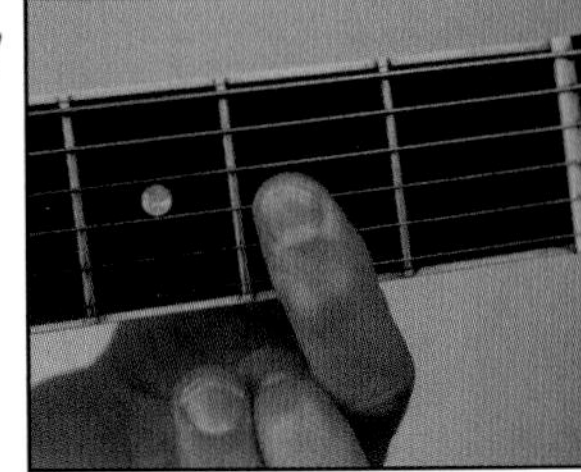

Chord diagrams for Cmaj7,Fmaj7, Amaj7, and Dmaj.

In moving between Cmaj7 and Fmaj7, notice that the second and third fingers move as a fixed shape across the strings in switching between these chords. The first finger doesn't fret any string in a Cmaj7 chord, but keep it curled and poised above the first fret of the 2nd string so that you can bring it down quickly for the switch to Fmaj7.

Practise moving back and forth (strumming four times each) between Cmaj7 and Fmaj7 and between Amaj7 and Dmaj7.

Playing Songs with 7th Chords

The moment you've been waiting for is here: You're equipped to play a song. And at your disposal are not one but two tunes that make use of the knowledge you've acquired (and no more). Here is some useful information about the songs to help you along:

- **Home on the Range**: To play "Home on the Range," you need to know how to play C, C7, F, D7, and G7 chords (see Chapter 4 for the C and F chords and the section "Dominant 7th Chords," earlier in this chapter, for the others); how to play a "bass strum strum" pattern; and how to wail like a coyote.

  In the music, you see the words "Bass strum strum" over the rhythm slashes. Instead of simply strumming the chord for three beats, play only the lowest note of the chord on the first beat and then strum the remaining notes of the chord on beats 2 and 3. The sim. means to keep on playing this pattern throughout.

- **Oh, Susanna**: To play "Oh, Susanna," you need to know how to play Cmaj7, Dm7, Em7, Fmaj7, Am7, D7, Dm7, G7, and C chords (see Chapter 4 for C and various sections earlier in this chapter for the different 7th chords) and how to balance a banjo on your knee while traveling the Southern United States.

  This arrangement of "Oh, Susanna" uses three types of 7th chords: dominant 7ths (D7 and G7), minor 7ths (Dm7, Em7, and Am7), and major 7ths (Cmaj7 and Fmaj7). Using minor 7ths and major 7ths gives the song a hip sound. Lest you think this attempt to "jazz up" a simple folk song comes from out of the blue, listen to James Taylor's beautiful rendition of "Oh, Susanna" on the 1970 album Sweet Baby James to hear a similar approach. He actually says "banjo" without sounding corny. Use all downstrokes on the strums.

Home on the Range

Oh, Susanna

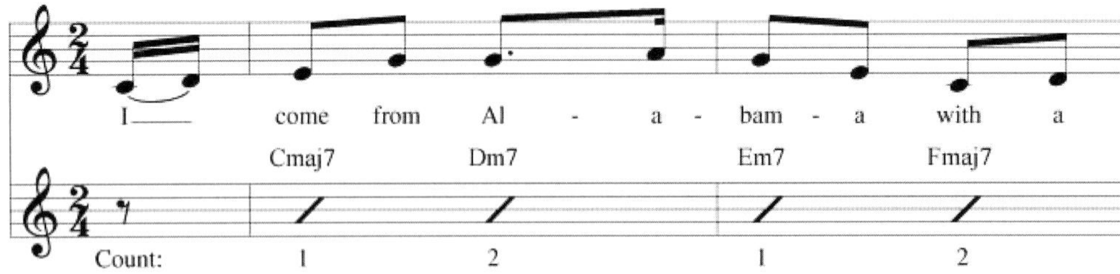
I___ come from Al - a - bam - a with a
Cmaj7 Dm7 Em7 Fmaj7
Count: 1 2 1 2

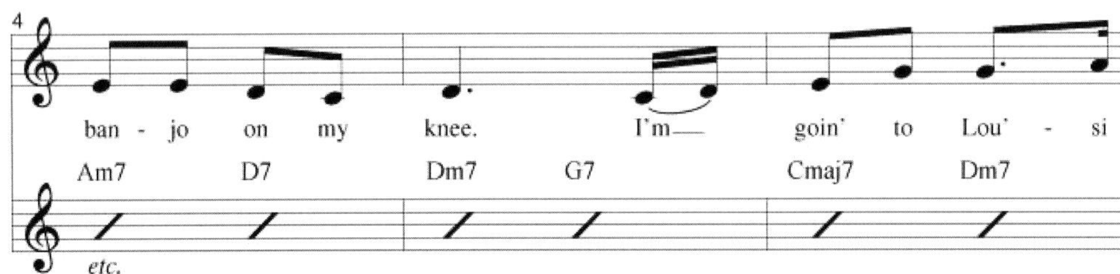
4
ban - jo on my knee. I'm___ goin' to Lou' - si
Am7 D7 Dm7 G7 Cmaj7 Dm7
etc.

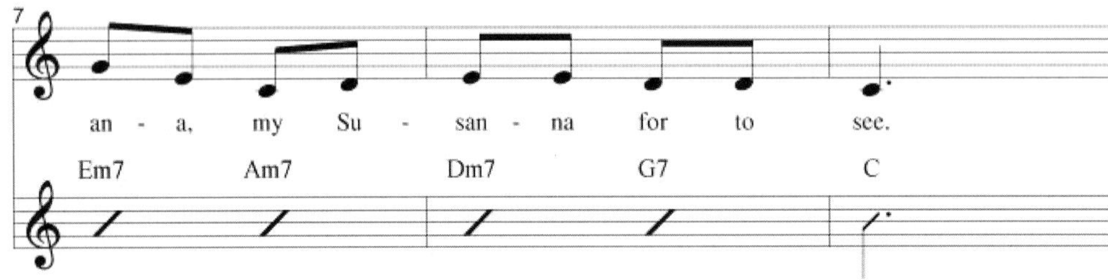
7
an - a, my Su - san - na for to see.
Em7 Am7 Dm7 G7 C

Fun with 7th Chords: The 12-Bar Blues

Playing the guitar isn't all about folk songs and nursery rhymes, you know. Sometimes you can pick up something really cool. And what's cooler than the blues? By knowing a few dominant 7th chords and being able to strum four beats per measure, you already have the basics down pat for playing 99 per cent of all blues songs ever written.

REMEMBER

Ninety-nine per cent?! That's right! The 12-bar blues follow a simple chord formula, or progression, that involves three dominant 7ths. In this progression, you don't need to know any new chords or techniques; you need to know only which three dominant 7th chords to play — and in which order.

Blues guitarist B.B.King.

Playing the 12-bar blues

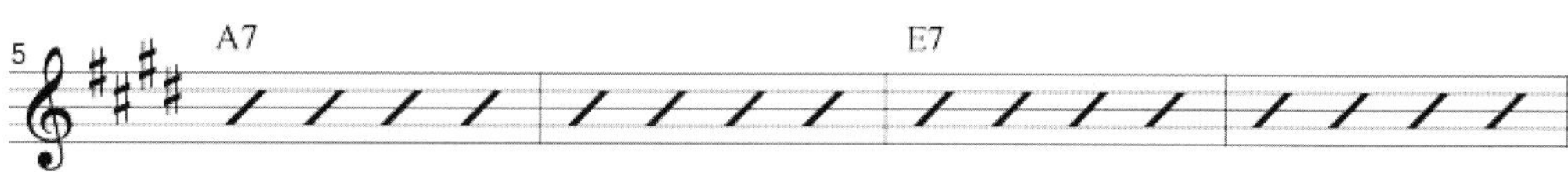

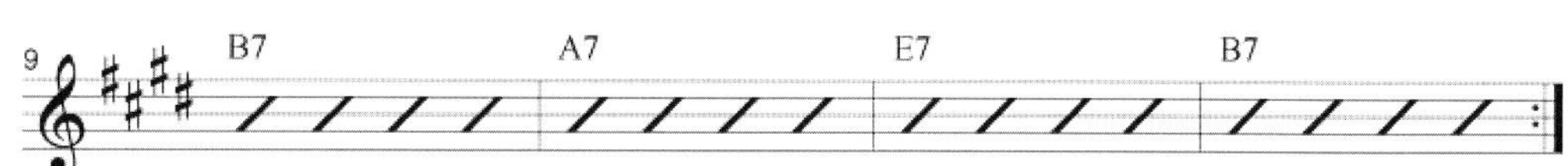

A 12-bar blues progression in E.

Famous 12-bar blues songs include "Rock Around the Clock," "Blue Suede Shoes," "Roll Over Beethoven," "Long Tall Sally," "Kansas City," "The Twist," "The Peppermint Twist," and "Johnny B. Goode." You can play any of these right now just by singing along and observing the 12-bar scheme.

The key of E is one of the best "guitar keys" for playing the blues. The image shows the chord progression to a 12-bar blues in E. Practise this pattern and become familiar with the way chords change in a blues progression.

Writing your own blues song

Blues songs are simple to write lyrics for. (Just think of any Little Richard song.) Usually you repeat lines and then finish off with a zinger — for example:

> My baby she done left me, and she stole my best friend Joe. My baby she done left me, and she stole my best friend Joe. Now I'm all alone and cryin', 'cause I miss him so.

Try composing some lyrics yourself, improvise a melody, and apply them to the blues progression that we outline here.

As a rule, a good blues song must include the following elements:

- A subject dealing with hardship or injustice.
- A locale or situation conducive to misery.
- Bad grammar.

Use the following table to find mix-and match elements for your blues songs

Song Element	Good Blues	Bad Blues
Subject	Treachery, infidelity, your mojo	Rising interest rates, an impending market correction, the scarcity of good help
Locale	Memphis, the Bayou, prison	Guildford, Regent Street, Wimpy
Grammar	"My baby done me wrong."	"My life-partner has been insensitive to my needs."

Why not compose one yourself? Call it the "Left-Hand Callus Blues" and talk about how them bad ol' strings put a big hurtin' on your fingertips.

Playing Melodies in Position and in Double-Stops

IN THIS ARTICLE

- *Playing single notes in position*
- *Playing double-stops as string pairs*
- *Playing double-stops across the neck*

One of the give-aways of beginning players is that they can play only down the neck, in open position, and that they play only single-string melodies. As you get to know the guitar better, you find you can use the whole neck to express your musical ideas, and that you're not limited to plunking out just single notes.

Venture out of open-position base camp into the higher altitudes of position playing! Here you find out how, and you also pick up the technique of playing in double-stops along the way.

Playing in Position

As you listen to complicated-sounding guitar music played by virtuoso guitarists, you may imagine their left hands leaping around the fretboard with abandon. But usually, if you watch those guitarists on stage or TV, you discover that their left hands hardly move at all. Those guitarists are playing in position.

REMEMBER

Playing in position means that your left hand remains in a fixed location on the neck, with each finger more or less on permanent assignment to a specific fret, and that you fret every note - you don't use any open strings. If you're playing in fifth position, for example, your first finger plays the fifth fret, your second finger plays the sixth fret, your third finger plays the seventh fret, and your fourth finger plays the eighth fret. A position, therefore, gets its name from the fret that your first finger plays.

In addition to enabling you to play notes where they feel and sound best on the fingerboard - not just where you can most easily grab available notes (such as the open-string notes in open position), playing in position makes you look cool - like a nonbeginner! Think of it this way: A tap-in and a thirty-yard volley are both worth one goal in football, but only in the latter case does the commentator scream, "And the crowd goes wild!"

Playing in position versus playing with open strings

Why play in position? Why not use open position and open strings all the time? We can give you two key reasons:

- **It's easier to play high-note melodies.** Playing in open position allows you to play only up to the fourth or fifth fret. If you want to play higher than that, position playing enables you to play the notes smoothly and economically.
- **You can instantly transpose any pattern or phrase that you know in position to another key simply by moving your hand to another position.** Because position playing involves no open strings, everything you play in position is movable.

People have the idea that playing guitar in lower positions is easier than playing in higher ones. The higher notes actually aren't harder to play; they're just harder to read in standard notation if you don't get too far in a conventional method book (where reading high notes is usually saved till last). But here, you're not focusing on music reading but on guitar playing — so go for the high notes whenever you want.

Playing exercises in position

The major scale (you know, the familiar do-re-me-fa-sol-la-ti-do sound you get by playing the white keys on the piano starting from C) is a good place to start practising the skills you need to play in position. Here's a C major scale in second position. Although you can play this scale in open position, play it as the tab staff in the figure indicates, because you want to start practising your position playing.

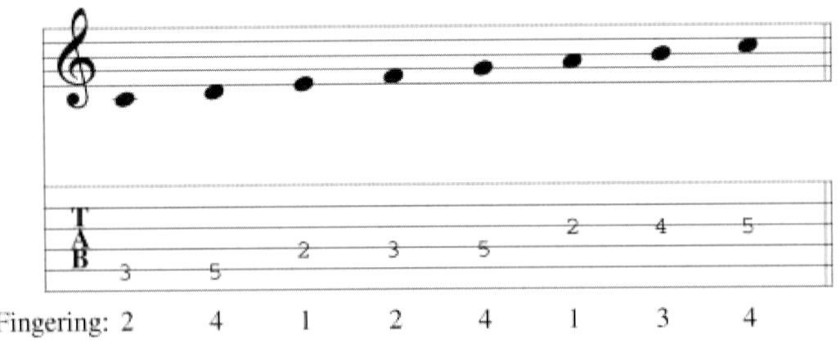

A one-octave C-major scale in second position.

The most important thing about playing in position is the location of your left hand — in particular, the position and placement of the fingers of your left hand. The following list contains tips for positioning your left hand and fingers:

- **Keep your fingers over the appropriate frets the entire time you're playing**. Because you're in second position for this scale, keep your first finger over the second fret, your second finger over the third fret, your third finger over the fourth fret, and your fourth finger over the fifth fret at all times — even if they're not fretting any notes at the moment.
- **Keep all your fingers close to the fretboard, ready to play.** At first, your fingers may exhibit a tendency to straighten out and rise away from the fretboard. This tendency is natural, so work to keep them curled and to hold them down over the frets where they belong for the position.
- **Relax!** Although you may think that you need to intensely focus all your energy on performing this manoeuvre correctly or positioning that finger just so, you don't. What you're actually working toward is simply adopting the most natural and relaxed approach to playing the guitar. Remember to take frequent deep breaths, especially if you feel yourself tightening up.

Notice that the score indicates left-hand fingerings under the tab numbers. These indicators aren't essential because the position itself dictates these fingerings. But if you want, you can read the finger numbers (instead of the tab numbers) and play the C scale that way (keeping an eye on the tab staff to check which string you're on). Then, if you memorize the fingerings, you have a movable pattern that enables you to play a major scale in any key.

Play the one-octave scale (one having a range of only eight notes) by using both up- and downstrokes - that is, by using alternate (up and down) picking. Try it descending as well (you should practice all scales ascending and descending). This scale is the familiar *do-re-mi-fa-sol-la-ti-do*.

Play scales slowly at first to ensure that your notes sound clean and smooth; then gradually increase your speed.

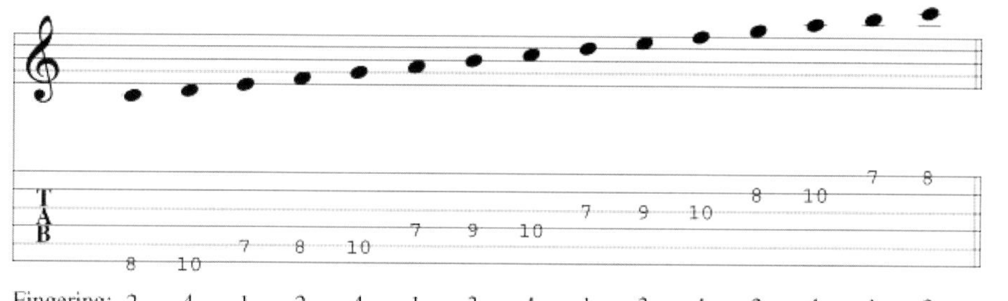

A two-octave C-major scale in seventh position.

Here's a two-octave C-major scale (one with a range of 15 notes) in the seventh position. Notice that this scale requires you to play on all six strings.

To help you remember to hold your fingers over the appropriate frets all the time, even if they're not playing at the moment, and keep your fingers close to the fretboard, we have a twist on an old expression: Keep your friends close, your enemies closer, and your frets even closer than that.

Practise playing the two-octave scale up and down the neck, using alternate picking. If you memorize the fingering pattern (shown under the tab numbers), you can play any major scale simply by moving your hand up or down to a different position. Try it. And then challenge the nearest piano player to a transposing (key-changing) contest using the major scale.

Shifting positions

Music isn't so simple that you can play it all in one position, and life would be pretty static if you could. In real-world situations, you must often play an uninterrupted passage that takes you through different positions. To do so successfully, you need to master the position shift with the aplomb of an old politician.

Andrés Segovia, legend of the classical guitar, devised fingerings for all 12 major and minor scales. Here's how Segovia played the two-octave C-major scale. It differs from the two scales in the preceding section in that it requires a position shift in the middle of the scale.

A two-octave C-major scale with a position shift.

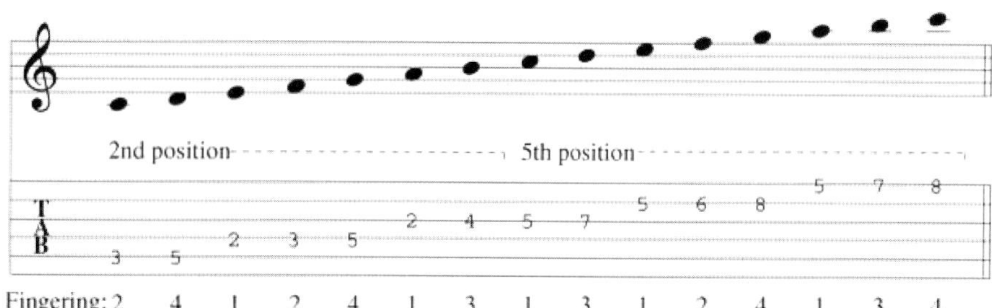

Play the first seven notes in second position and then shift up to fifth position by smoothly gliding your first finger up to the fifth fret (third string). As you play the scale downward, play the first eight notes in fifth position, and then shift to second position by smoothly gliding your third finger down to the fourth fret (third string). The important thing is that the position shift sounds seamless.

Someone listening shouldn't be able to tell that you shift positions. The trick is in the smooth gliding of the first (while ascending) or third (while descending) finger.

You must practise this smooth glide to make it sound uninterrupted and seamless. Isolate just the two notes involved (3rd string, fourth fret, and 3rd string, fifth fret) and play them over and over as shown in the scale until you can make them sound as if you're making no position shift at all.

Building strength and dexterity by playing in position

Some people do all sorts of exercises to develop their position playing. They buy books that contain nothing but position-playing exercises. Some of these books aim to develop sight-reading skills, and others aim to develop left-hand finger strength and dexterity.

But you don't really need such books. You can make up your own exercises to build finger strength and dexterity. (And sight-reading doesn't concern you now anyway, because you're reading tab numbers.)

To create your own exercises, just take the two-octave major scale shown earlier in this article and number the 15 notes of the scale as 1 to 15. Then make up a few simple mathematical combinations that you can practise playing. Following are some examples:

- **1-2-3-1, 2-3-4-2, 3-4-5-3, 4-5-6-4, and so on.**
- **1-3-2-4, 3-5-4-6, 5-7-6-8, 7-9-8-10, and so on.**
- **15-14-13, 14-13-12, 13-12-11, 12-11-10, and so on.**

Here's how these numbers look in music and tab. Remember, these notes are just suggested patterns to memorise and help build dexterity.

Three examples of patterns to help build up the left hand.

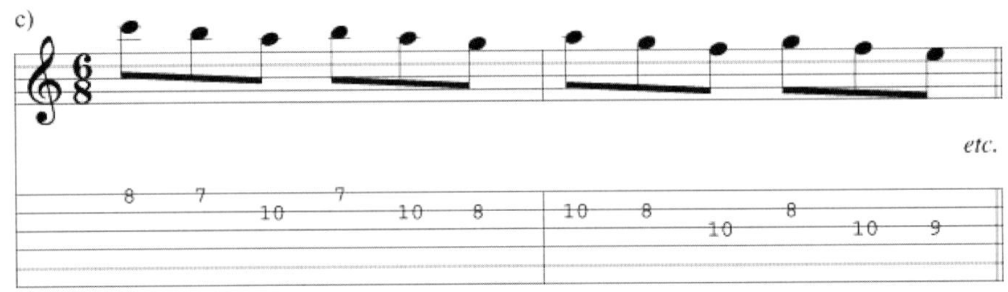

You get the idea. You can make up literally hundreds of permutations and practise them endlessly — or until you get bored.

Double-Stops

The term double-stop doesn't refer to going back to the shop because you forgot milk. Double-stop is guitar lingo for playing two notes at once - something the guitar can do with relative ease but that's impossible on woodwinds and only marginally successful on bowed string instruments. By the way, you do nothing special in fretting the notes of a double-stop. Fret them the same way that you do chords or single notes.

You experience the guitar's capability to play more than one note simultaneously as you strum a chord, but you can also play more than one note in a melodic context. Playing double-stops is a great way to play in harmony with yourself. So adept is the guitar at playing double-stops, in fact, that some musical forms - such as 50s rock 'n' roll, country, and Mariachi music (you know, the music that Mexican street bands play) - use double-stops as a hallmark of their styles.

Understanding double-stops

A double-stop is nothing more than two notes that you play at the same time. It falls somewhere between a single note (one note) and a chord (three or more notes). You can play a double-stop on adjacent strings or on nonadjacent strings (by skipping strings). The examples here involve only adjacent-string double-stops, because they're the easiest to play.

If you play a melody in double-stops, it sounds sweeter and richer, fuller and prettier than if you play it by using only single notes. And if you play a riff in double-stops, it sounds gutsier and fuller — the double-stops just create a bigger sound. Check out some Chuck Berry riffs — "Johnny B. Goode," for example — and you can hear that he uses double-stops all the time.

Playing exercises in double-stops

You can play double-stop passages using only one pair of strings (the first two strings, for example) — moving the double-stops up and down the neck — or in one area of the neck by using different string pairs and moving the double-stops across the neck (first playing the 5th and 4th strings, for example, and then the 4th and 3rd, and so on).

Playing double-stops up and down the neck

Start with a C-major scale that you play in double-stop thirds (notes that are two letter names apart, such as C-E, D-F, and so on), exclusively on the first two strings, moving up the neck. Check out this type of double-stop pattern here.

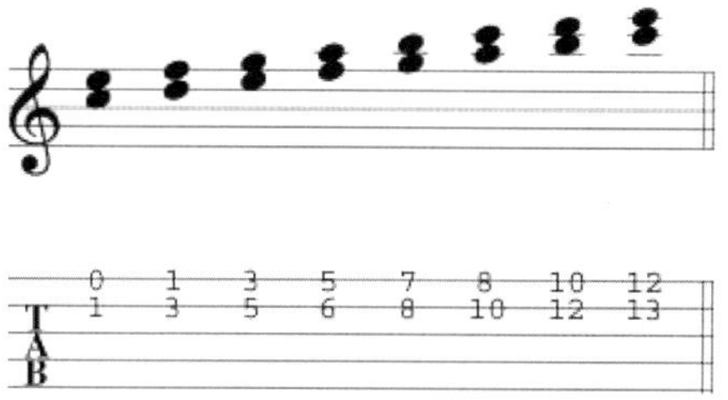

A C-major scale that you play in double-stops, moving up the neck on one pair of strings.

The left-hand fingering doesn't appear below the tab numbers in this score, but that's not difficult to figure out. Start with your first finger for the first double-stop. (You need only one finger to fret this first double-stop because the 1st string remains open.) Then, for all the other double-stops in the scale, use fingers 1 and 3 if the notes are two frets apart (the second and third double-stops, for example) and use fingers 1 and 2 if the notes are one fret apart (the fourth and fifth double-stops, for example). With your right hand, strike only the 1st and 2nd strings.

Playing double-stops across the neck

Playing double-stops across the neck is probably more common than playing up and down the neck on a string pair. Here's a C-major scale that you play in thirds in open position, moving across the neck.

A C-major scale that you play in double-stops, moving across the neck in open position.

What's especially common in rock and blues songs is playing double-stops across the neck where the two notes that make up the double-stop are on the same fret (which you play as a two-string barre).

Again, the example doesn't show the fingerings for each double-stop. But you can use fingers 1 and 2 if the notes are one fret apart and fingers 1 and 3 if the notes are two frets apart.

To hear double-stops in action, listen to the opening of Jimmy Buffett's "Margaritaville," Leo Kottke's version of the Allman Brothers' "Little Martha," Van Morrison's "Brown-Eyed Girl," Chuck Berry's "Johnny B. Goode," and the intros to Simon and Garfunkel's "Homeward Bound" and "Bookends."

10 Guitarists you should know

Regardless of style, certain guitarists have made their mark on the world of guitar so that any guitarist who comes along after them has a hard time escaping their legacy. We present here, in chronological order, ten who mattered and why they mattered.

CHARLIE CHRISTIAN *(1916-1942)*

Charlie Christian invented the art of electric jazz guitar. His fluid solos with Benny Goodman's big band and smaller combos were sophisticated, scintillating, and years ahead of their time. After hours, he used to jam with fellow jazz rebels at Minton's in New York, where his adventurous improvisations helped create the genre known as bebop. Christian played the guitar like a horn, incorporating intervallic (non-stepwise) motion into his lines. His signature tunes include "I Found a New Baby" and "I Got Rhythm."

B.B. KING *(1925-)*

Although he wasn't the first electric bluesman, B.B. King is easily the most popular: His swinging, high-voltage guitar style complements charismatic stagemanship and a huge, gospel-fueled voice. Along with his trademark ES-355 guitar, nicknamed "Lucille," King's minimalist soloing technique and massive finger vibrato has cemented his place in the annals of electric blues history. His signature tunes include "Every Day I Have the Blues" and "The Thrill Is Gone."

JIMI HENDRIX *(1942-1970)*

Considered the greatest rock guitarist of all time, Hendrix fused R&B, blues, rock, and psychedelia into a mesmerizing sonic soup. His 1967 breakthrough at the Monterey Pop Festival instantly rewrote the rock guitar textbook, especially after he whipped off his Stratocaster and lit it on fire. Young guitarists religiously copy his licks to this day. Hendrix was known for his fiery abandon (even when his guitar wasn't actually on fire) and innovative work with feedback and the whammy bar. His signature tunes include "Purple Haze" and "Little Wing."

EDDIE VAN HALEN *(1955-)*

Rock guitar's equivalent to Jackson Pollock, Eddie Van Halen's splatter-note approach to metal guitar completely reinvented the style starting in the late '70s. He turned two-handed tapping into a common guitar technique (thanks to his groundbreaking "Eruption"), while pushing the limits of whammy-bar and hammer-on expertise. He is also a master at fusing blues-based rock with modern techniques, and his rhythm playing is one of the best examples of the integrated style (combining low-note riffs with chords and double-stops). A guitar hero in every sense of the term, his signature tunes include "Eruption" and "Panama."

JIMMY PAGE *(1944-)*

Page succeeded Eric Clapton and Jeff Beck in the Yardbirds, but he didn't really find his niche until forming Led Zeppelin, one of the great '70s rock bands. Page's forte was the art of recording guitars, layering track upon track to construct thundering avalanches of electrified tone. Yet he could also play sublime acoustic guitar, regularly employing unusual tunings and global influences. In rock circles, his six-string creativity in the studio is unmatched. His signature tunes include "Stairway to Heaven" and "Whole Lotta Love."

ANDRES SEGOVIA *(1893-1987)*

Not only was Segovia the most famous classical guitarist of all time, but he also literally invented the genre. Before his arrival, the guitar was a lowly instrument of the peasant classes. Segovia began performing Bach pieces and other serious classical music on the guitar (writing many of his own transcriptions), eventually elevating this "parlour" activity to a world-class style. His incredible performing career lasted more than 70 years. His signature pieces include Bach's "Chaconne" and Albeniz's "Granada."

CHET ATKINS *(1942-2001)*

Known as "Mr. Guitar," Atkins is the definitive country guitarist. Building on Merle Travis' fast fingerpicking technique, Atkins refined the style, adding jazz, classical, and pop nuances to create a truly sophisticated country-guitar approach. He's played with Elvis Presley, the Everly Brothers, and countless country stars over the decades. His signature tunes include "Stars and Stripes Forever" and "Yankee Doodle Dixie."

WES MONTGOMERY *(1925-1968)*

A legendary jazz player, Wes's brand of cool jazz was based on the fact that he used his thumb to sound notes, instead of a traditional guitar pick. Another of his innovations was the use of octaves (that is, two identical notes in different ranges) to create fat, moving, unison lines. He died young, but his proponents still call him one of the all-time jazz greats. His signature tunes include "Four on Six" and "Polka Dots and Moonbeams."

CHUCK BERRY *(1926-)*

Perhaps rock's first real guitar hero, Berry used fast, rhythmic double-stops to create his signature guitar style. Although some regard him equally for his songwriting and lyric-writing skills, his fire-breathing breaks made his signature tunes "Johnny B. Goode," "Rockin' in the U.S.A.," and "Maybelline," bona fide guitar classics.

ERIC CLAPTON *(1945-)*

In many ways, Clapton is the father of contemporary rock guitar. Before Hendrix, Beck, and Page showed up, the Yardbirds-era Clapton was already fusing electric Chicago blues with the fury of rock 'n' roll. He later expanded upon this style in Cream, Blind Faith, and the legendary Derek and the Dominoes. Clapton eventually went solo, turning into one of the most popular recording artists of the last 20 years. A true living legend, his signature tunes include "Crossroads" and "Layla."

Stretching Out: The E-Based Barre Chords

IN THIS ARTICLE

- *Playing major barre chords based on E*
- *Playing more E-based barre chords*

Unlike open-position chords, which can be played only in one place, movable chords can be played at any fret. In most of these movable chords, you play what's called a barre (pronounced "bar"). Movable barre chords are either E-based, getting their names from the notes that you play on the 6th (low E) string, or A-based, getting their names from the notes that you play on the 5th (A) string. (The next article shows you A-based barre chords.)

As you play a barre, one of your left-hand fingers (usually the index) presses down all or most of the strings at a certain fret, enabling the remaining fingers to play a chord form immediately above (toward the body of the guitar) the barre finger. Think of your barre finger as a sort of movable nut or capo and your remaining fingers as playing certain open-position chord forms directly above it. A movable barre chord contains no open strings - only fretted notes. You can slide these fretted notes up or down the neck to different positions to produce other chords of the same quality.

Playing Major Barre Chords Based on E

One of the most useful movable barre chords is the one based on the open E chord. The best way to get a grip on this barre chord is to start out with an open-position E chord.

Follow these steps:

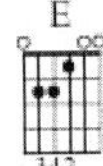

1. **Play an open E chord, but instead of using the normal 2-3-1 left-hand fingering, use fingers 3-4-2.**

   This fingering leaves your first (index) finger free, hovering above the strings.

2. **Lay your first finger down across all six strings on the other side of the nut (the side toward the tuning pegs).**

   Placing your index finger across the strings at this location doesn't affect the sound of the chord because the strings don't vibrate on that side of the nut. Extending your first finger across the width of the nut, however, helps you get the "feel" of a barre chord position. Don't press too hard with any of your fingers, because you're going to move the chord.

3. **Take the entire left-hand shape from Step 2 and slide it up (toward the body of the guitar) one fret so that your first finger is barring the first fret and your E-chord fingers have all advanced up a fret as well.**

   You're now in an F-chord position (because F is one fret higher than E), and you can press down across all the strings with your index finger.

4. **Try playing the notes of the chord one string at a time (from the 6th string to the 1st) to see whether all the notes ring out clearly.**

   The first few times you try this chord, the chances are pretty good that some of the notes aren't going to ring clearly and that your left-hand fingers are going to hurt.

The photo shows how you end up.

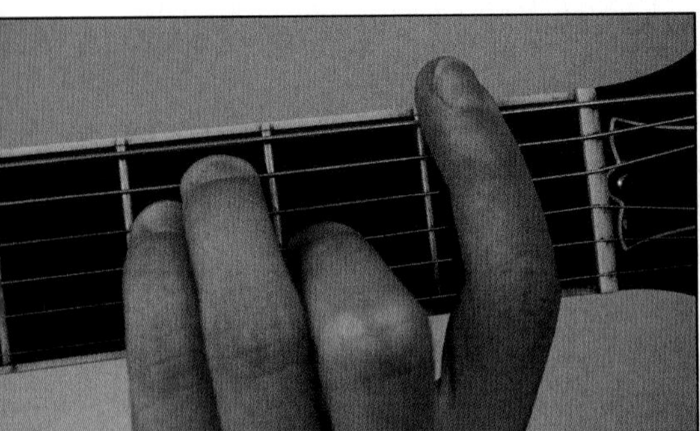

The insidious F barre chord.

You can use this "sliding up from an open-position chord" technique to form all the barre chords in this chapter. (But we also provide you with another approach in later sections.)

Having difficulty at first in creating a barre F is normal (discouraging maybe, but normal). So before you give up on the guitar and take up the sousaphone, here are some tips to help you nail this vexing chord:

- **Make sure that you line up your left-hand thumb on the back of the guitar neck under the spot between your first and second fingers.** This position gives you maximum leverage while exerting pressure.
- **Instead of holding your first finger totally flat, rotate it a little onto its side.**
- **Move the elbow of your left arm in close to your body, even to the point that it's touching your body at the waist.** As you play open-position chords, you find that you usually hold your elbow slightly away from your body. Not so with full barre chords.
- **If you hear muffled strings, check to see that your left-hand fingers are touching only the appropriate strings and not preventing adjacent ones from ringing.** Try exerting more pressure with the fingers and make sure to play on the very tips for extra clearance. Calluses and experience help you get a clear sound from a barre chord.

You need to exert more pressure to fret at the bottom of the neck (at the first fret) than you do at, say, the fifth fret. Try moving your F chord up and down the neck to different frets on the guitar to prove to yourself that playing the chord gets easier as you move up the neck. Remember that the essence of this chord form is that it's movable. Unlike what your elementary school teachers may have told you, don't sit so still! Move around already!

Playing barre chords on an electric guitar is easier than playing them on an acoustic guitar. The string gauges (the thickness of the strings) are lighter on an electric guitar and the action (distance of the strings to the fretboard) is lower than on an acoustic. If you're using an acoustic and you're having trouble with barre chords, try playing them on an electric (but not one of those el-cheapo ones from the second-hand shop) and take note of the difference. Doing so may inspire you to keep at it.

Finding the right fret

Because you can play an F chord as a barre chord, you can now, through the miracle of movable chords, play every major chord — all 12 of them — simply by moving up the neck. To determine the name of each chord, you simply have to know what note name you're playing on the 6th (low E) string — because all E-based barre chords get their name from the 6th string (just as the open E chord does).

Remember that each fret is a half step away from each adjacent fret. So if a first-fret barre chord is F, the second-fret barre chord is F♯; the third-fret chord is G; the fourth fret is G♯; and so on through to the twelfth fret.

After you reach the twelfth fret, the notes — and thus the barre chords that you play at those frets — repeat: The thirteenth-fret barre chord is the same as the first (F); the fourteenth is the same as the second (F♯); and so on. The frets work sort of like a clock: 13 equals 1, 14 equals 2, and so on.

Playing progressions using major barre chords based on E

A good way to build your comfort and confidence in playing barre chords is by practising a progression, which is a series of chords. The notation shows a four-measure progression using E-based major barre chords. Below the staff, you see the correct first-finger fret for each chord.

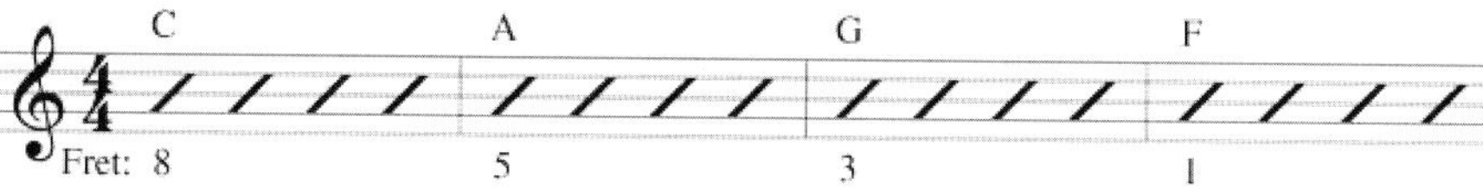

A progression using E-based major barre chords.

Use only barre chords for this exercise (and for all the exercises in this article), even if you know how to play these chords as open-position chords. Play the C chord, for example, by barring at the eighth fret. Then play A at the fifth fret, G at the third fret, and F at the first fret. Use the F-chord fingering for all these chords.

Trying to make all six strings ring out clearly on each chord can get a little tiring. You can give your left-hand fingers a break by releasing pressure as you slide from one chord to the next. This action of flexing and releasing can help you develop a little finesse and keep you from tiring so easily. You don't need to keep a Vulcan Death Grip on the neck all the time - only while you're strumming the chord.

Although you can stop altogether if your hand starts to cramp, try to keep at it; as with any physical endeavour, you eventually build up your strength and stamina. Without question, barre chords are the triathlon of guitar playing, so strap on your best Ironman regalia and feel the burn.

To demonstrate the versatility of barre-chord progressions, here's an example that has a syncopated strum and sounds a little like the music of the Kinks. In syncopation, you either strike a chord (or note) where you don't expect to hear it or fail to strike a chord (or note) where you do expect to hear it. (The Kinks, in case you don't recall, were the English proto-punk band of the '60s, who gave us such classic hits as "You Really Got Me," "So Tired," and "Lola.").

The notation shows you how to play this progression by using major barre chords. Because the two chords move back and forth so quickly, the release time (the period during which you can relax your fingers) is very short.

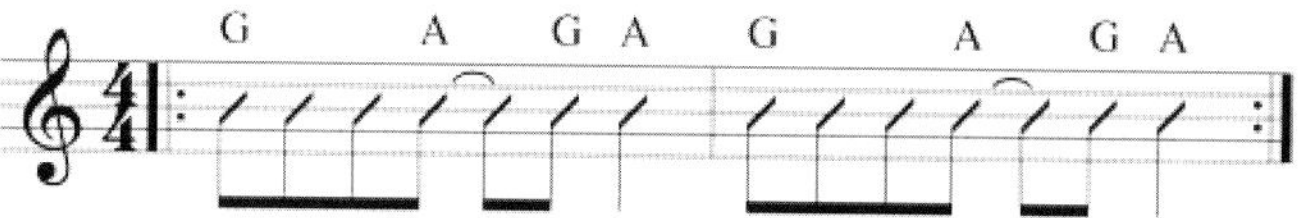

A syncopated progression using E-based major barre chords.

Playing Minor, Dominant 7th, and Minor 7th Barre Chords Based on E

After you're familiar with the basic feel and movement of the major barre chords, start adding other chord qualities into your repertoire (which is a fancy French word for "bag of tricks" that musicians frequently use in discussing their music).

The good news is that everything you know about moving chords around the neck — getting a clear, ringing tone out of the individual notes in the chord (you are practising, aren't you?) and the flex-and-release action that you use in playing major barre chords — carries over to the other forms of barre chords. Playing a minor, a 7th, or a minor 7th barre form is no more physically difficult than playing a major barre, so as you practise all the various barre chords, you should start to notice things getting a little easier.

Minor chords

Forming an E-based minor barre chord is similar to forming a major barre chord, as we explain in the steps in the section "Playing Major Barre Chords Based on E," earlier in this article. You can follow that set of steps, starting with an open Em chord but fingering it with fingers 3-4. Next, lay your first finger across all the strings on the other side of the nut and then slide the shape up one fret, producing an Fm chord.

The following simple steps describe another way to approach the Fm barre chord:

F
134211

1. **Play an F major barre chord.**

   See the section "Playing Major Barre Chords Based on E," earlier in this article.

Fm
134111

2. **Remove your second finger from the 3rd string.**

   The first-finger barre, which is already pressing down all the strings, now frets the new note on the 3rd string.

That's all you need to do. You instantly change a major barre chord to a minor barre chord by removing just one finger. Now you can play any of the 12 minor chords by moving the Fm chord to the appropriate fret. To play an Am barre chord, for example, you just move the barre to the fifth fret.

If you're not sure whether you're playing a barre chord on the correct fret, try alternating the chord with its open-position form, playing first the barre and then the open form. Play the two versions in rapid succession several times. You can then hear whether the two chords are the same or different.

Try playing this simple progression, which uses both major and minor barre chords.

A progression using both major and minor barre chords.

The dots above the slashes in bars 2 and 4 are called staccato marks. They tell you to cut the notes short. (Instead of playing daahh-daahh-daahh, play di-di-di.) The best way to cut these notes short is to slightly release your left-hand finger pressure right after you strum the chord. The symbols at the end of the measures 2 and 4 are called rests. Don't play during a rest.

Now try playing the progression two frets higher than the figure indicates. This two-fret variation gives you a D-Bm-Gm-A progression. You've just transposed (changed the key of) the progression quickly and easily — through the magic of movable chords!

Dominant 7th chords

Dominant 7th chords have a sharper, more complex sound than do straight major chords. Switching to a barre dominant 7th chord from a major barre chord, however, is just as easy as switching from a major to a minor barre chord — you just lift a single (although different) finger.

To change an F major barre chord into an F7 barre chord, follow these steps:

1. **Finger an F major barre chord, as we describe in the section "Playing Major Barre Chords Based on E," earlier in this article.**

2. **Remove your fourth finger from the 4th string.**

   The first-finger barre now frets the chord's new note.

Try playing this simple progression using major and dominant 7th barre chords

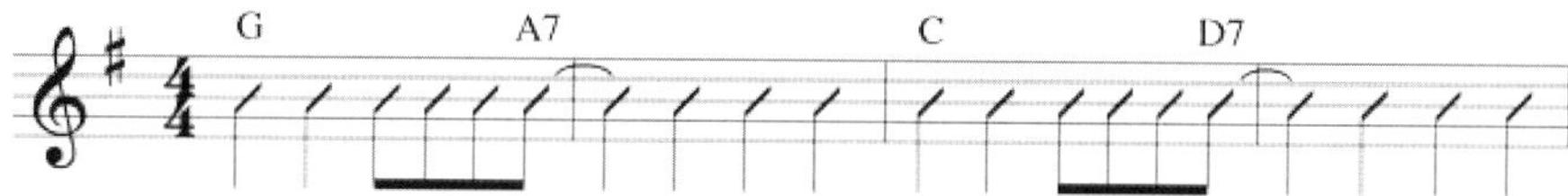

A progression using major and 7th barre chords.

Playing the progression in different keys is as simple as starting in a different location from the third fret and moving the same distance. From wherever you start, simply move up two frets for the second chord, up three more frets for the third chord, and then up two more frets for the fourth and last chord.

Minor 7th chords

Minor 7th chords have a softer, jazzier, and more complex sound than straight minor chords do. You can form a minor 7th E-based barre chord by simply combining the actions you take to change major to minor and major to dominant 7th.

To change an F major barre chord into an Fm7 barre chord, follow these steps:

1. **Play an F major barre chord, as we describe in the section "Playing Major Barre Chords Based on E," earlier in this chapter.**

2. **Remove your second finger from the 3rd string and your fourth finger from the 4th string.**

   The first-finger barre, which is already pressing down all the strings, frets the new notes on the 3rd and 4th strings.

To help you get accustomed to minor 7th barre chords, we put together the following exercise.

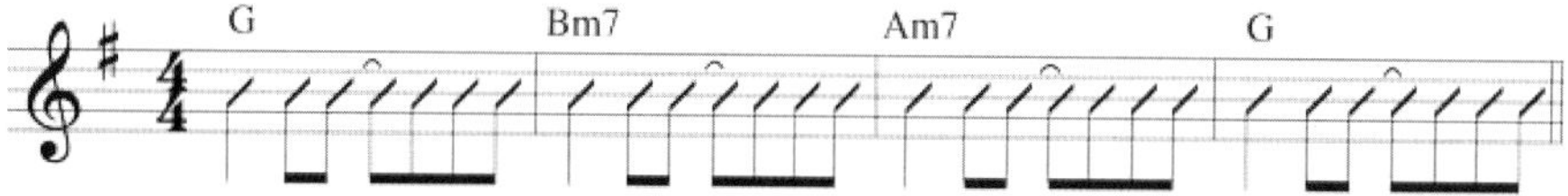

A progression using major and minor 7th barre chords.

You can play this progression in different keys simply by starting from chords other than G and moving the same relative number of frets to make the next chord. After the first chord, simply move up four frets for the second chord and then down two for the third chord; then move down another two for the last chord. (You can transpose the other progressions in this section in a similar manner.)

Say the names of the chords as you play them. Say them out loud. We're not kidding. You want to get so sick of hearing your own voice say the names of these chords at their correct locations that you can never forget that you play Am7 - the third chord of this progression - at the fifth fret.

Moving Through the Barre Chords Based on A

IN THIS ARTICLE

- *Playing major barre chords based on A*
- *Playing other A-based barre chords*

The A-based movable barre chords get their names from the notes that you play on the 5th (A) string. Like the E-based barre chords we show you in the previous article, you can play these chords at any fret.

Playing Major Barre Chords Based on A

The A-based major barre chord looks like an open A chord (but with different fingering, which we give you in the following section). The theory seems simple enough, but you may find that this chord is a little more difficult to play than the E-based major barre chord. Don't worry, however, because we have a substitute waiting for you that involves only two fingers. But for now, humour us and create the A-based barre chord according to the directions in the following section.

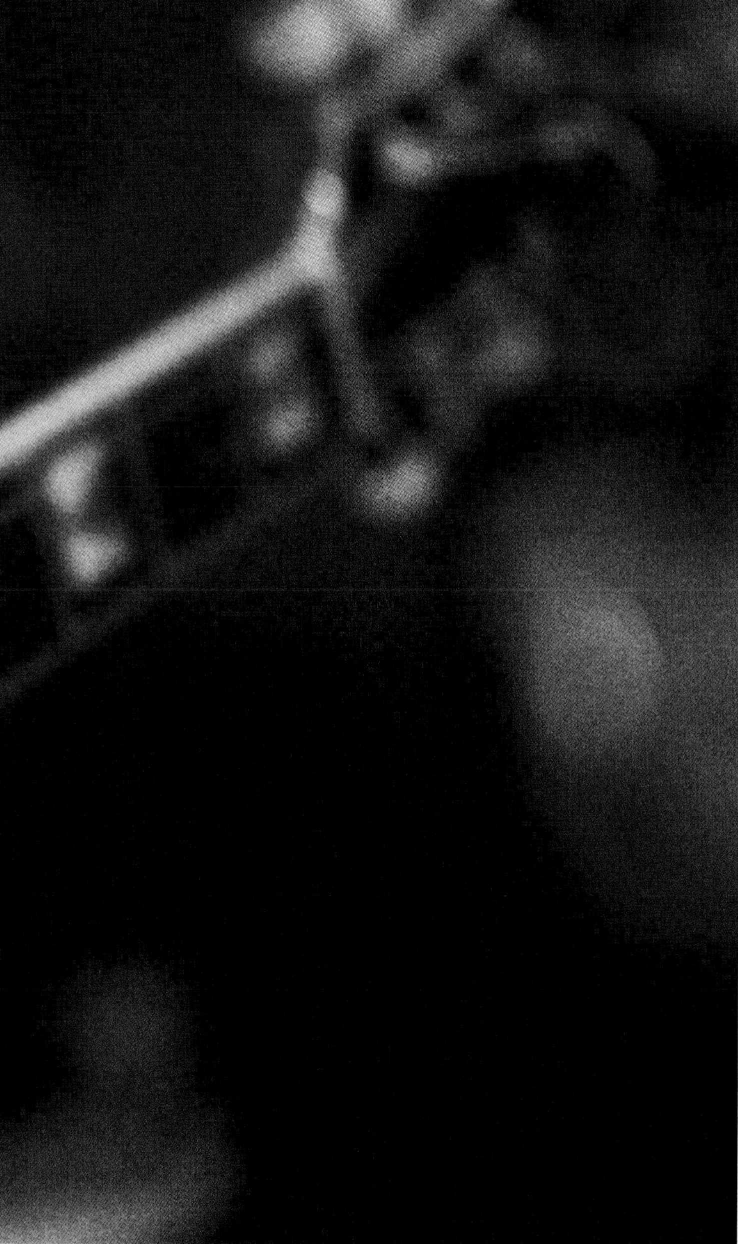

Fingering the A-based major barre chord

To finger an A-based major barre chord, follow these steps:

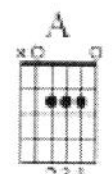

1. Finger an open A chord, but instead of using the normal fingering of 1-2-3, use 2-3-4.

   This fingering leaves your first (index) finger free and ready to act as the barre finger.

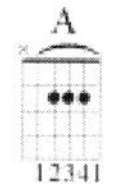

2. **Lay your first finger down across all six strings, just behind the nut (the side toward the tuning pegs).**

   Because you strum only the top five strings for A-based barre chords, you could lay your finger down across just five strings. But most guitarists cover all six strings with the barre because it feels more comfortable and it prevents the open 6th string from accidentally sounding.

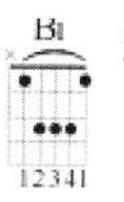

3. **Take the entire left-hand shape from Step 2 and slide it up one fret so that your first finger barres the first fret, producing a B♭ chord, as the photo shows.**

TIP

Placing your index finger across the strings at this point doesn't affect the sound of the chord because the strings don't vibrate on this side of the nut. Right now, you're just getting the feel of the chord position. Don't press too hard with any of your fingers because you're going to move the chord.

The barre B♭ chord.

After you finger the B♭ chord, try playing the notes of the chord one string at a time (from the 5th string to the 1st) to see whether all the notes ring out clearly. If you encounter any muffled notes, check to see that your left-hand fingers are touching only the appropriate strings and aren't preventing adjacent ones from ringing. If the sound is still muted, you need to exert more pressure with your fingers.

Finding the right fret

Because you can play a B♭ chord as a barre chord, you can now play all 12 A-based major barre chords — but only if you know the names of all the notes on the 5th string. All A-based barre chords get their name from the 5th string (just as the open A chord does).

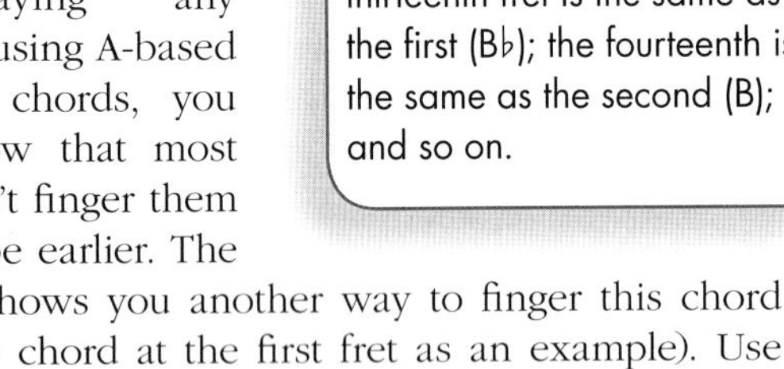

The notes and frets work sort of like a clock. After you get past 12, they repeat, so the thirteenth fret is the same as the first (B♭); the fourteenth is the same as the second (B); and so on.

Progressions using A-based major barre chords

Before playing any progressions using A-based major barre chords, you need to know that most guitarists don't finger them as we describe earlier. The photograph shows you another way to finger this chord (using the B♭ chord at the first fret as an example). Use your ring finger to barre the three notes at the third fret.

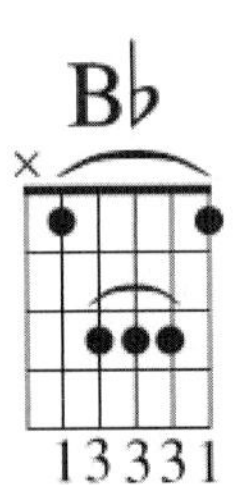

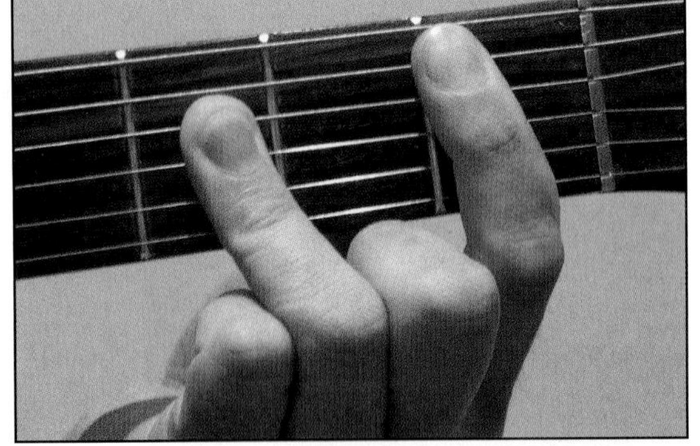

Alternative fingering for the A-based major barre chord.

The tricky thing about the fingering in the previous photo is that, for the 1st string to ring, you need to engage in a mean contortion with your third finger, elevating the middle knuckle out of the way (see photo). Some people can accomplish this position and some can't — it's kind of like wiggling your ears. The people who can't (lift their finger, not wiggle their ears) can use the fingering shown here.

Another alternative fingering for the A-based major chord.

If you play the B♭ barre chord as shown in the latter photo (with the 1st string not played), make sure that the 1st string doesn't accidentally sound. To keep the 1st string quiet either avoid striking it with your right hand or mute it (deaden it by lightly touching it) with the third finger.

Experiment with all three fingerings and pick the one that feels best for you.

The following exercise uses A-based major barre chords and has a light, early rock sound. You can give your left-hand fingers a break by releasing pressure as you slide from one chord to the next. Don't forget that you can (and should) transpose this progression to other keys by moving the entire pattern to a new starting point. Do so for all the exercises in this article. Notice, too, the staccato marks in measure 4 (play it di-di-di).

C F G

Fret: 3 8 10

A progression using A-based major barre chords.

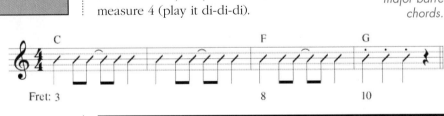

Playing Minor, Dominant 7th, Minor 7th, and Major 7th Barre Chords Based on A

We admit that the A-based major barre chord is something of an oddball with respect to left-hand fingering. But all the other A-based forms are much more logical and comfortable in terms of left-hand fingering.

For the rest of the A-based forms, you don't encounter any weird hand contortions or new techniques. All you do is pick up a variety of different forms to enrich your chord vocabulary.

Minor chords

To form an A-based minor barre chord you could follow steps similar to the ones that we describe in the section "Playing Major Barre Chords Based on A," earlier in this article: Play an open Am chord by using a 3-4-2 fingering instead of 2-3-1; lay your first finger down across all the strings on the other side of the nut; and then slide the shape up one fret and press down firmly, producing a B♭m chord.

But if you want, you can form the B♭m chord by skipping the "sliding up from an open chord" process and just placing your fingers directly on the frets, as indicated by the first chord diagram below. Check your strings individually to see that they're clear and buzz-free. (Notice that we've gone ahead and also given you the fingerings for B♭7, B♭m7, and B♭maj7. More on these in the following sections.)

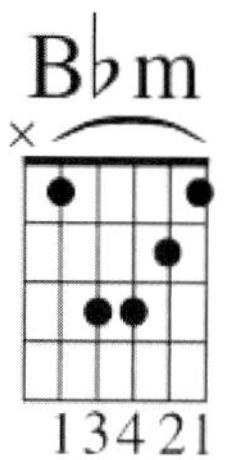

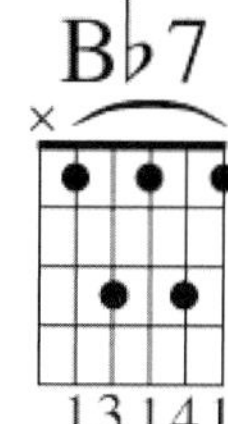

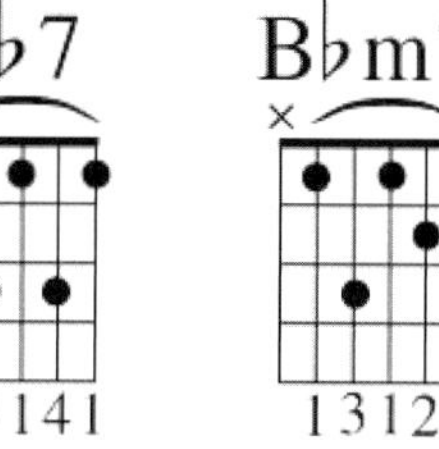

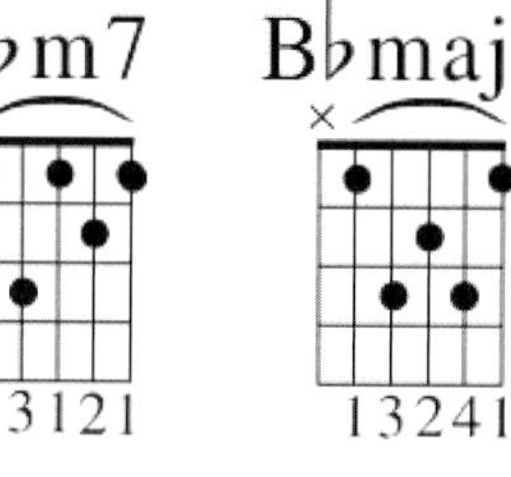

B♭m, B♭7, B♭m7, and B♭maj7 barre chords.

The following progression is typical of a rock, folk, or country song and uses both major and minor A-based barre chords.

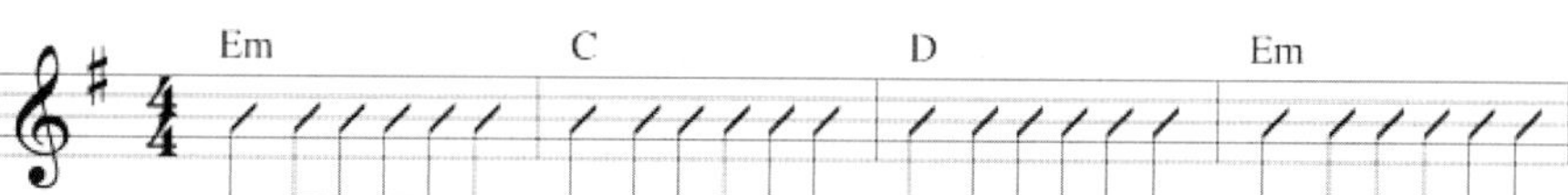

A progression using both major and minor A-based chords.

Dominant 7th chords

Dominant 7th chords sound bluesy and funky compared to major chords. Check out the chord diagram above to see the fingering for the B♭7 barre chord (A-based). Remember that you can "slide up" to this chord from a two-finger, open-position A7 chord (but only if you use a 3-4 fingering for the A7).

Now, using any A-based barre chord, try playing the simple progression below, which uses major, minor, and dominant 7th A-based barre chords.

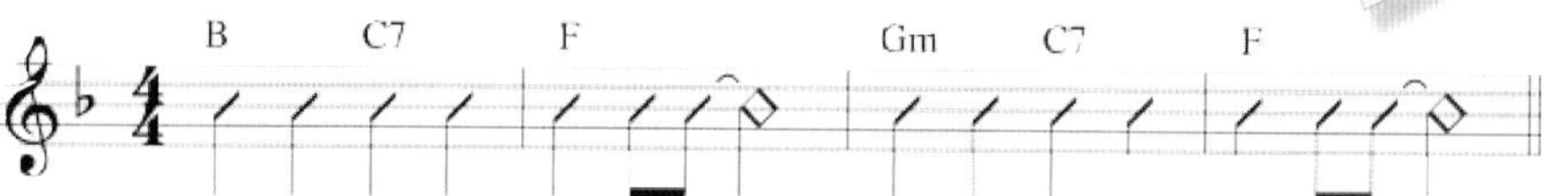

A progression using major, minor, and dominant 7th barre chords.

Minor 7th chords

Minor 7th chords sound soft and jazzy compared to major chords. You can form the B♭m7 chord by "sliding up" from an open-position Am7 chord (using a 3-2 fingering), or you can refer to the example shown on the left and place your fingers directly on the frets for the B♭m7.

The simple progression that follows uses A-based minor 7th chords exclusively.

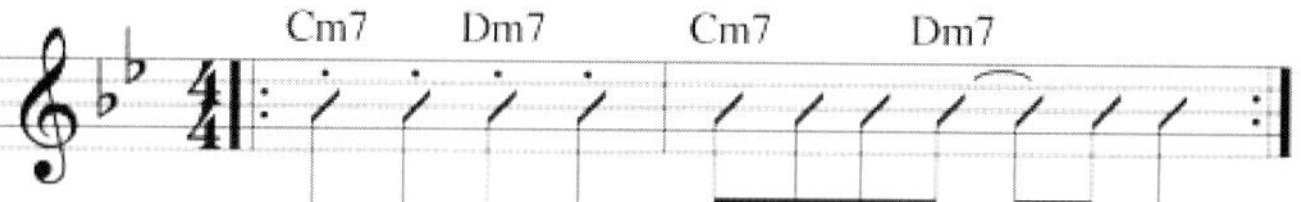

A progression using minor 7th barre chords.

Major 7th chords

Major 7th chords have a bright and jazzy sound compared to major chords. (You may notice that, in the section on E-based barre chords earlier in this chapter, we don't include the major 7th chord. That's because you don't play such chords in a barre form.)

You can form the B♭maj7 chord by "sliding up" from an open-position Amaj7 chord (using a 3-2-4 fingering), or you can refer to the example shown to the left and place your fingers to the left directly on the frets for the barre chord, as the figure shows you.

The simple progression here uses A-based minor 7th and major 7th barre chords.

A progression using minor 7th and major 7th barre chords.

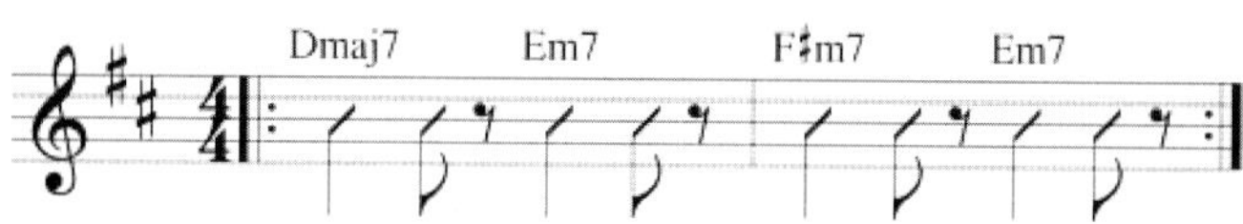

Special Articulation: Putting the Play in Your Playing

IN THIS ARTICLE

- *Playing hammer-ons*
- *Playing pull-offs*

Articulation refers to how you play and connect notes on the guitar. Look at it this way: If pitches and rhythms are what you play, articulation is how you play. Articulation gives your music expression and enables you to make your guitar talk, sing, and even cry.

From a technical standpoint, such articulation techniques as hammer-ons and pull-offs enable you to connect notes smoothly, giving your playing a little "grease" (a good thing, especially in playing the blues).

As you start to incorporate articulation in your playing, you begin to exercise more control over your guitar. You're not merely playing "correctly" - you're playing with individual style.

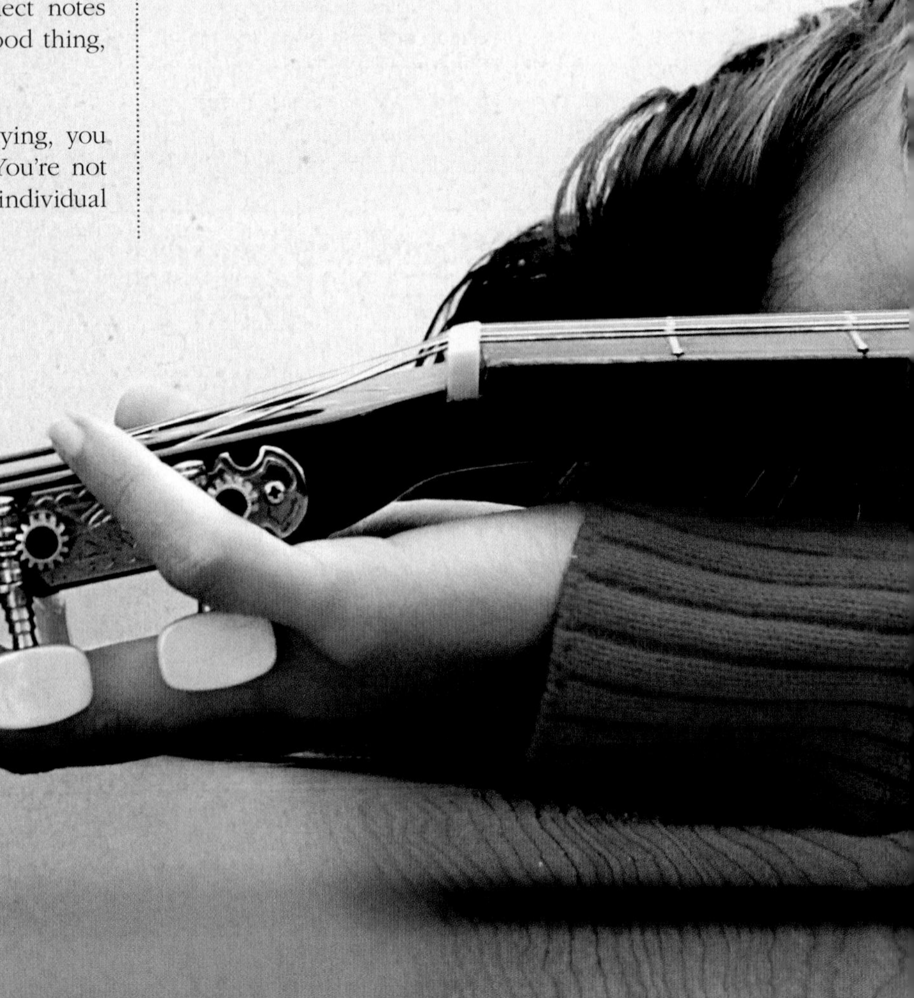

10

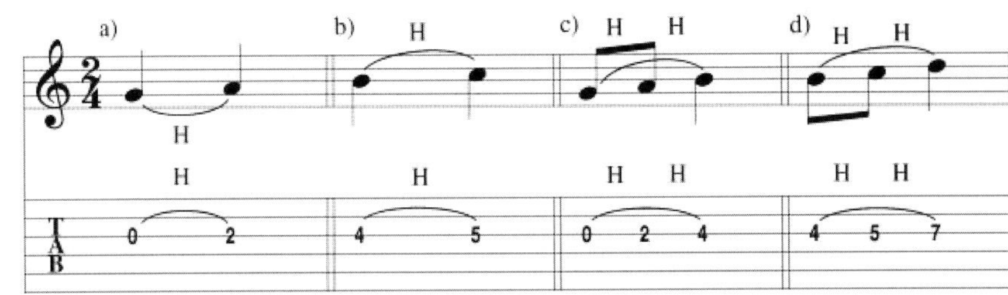

Four kinds of hammer-ons.

Getting the Hang of Hammer-Ons

A hammer-on doesn't refer to playing the guitar while wearing a tool belt; a hammer-on is a left-hand technique that enables you to play two consecutive ascending notes by picking only the first note. The hammer-on derives its name from the action of your left-hand finger, which acts like a hammer striking the fretboard, causing the note of that fret to sound out. This technique makes the connection between the notes sound smooth — far smoother than if you simply pick each note separately.

In the tab (and standard) notation in this book, the letter H with a slur (a curved line) indicates a hammer-on. (The slur connects the first fret number, or note, of the hammer-on with the last, and the H appears centered over the slur. If two Hs appear over the slur, the hammer-on involves three notes.)

Playing a hammer-on

An open-string hammer-on (or just hammer, for short) is the easiest kind to play. Following are the steps for the open-string hammer-on:

1. **Pick the open G string (the 3rd string) as you normally do.**

2. **While the open string is still ringing, use a finger of your left hand (say, the first finger) to quickly and firmly strike (or slam or smack, as you prefer) the second fret of the same string.**

   If you bring your finger down with enough force, you hear the new note (the second fret A) ringing. Normally, your left hand doesn't strike a fret; it merely presses down on it. But to produce an audible sound without picking, you must hit the string pretty hard, as though your finger's a little hammer coming down on the fretboard.

The first measure in the notation above shows how you play the steps; the second shows a hammer-on from a fretted note on the 3rd string. Use your first finger to fret the first note at the fourth fret and strike the string; then, while that note's still ringing, use your second finger to hammer down on the fifth fret.

Double hammer-on

The third measure in the notation above shows a double hammer-on on the 3rd string. Play the open string and hammer the second fret with your first finger; then, while that note's still ringing, hammer the string again (at the fourth fret) with your third finger, producing a super-smooth connection between all three notes.

The last measure of the notation shows a double hammer-on on the same string using three fretted notes. This type of hammer-on is the most difficult to play and requires some practice. Play the note at the fourth fret, fretting with your first finger; hammer-on the fifth-fret note with your second finger; then hammer the seventh-fret-note with your fourth finger.

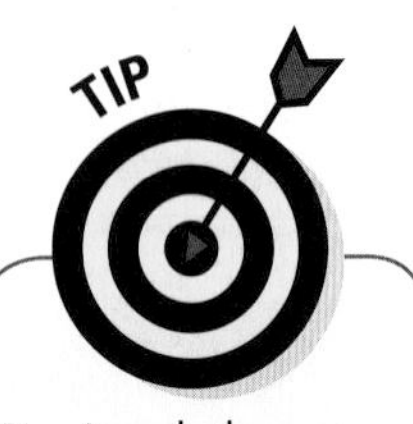

Don't rush the notes together; rushing is a tendency as you first work with hammer-ons.

Double-stop hammer-on

You can also play hammer-ons as double-stops. The most common double-stop hammer-ons - and the ones that are the easiest to play - are the ones where both double-stop notes lie on the same fret, enabling you to barre them (play them with one finger).

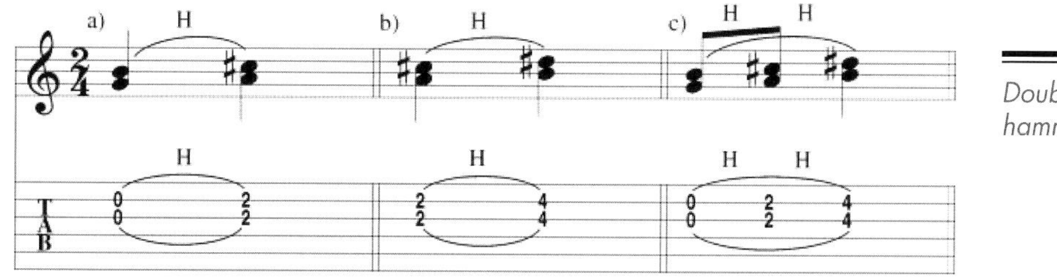

Double-stop hammer-ons.

The first measure of the notation above shows a double-stop hammer-on from open strings (the 2nd and 3rd). After striking the two open strings with the pick, and while the open strings are still ringing, slam down your first finger at the second-fret, across both strings at the same time.

Next, try a double-stop hammer-on from the second fret to the fourth fret, also on the 2nd and 3rd strings, as shown in the second measure. Use your first finger to barre the second fret and your third finger to barre the fourth fret.

Now, to get really fancy, try a double double-stop hammer-on, on the same strings, as shown in the last measure. Start with the open strings; hammer the second-fret barre with your first finger; then hammer the fourth-fret barre with your third finger.

Hammer-on from nowhere

The notation below shows what we call a hammer-on from nowhere. It's not a typical hammer-on in that the hammered note doesn't follow an already-ringing lower note. In fact, the hammered note is on an entirely different string than the previous note. Sound the hammered note by fretting it very hard (hammering it) with a left-hand finger — hard enough that the note rings out without your striking it with the pick.

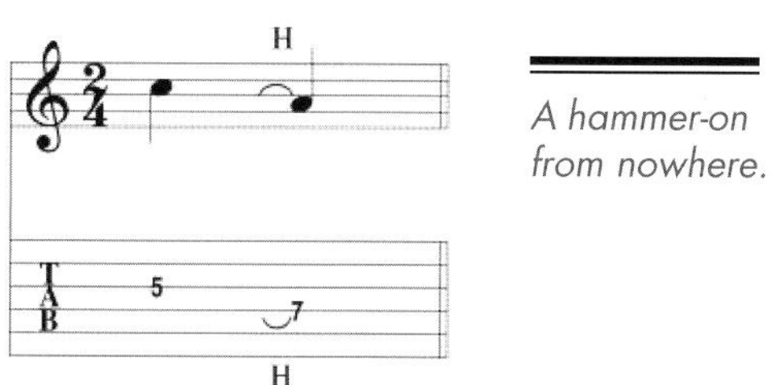

A hammer-on from nowhere.

Why would you even use this type of hammer-on? Sometimes, in fast passages, your right-hand picking pattern just doesn't give you time for that one extra pick attack when you need it. But you can sound the note anyway by fretting it hard enough with a finger of the left hand — hammering it from nowhere.

Getting idiomatic with hammer-ons

In this section, you find some idiomatic licks using hammer-ons. The little numbers next to the noteheads in the standard notation indicate left-hand fingerings. The first lick uses single-note hammer-ons from open strings. You may hear this kind of lick in a rock, blues, or country song. Try it out for a bit more practice with hammer-ons.

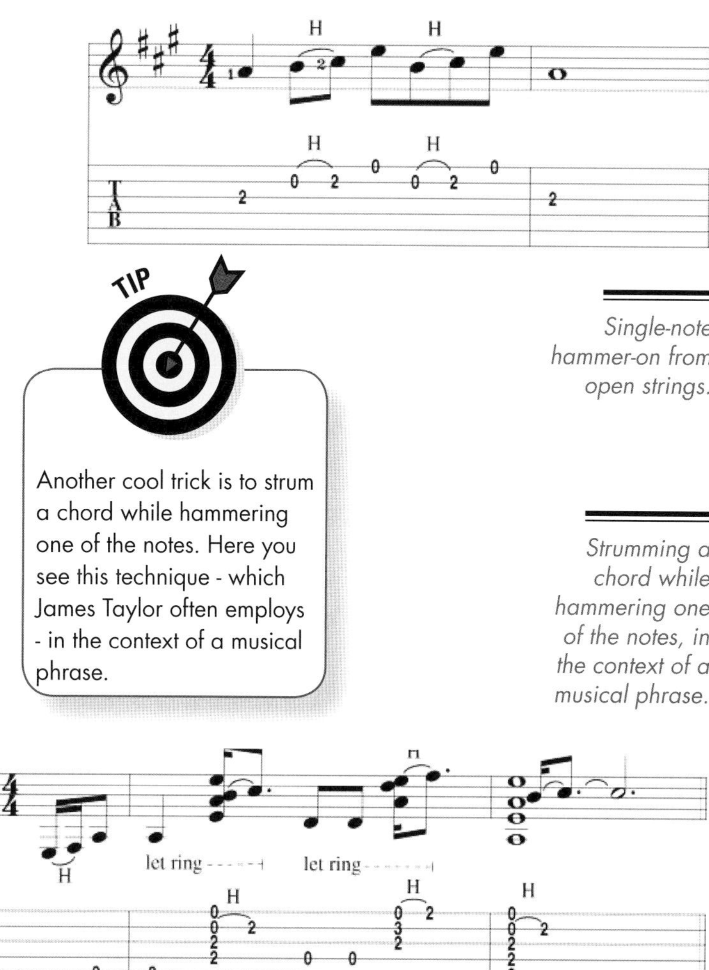

Single-note hammer-on from open strings.

TIP: Another cool trick is to strum a chord while hammering one of the notes. Here you see this technique - which James Taylor often employs - in the context of a musical phrase.

Strumming a chord while hammering one of the notes, in the context of a musical phrase.

The following notation shows single-note hammer-ons involving only fretted notes. You can hear this kind of lick in many rock and blues songs. Down-picks are indicated by the ⊓ symbol, and up-picks are indicated by the V symbol. (The sim. means to keep playing in a similar manner — here referring to the picking pattern indicated.)

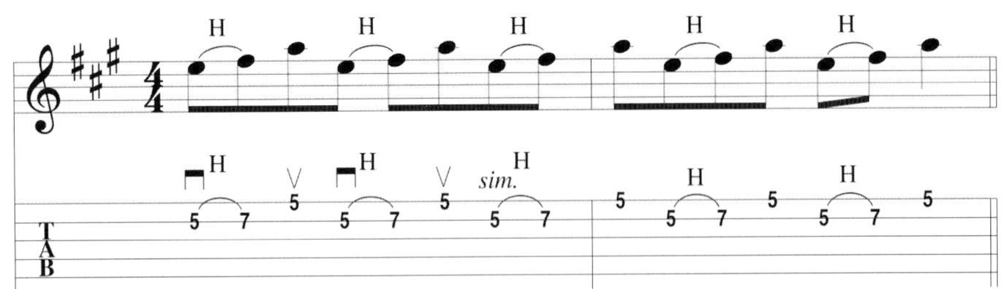

Single-note hammer-ons from fretted notes.

Keep your first finger barring the fifth fret for this lick as you play it. You get a smoother sound, and you find that it's easier to play, too.

This last notation combines a double-stop hammer-on with a hammer-on from nowhere in fifth position. Try picking that last note, and you can easily see that the hammer-on from nowhere feels more comfortable than the picked version of the note.

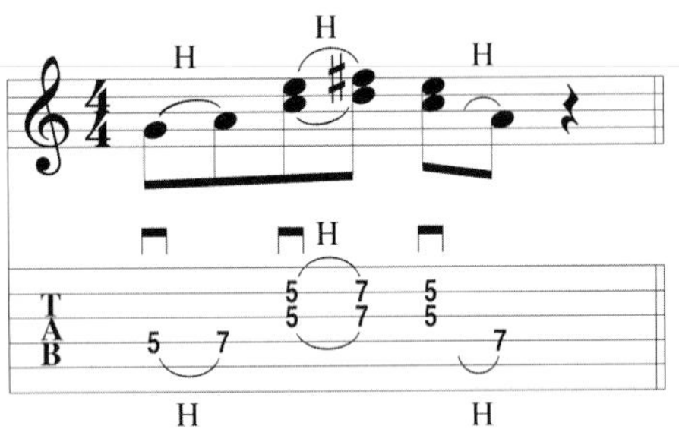

A double-step hammer-on plus a hammer-on from nowhere.

Getting Playful with Pull-Offs

A pull-off is another technique that enables you to connect notes more smoothly. To execute a pull-off, you play two consecutive descending notes by picking only once with the right hand and, as the first note rings, pulling your finger off that fret. As you pull your finger off one fret, the next lower fretted (or open) note on the string then rings out instead of the first note. You can sort of think of a pull-off as the opposite of a hammer-on, but that particular contrast doesn't really tell the whole story. A pull-off also requires that you exert a slight sideways pull on the string where you're fretting the picked note and then release the string from your finger in a snap as you pull your finger off the fret — something like what you do in launching a tiddly-wink.

The tab (and standard) notation in this book indicates a pull-off by showing the letter P centered over a slur (short curved line) connecting the two tab numbers (or notes).

Playing pull-offs

A pull-off (or pull, for short) to an open string is the easiest kind to play. Following are the steps for the open-string pull-off that the first measure of the notation shows:

1. **Press down the 3rd string at the second fret with your first or second finger (whichever is more comfortable) and pick the note normally with your right hand.**
2. **While the note is still ringing, pull your finger off the string in a sideways motion (toward the 2nd string) in a way that causes the open 3rd string to ring — almost as if you're making a left-hand finger pluck.**

   If you're playing up to speed, you can't truly pluck the string as you remove your finger — you're half lifting and half plucking . . . or somewhere in between. Experiment to find the left-hand finger motion that works best for you.

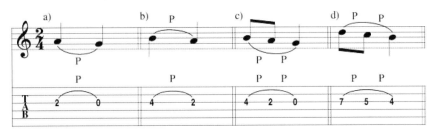

Four kinds of pull-offs.

The notation's second measure shows a pull-off involving only fretted notes. The crucial factor in playing this kind of pull-off is that you must finger both pull-off notes ahead of time.

We put that last part in italics because it's so important. This requirement is one of the big differences between a hammer-on and a pull-off. You must anticipate, or set up, a pull-off in advance. Following are the steps for playing the fretted pull-off in the second measure:

1. **Press down both the second fret of the 3rd string with your first finger and the fourth fret of the 3rd string with your third finger at the same time.**

2. Strike the 3rd string with the pick and, while the fourth-fret note is still ringing, pull your third finger off the fourth fret (in a half pluck, half lift) to sound the note of the second fret (which you're already fingering).

Try to avoid accidentally striking the 2nd string as you pull off. Also, you can see that if you aren't already pressing down that second-fret note, you end up pulling off to the open string instead of the second fret!

Double pull-off

The third measure shows a double pull-off to the open 3rd string. Start by simultaneously fretting the first two notes (with your first and third fingers). Pick the string and then pull off with your third finger to sound the note at the second fret; then pull off with your first finger to sound the open string. (Notice that two Ps appear over the slur connecting the three notes; these indicate that you're pulling off two notes and not just one.)

In the last measure, you see a double pull-off on the 3rd string using only fretted notes. Start with all three notes fretted (using your first, second, and fourth fingers). Pick the string and then pull off with your fourth finger to sound the fifth-fret note; then pull off with your second finger to sound the fourth-fret note.

Double-stop pull-off

You can also play pull-offs as double-stops. As is true with hammer-ons, the double-stop pull-offs that are the most common and are the easiest to play are those where both double-stop notes lie on the same fret, enabling you to barre them.

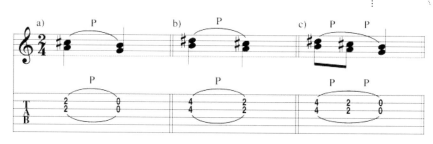

Double-stop pull-offs.

The first measure of the above notation shows a double-stop pull-off to open strings on the 2nd and 3rd strings. After striking the notes at the second fret, and while the strings are still ringing, pull off your first finger (in a half pluck, half lift) from both strings at the same time (in one motion) to sound the open strings.

Next, try a double-stop pull-off from the fourth fret to the second fret, as shown in the second measure. Place your first finger at the second fret, barring the 2nd and 3rd strings, and place your third finger at the fourth fret (also barring the 2nd and 3rd strings) at the same time. Pick the strings and then pull your third finger off the fourth fret to sound the notes at the second fret of both strings.

Now try a double double-stop pull-off, on the same strings, as shown in the last measure. This type of pull-off is similar to what you play in the example shown in the middle measure except that, after the notes on the second fret sound, you pull your first finger off the second fret to sound the open strings.

Getting idiomatic with pull-offs

In the following notations, you see two idiomatic licks using pull-offs. The first involves single-note pull-offs to open strings. You can hear this kind of lick in many rock and blues songs.

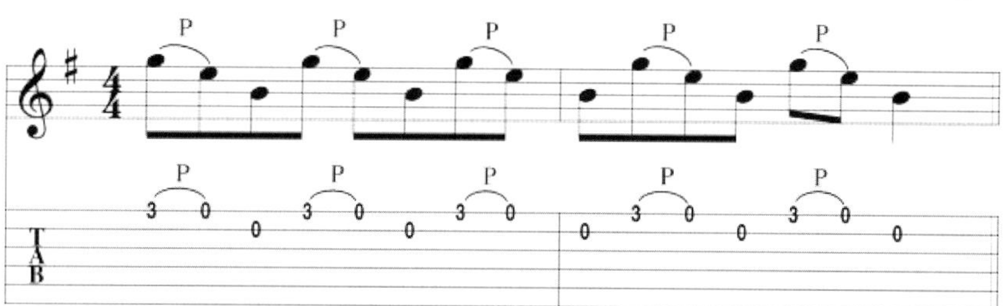

Single-note pull-offs to open strings.

Notation in the section "Getting idiomatic with hammer-ons," earlier in this article, shows you how to strum a chord while hammering on a note of that chord. The notation here shows the opposite technique: strumming a chord while pulling off one note. The passage in this figure leads off with two single-note pull-offs, just to get you warmed up.

Strumming a chord while pulling off one of the notes.

10 Guitars you should know

No musical instrument offers a greater variety of appearance, function, and sound than a guitar. Whether it's the quietly elegant Ramirez, the smoothly debonair D'Angelico, or the raucously funky Telecaster, each guitar presented below has left an indelible mark on the guitar-playing canon and will forever be known as a classic.

Gibson J-200

Manufactured: 1937–

For a booming acoustic tone and stylish looks, look no farther than Gibson's venerable J-200. This "jumbo" steel-string was targeted toward country guitarists and quickly became a Nashville classic. Of special note is its highly ornamental rosewood and mother-of-pearl inlaid bridge, which is shaped something like a mustache.

Fender Telecaster

Manufactured: 1951–

Fender's other great contribution to electric guitar lore is the Telecaster, which was also the first commercially made solid-body (1950). The Tele made its mark in the country world, adding a bright, twangy sound to countless recordings. A simple guitar made out of a plank of ash or alder, basic electronics, and a maple neck, it set the standard for electric guitar design and remains a classic today.

Martin D-28

Manufactured: 1931–

Martin first mass-produced "dreadnought" (named after a class of battleship) acoustic guitars in 1931 and its D-28 is the quintessential example of that great design. With a fat waist and bass-heavy tone, this big guitar became integral to the sounds of country, bluegrass, and, indeed, just about all steel-string acoustic music.

Gibson Les Paul

Manufactured: 1952–

Named after Les Paul, the '50s jazz-pop sensation, the Gibson Les Paul model ironically went on to become one of the definitive rock 'n' roll instruments. Championed by Jimmy Page and Jeff Beck, this single-cutaway electric exudes the fat, bassy tone that helped define the sound of hard rock and heavy metal. Some original models from the late 1950s — notably the 1959 Standard — can now fetch more than £50,000.

Gretsch 6120

Manufactured: 1954–

Best known as country virtuoso Chet Atkins's main electric guitar, the big, funky tones of this hollow-body were common on many '50s and '60s rock and country records. With its unusual FilterTron pickups and warbly Bigsby vibrato bar, the 6120 also gave early rocker Duane Eddy his signature twangy guitar sound.

Gibson ES-335

Manufactured: 1958–

Introduced in the late 1950s, this axe is a thin "semihollow-body" design, which sought to combine the acoustic qualities of a big archtop with the compactness of a solid-body electric. The result was a superb guitar with a smooth woody tone, good for both clean jazz and heavy rock 'n' roll. This guitar's most famous advocate was '70s jazz-popper Larry Carlton, also known as "Mr. 335."

Ramirez Classical

Manufactured: mid-1800s

Serious classical and flamenco guitarists often consider playing only one kind of guitar — a Ramirez. First built in the mid-19th century, Jose Ramirez's classical guitars helped define the style, with soft gut (later, nylon) strings, superb workmanship, and a luscious tone. Among Ramirez's earliest champions was none other than the master, Andrés Segovia, himself.

D'Angelico Archtop

Manufactured: 1932–1964

Considered by many to be the greatest jazz guitar ever made, D'Angelicos were custom archtop (the tops were arched slightly instead of flat like steel-string folk guitars) hollow-bodies built by the grand master of the genre, John D'Angelico (1905–64). In addition to their warm, lush tone, these guitars were meticulously constructed and graced with some of the most elegant decorations of all time.

Fender Stratocaster

Manufactured: 1954–

The world's most famous electric guitar, the Stratocaster was designed as a space-age instrument in the early '50s, featuring sleek lines, trebly tone, and small body dimensions (at least compared to the huge jazz archtops of the day). In the hands of masters such as Buddy Holly, Jimi Hendrix, Stevie Ray Vaughan, and Eric Clapton, this solid-body ax became ubiquitous, and today, you can't go into any guitar store without seeing at least a few Strats on the wall.

Rickenbacker 360-12

Manufactured: 1963–

The ringing guitar tone on early Beatles and Byrds records came from one great guitar: the Rickenbacker 360-12. A semihollow-body electric with 12 strings, this classic has a completely distinctive tone in the guitar universe. The timeless Rick sound later resurfaced in the '80s on smash records by Tom Petty and R.E.M., among many others.

Making the Guitar Talk by Bending Strings

IN THIS ARTICLE

- *Playing bends*
- *Playing vibratos*

The string bend is what makes your guitar talk (or sing or cry), giving the instrument almost voicelike expressive capabilities. Bending is nothing more than using a left-hand finger to push or pull a string out of its normal alignment, stretching it across the fingerboard toward the 6th or 1st string. (More later on how to tell in which direction to stretch the string.)

As you bend a string, you raise its pitch by stretching that string. This rise in pitch can be slight or great, depending on exactly how far you bend the string. Between the slightest and greatest bends possible are infinite degrees of in-between bends. It's those infinite degrees that make your guitar sing.

The tab notation in this book indicates a bend by using a curved arrow and either a number or a fraction (or both) at the peak of the arrow. The fraction 1/2, for example, means that you bend the string until the pitch is a half step (the equivalent of one fret) higher than normal. The numeral 1 above a bend arrow means that you bend the string until the pitch is a whole step (the equivalent of two frets) higher than normal. You may also see fractions such as 1/4 and 3/4 or bigger numbers such as 1 1/2 or 2 above a bend arrow. These fractions or numbers all tell you how many (whole) steps to bend the note. But 1/2 and 1 are the most common bends that you see in most tab notation.

You can check to see that you're bending in tune by fretting the target note normally and comparing that to the bent note. If the bend indicates a whole step (1) on the seventh fret of the 3rd string, for example, play the ninth fret normally and listen carefully to the pitch. Then try bending the seventh-fret note to match the ninth-fret pitch in your head.

Although nearly all publishers of printed guitar music use curved arrows and numbers to indicate bends in tablature, not all publishers use these indications on the standard notation staff as well. Some publishers instead show the pitch of both the unbent and bent notes, with one of them in parentheses or one of them very small. To avoid confusion, make sure that you establish how each system treats the issue of bent notes before you start playing that music.

Developing a Feel for Bends

You don't normally do a lot of string bending on acoustic guitars, because the strings are too thick. In electric guitar playing, where string bending is an integral technique, the strings are thinner.

Here you play your first bend on the 3rd string with the third finger, which represents a very common bending situation — probably the most common.

Follow these steps:

1. **Place your third finger at the seventh fret but support the third finger by placing the second finger at the sixth fret and the first finger at the fifth fret, all at the same time.**

The first and second fingers don't produce any sound, but they add strength to your bend. Supporting your bends with any other available fingers is always a good idea.

2. **Pick the 3rd string with your right hand.**

3. **After picking, use all three fingers together to push the string toward the 6th string, raising the pitch a whole step (to the pitch you normally get at the ninth fret).**

Before bending (top) and after bending (above).

Pushing your hand into the neck as you execute the bend gives you added leverage. Also, using light-gauge, or thin, strings on your guitar also makes bending easier.

Here's what bends look like in standard notation and tab. From left to right, this figure shows

- An **immediate bend**, in which you pick the note and then immediately bend it up.

- A **bend and release**, meaning that you pick the note, bend it (without repicking), and unbend it (release it without repicking) to its normal position. Unlike the bend to its left, this bend isn't immediate; instead, you see it notated in a specific rhythm. You can refer to this type of bend as a bend in rhythm, or a measured bend.

- A **prebend and release**, which changes up the order of things. You prebend the note, or bend it before you strike it with the pick. Bend the note as you do in Step 1, but don't pick the string until after you bend it. After you pick the note, unbend (release without repicking) the string to its normal position.

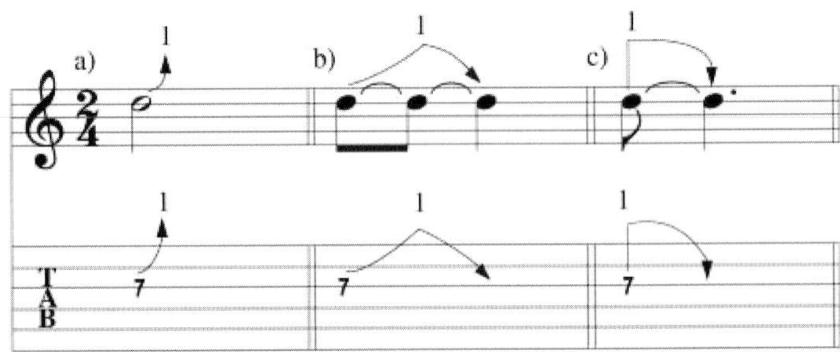

Three types of bends.

Most often, as the examples show, you push the string toward the 6th string (or toward the ceiling). But if you bend notes on the bottom two strings (the 5th and 6th strings), you pull the string toward the 1st string (or toward the floor) — otherwise the string slides right off the fretboard.

Getting Idiomatic with Bends

The notation shows a very common bend figure that you can use in rock soloing. Notice the fingering that the standard notation staff indicates to use. Your left hand hardly moves — it's locked in fifth position, with the first finger barring the 1st and 2nd strings at the fifth fret. The second note of the figure (fifth fret, 2nd string) happens to be the same pitch (E) as your target bend, so you can use that second note to test the accuracy of your bend. Soon, you start to feel just how far you need to bend a string to achieve a whole-step or half-step rise in pitch. All the bends in this example are immediate bends.

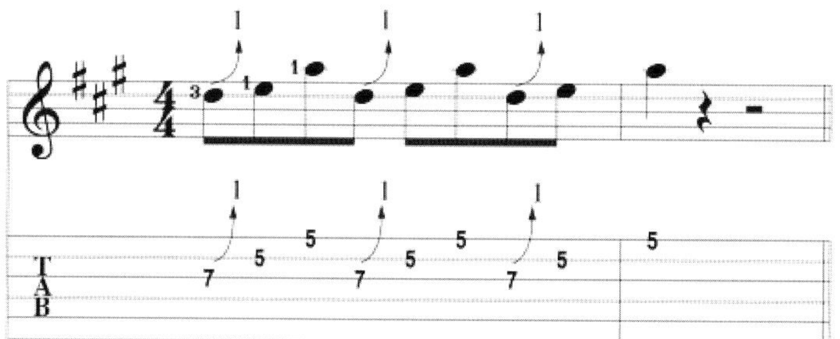

Bending the 3rd string in a classic rock 'n' roll lead lick.

After you play each 3rd-string bend, just before you pick the 2nd-string note, reduce your finger pressure from the bent note. This action causes the 3rd string to stop ringing as you pick the 2nd string.

In the following notation, you bend the 2nd string, once as an immediate bend and once as a bend in rhythm. Strictly speaking, because you're in twelfth position, you should be using your fourth finger to play the fifteenth fret. But we indicate for you to use the third finger, because if you're up at the twelfth fret, the frets are closer together, so your third finger can easily make the reach and is stronger than your fourth finger.

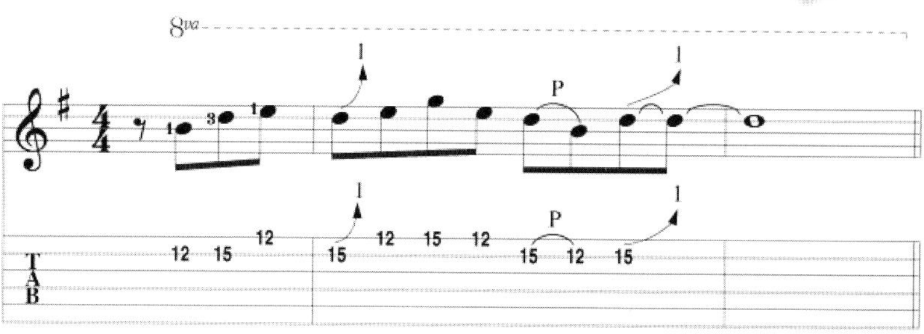

Bending the 2nd string in the lead lick.

Note: The 8va indication above the standard music notation tells you to play the notes an octave higher than written.

You play both of the previous examples in what lead guitarists call a box pattern — a group of notes in one position that vaguely resembles the shape of a box. You can use this pattern for improvising lead solos.

The following notation shows a small box pattern in the eighth position. This example features a bend and release, in which the bend is immediate and the release is in rhythm.

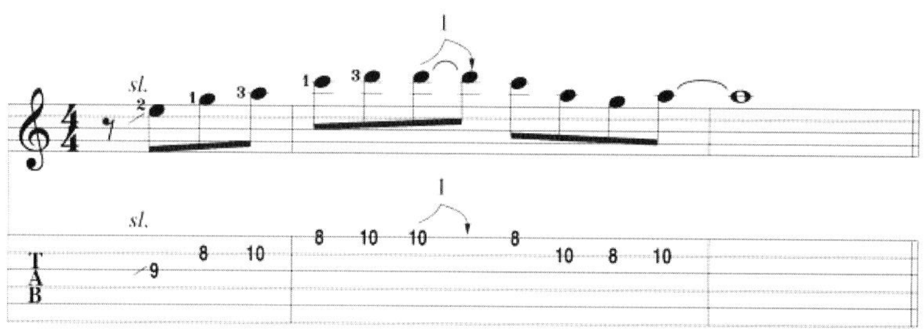

Bending and releasing a note in a lead lick.

Although you bend most notes by pushing a string toward the 6th string, you may sometimes need to bend a string the other way, even on a middle or upper string (but not on the 1st string because it slides off the neck if you do). You need to use this type of opposite-direction bend if the note that follows a bend is on a string that's adjacent to the bent string. You need to bend away from the upcoming string; otherwise, your bending finger may accidentally touch it, inadvertently muting it.

Here are two first-finger, half-step bends on the 3rd string. The first one bends toward the 6th string because the following note is on the 2nd string. (Remember that you're bending away from the following note.) The second one, however, bends toward the floor because the following note is on the adjacent 4th string. Again, you're bending away from the next note.

Bending the same string in two different directions. The asterisks and footnotes tell you which direction to bend towards.

You can create an interesting effect by bending a note, letting it ring in its bent state, striking a note on another string, and then restriking the bent string and releasing it. Many southern-rock and country-rock guitarists are fond of this kind of bend.

The following notation shows this "held-bend" technique. In the notation, the dotted line after the arrow indicates that you hold the bend not only as you strike the 2nd string, but also as you restrike the 3rd string; the downward-curved solid line shows the release of the bend. Make sure that you bend the 3rd string toward the ceiling so that your bending finger is out of the way of the 2nd string.

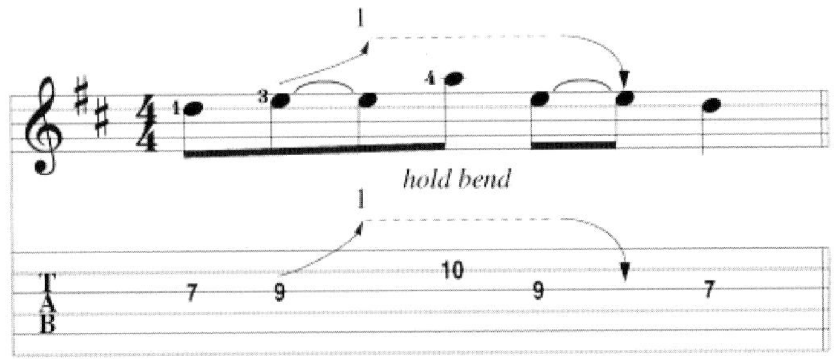

Bending and holding a note while striking another string and then restriking and releasing the bent note.

You can also play bends as double-stops - you just bend two strings at the same time, usually by barring the two strings with one finger. Here's a double-stop bend of the 2nd and 3rd strings in the box pattern at the fifth fret. Use your first finger to play the fifth-fret double-stop; then use your third finger to play the double-stop bend and release at the seventh fret. The double arrow in the notation tells you to bend both notes. By the way, it's shown as a single arrow on the release of the bend only to avoid messiness in the notation - so go ahead and release both notes.

A double-stop bend and release.

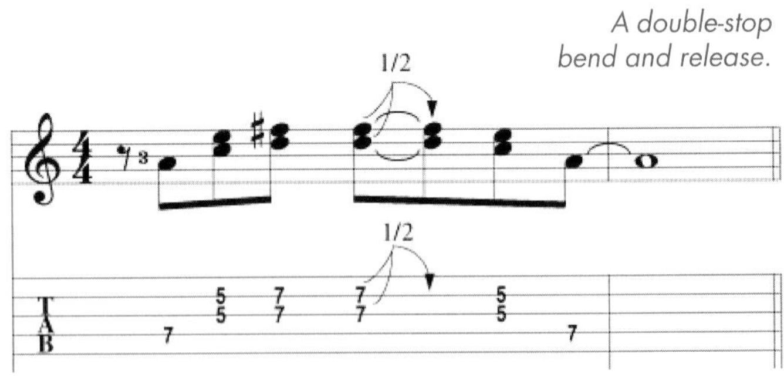

Using Bends (and More) to Go Vibrato

Think of the term vibrato, and you may imagine a singer's wavering voice or a violinist's twitching hand. On the guitar, however, vibrato is a steady, even (and usually slight) fluctuation of pitch, most often achieved by rapidly bending and releasing a note a slight degree. A vibrato can add warmth, emotion, and life to a held, or sustained, note.

The most obvious time to apply vibrato is whenever you hold a note for a long time. Vibrato not only gives the note more warmth, but it also increases the sustain period of the note. Some guitarists, such as blues great B.B. King, are renowned for their expressive vibrato technique. Both the tab and standard notation indicate a vibrato by placing a wavy line at the top of the staff over the note you're playing.

You can produce a vibrato in several ways, as the following list describes:

- **You can slightly bend and release a note over and over again, creating a wah-wah-wah effect.** The average pitch of the vibrato is slightly higher than the unaltered note. The left-hand technique for this method is the same as the technique for bending — you move a finger back and forth, perpendicular to the string, creating a fluctuation of pitch.
- **You can very rapidly slide your finger back and forth along the length of a string, within one fret.** Although you're not actually moving your finger out of the fret, the pitch becomes slightly sharper as you move toward the nut and slightly flatter as you move toward the bridge. Consequently, the average pitch of the vibrato is the same as the unaltered note. This type of vibrato is reserved almost exclusively for playing classical guitar with nylon strings.
- **If your electric guitar has a whammy bar mounted on it, you can move the bar up and down with your right hand, creating a fluctuation in pitch.** In addition to giving you greater rhythmic flexibility and pitch range, the whammy bar enables you to add vibrato to an open string.

The bend-and-release type of vibrato is the most common, by far. To play it, support your vibrato finger with other available fingers by placing them all on the string at the same time. You can either move your whole hand by rotating it at the wrist and keeping the finger fixed, or you can move just your finger(s). Try both ways and see which feels most comfortable.

You may find that playing a vibrato is easier if you anchor your left hand on the neck as you play. Squeeze the neck a little between the side of your thumb and the part of your palm that's about half an inch below your first finger. This action gives you better leverage and helps you control the evenness of the fluctuation.

The figure shows a vibrato at the ninth fret of the 3rd string. Anchor your hand, as we describe in the preceding paragraph, and slightly bend and release the note over and over. Try the vibrato with each finger. Try it at different frets and on different strings.

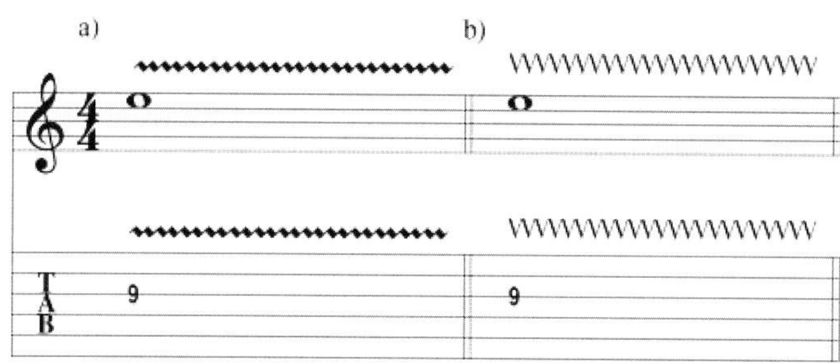

Narrow and wide vibration.

The notation for a vibrato never tells you how fast or slowly to bend and release — that's up to you. But whether you play a fast vibrato or a slow one, make sure that you keep the fluctuations steady and even. The notation does tell you, however, whether to make the vibrato narrow (that is, you bend the string only slightly — less than a half step — for each pulsation) or wide (you bend the string to a greater degree — about a half step or more). The measure on the left shows a regular (narrow) vibrato, and the one on the right shows a wide vibrato, indicating the latter by using an exaggerated wavy line (with deeper peaks and valleys). Try playing a wide vibrato with each finger. Try it at different frets and on different strings.

If the note that you're holding is a bent note, you create the vibrato by releasing and bending (instead of bending and releasing) — because the note's already bent as you start the vibrato. This action makes the average pitch lower than the held (bent) note, which itself produces the highest pitch in the vibrato.

After a long vibrato, guitarists often play a descending slide, gradually releasing finger pressure as they go, to give the vibrato a fancy little ending. Another trick is to play a long note without vibrato for a while and then add some vibrato toward the end of the note. This "delayed vibrato" is a favourite technique that singers often use.

Playing Rock Guitar

IN THIS ARTICLE

- *Playing classic rock 'n' roll rhythm guitar*
- *Playing rock 'n' roll lead guitar*
- *Building solos*

With the volume turned up and your adrenaline flowing, nothing's quite like laying down a chunking rhythm or ripping through a searing lead to screaming, adoring fans — or even to your own approving smile coming back at you from the mirror. All you need to do is figure out how to play a couple of simple patterns and you can be gyrating like Elvis, duck-walking like Chuck Berry, and windmilling like Pete Townshend in no time.

Classic rock 'n' roll is defined here as the straightforward style pioneered by Chuck Berry and heard in the music of the early Beatles, the Rolling Stones, the Who, the Beach Boys, and others who based their sound on a solid, chord-based rhythm guitar groove. It also includes the sound of the blues-based rockers, such as Jimi Hendrix, Led Zeppelin's Jimmy Page, and Cream's Eric Clapton.

Laying the Groundwork: Rhythm Guitar

About 99 per cent of all rock guitar playing involves rhythm guitar playing. To a guitarist, playing rhythm means supplying the accompaniment or backing part to a vocalist or other featured instrument. Mostly, this accompaniment involves strumming chords and, to a lesser extent, playing single-note or double-stop (two notes played at once) riffs in the lower register (the bottom two or three strings).

Listen to the verses of Chuck Berry's "Johnny B. Goode" or the Beatles' "I Saw Her Standing There" for some good, unadulterated rhythm guitar, and check out the Beatles' "Day Tripper" for low-note riffing. Listen also to almost anything by the Who's Pete Townshend, who's (no pun intended) the quintessential rock rhythm guitarist and who immortalized the "windmill" technique — the sweeping circular motion of the right hand that you can use for strumming chords. And although he's mostly known for his innovative lead work, Eddie Van Halen is one of the best rhythm guitarists in the modern-rock genre.

Open-position accompaniment

The Chuck Berry style, a simple rhythm figure (accompaniment pattern) in open position (using open strings), gains its name from the fact that almost all of Berry's songs use this pattern. Here's the pattern for this style.

The classic Chuck Berry rock 'n' roll accompaniment riff for A,D and E chords.

To play this rhythm (called the 5-to-6 pattern) effectively, use the following techniques:

- Anchor the first finger (at the second fret) and add the third finger (at the fourth fret) as you need it.
- Pick the notes using all downstrokes.
- Don't lift the first finger while adding the third finger.

Notice that all three chords, A, D, and E, use the exact same fingering and that the open strings make the pattern easy to play.

Jimmy Page is one of rock music's most influential guitarists.

The 12-bar blues pattern

The 5-to-6 pattern sounds great, but to make it work for you, you need to put it into a progression. The following notation shows what's known as a 12-bar blues progression, a common chord progression in tons of rock songs: "Johnny B. Goode," "Roll Over Beethoven," "Tutti Frutti," "At the Hop," and "Blue Suede Shoes," to name but a few.

Notice that this 12-bar blues progression is in the key of A, uses the 5-to-6 movement, and has major chord symbols above the notes. The 12-bar blues progression can occur in any key, and often uses dominant-seventh chords instead of major chords.

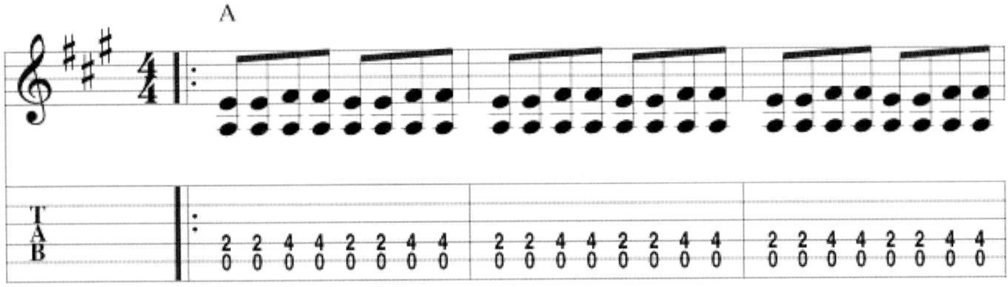

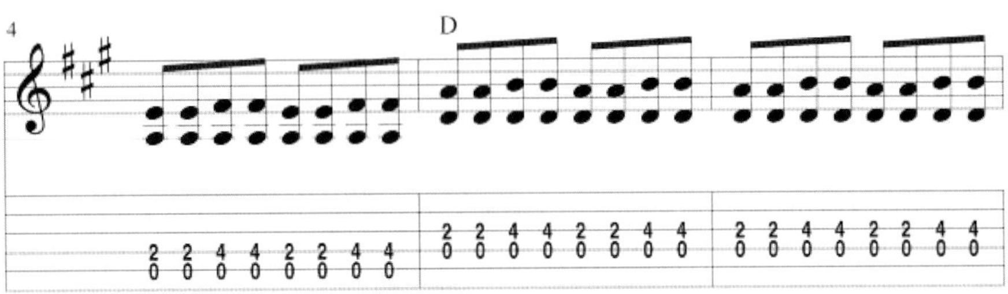

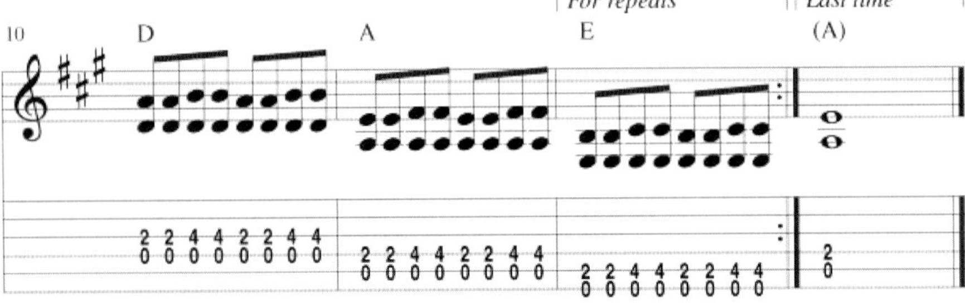

A 12-bar blues progression in A.

Enter the Licks: Lead Guitar

After you gain a solid feel for a basic rock 'n' roll rhythm, you may want to try some lead guitar, which simply involves playing single notes over an underlying accompaniment. You can play memorized licks, which are short, self-contained phrases, or you can improvise by making up melodies on the spot. In this section, we provide you with the building blocks for great classic rock solos, help you mix in some articulation, show you how to string it all together, and finish up with some tips on building your own solos.

What's behind Box I? The pentatonic minor scale

You can play lead right away by memorizing a few simple patterns on the guitar neck, known as boxes, that produce instant results. Basically, guitarists memorize a finger pattern that vaguely resembles the shape of a box — hence the term box position — and use notes from that pattern (in various orders) over and over pretty much throughout a solo or a section of a solo. In soloing over a basic chord progression, you can keep using this one pattern even if the chords change.

The first box we're going to show you is made up of notes from the pentatonic minor scale, and it's the most useful box for rock music. You don't need to think about theory, scales, or chords — only the fingering, which you memorize. These patterns contain no "wrong notes," so by virtue of just moving your fingers around in time to a rhythm track, you can play instant rock 'n' roll lead guitar.

The notation shows a two-octave A pentatonic minor scale in fifth position. This example is your first box, here called Box I.

*Box 1:
A two-octave
A pentatonic
minor scale in
fifth position.*

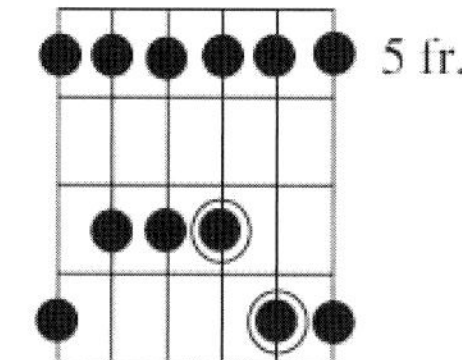

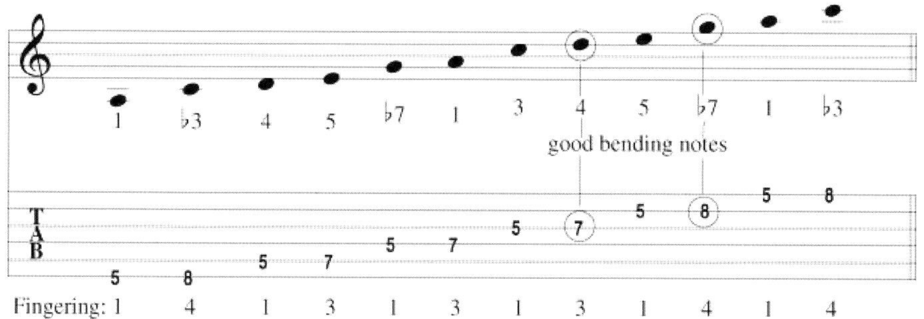

Adding articulations

The box pattern shows you what to play, but articulations show you how to play. Articulations include hammer-ons, pull-offs, slides, bends, and vibrato. These elements are what make a solo sound like a solo, give the solo expression, and personalize it.

The following notation shows a four-bar lick using notes of Box I (the pentatonic minor scale) in ascending and descending order that you connect by using hammer-ons and pull-offs. Notice how much smoother and more flowing the sound is, as opposed to what you hear if you pick every note separately.

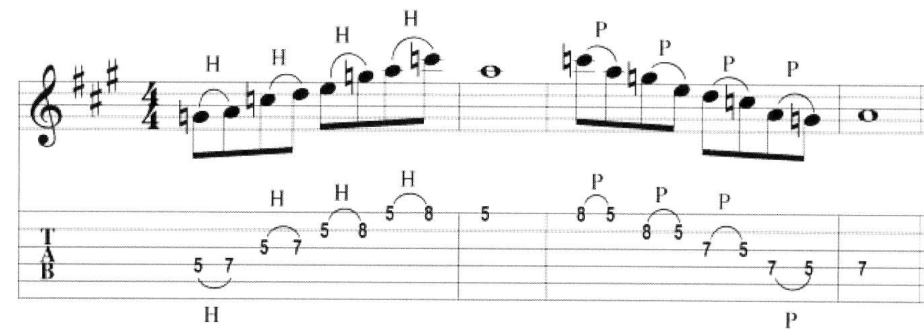

Using hammer-ons and pull-offs in Box 1.

Before proceeding, make sure you understand how the neck diagrams and staff correspond. Note that the neck diagram does not show a chord, but a scale, where the notes are played one at a time, from lowest to highest (as shown in the standard notation and tab below).

Notice that in the figure we show you (beneath the notes in the standard notation) the scale degree (not so important) and (beneath the tab numbers) the fingering (very important) for each note; we also show you which notes are good for bending. Memorize the fingering until you can play it in your sleep. This pattern is essential to know if you want to play rock guitar. Memorize it. Really do it. Play it over and over, up and down. Really. (We mean it. Honest!)

We use the key of A for all the examples in this section, but if you'd like to play lead in other keys, move your box patterns up or down the neck the appropriate number of frets. For example, to play in the key of B, move your boxes up two frets.

Having a box to use in improvising lead guitar is what makes playing classic rock 'n' roll (or blues) so much fun; you don't need to think - you just gotta feel. Of course, you can't just play the five notes of the scale up and down, over and over - that would get boring very fast. Instead, you use your creativity to create licks by using the scale and adding articulations such as bends and hammer-ons until you have a complete solo.

Bending notes is probably the coolest sound in lead soloing, but the trick is knowing which notes to bend and when to do so. When using Box I, guitarists really like to bend notes on the 2nd and 3rd strings because the tension feels right, and they get to bend toward the ceiling - their favorite direction. Start off by bending the third-finger note on the 3rd string and the fourth-finger note on the 2nd string.

Here's a typical four-bar phrase featuring a 3rd- and 2nd-string bend in Box I.

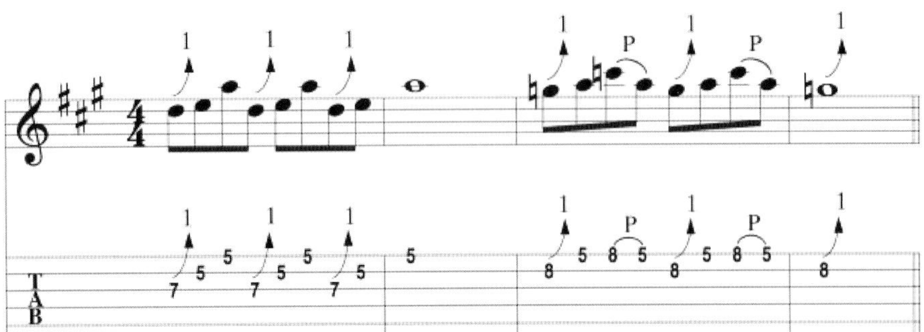

Bending the 3rd and 2nd strings in Box 1.

Add some vibrato to the final note to give it some expression.

Here's a typical two-bar phrase featuring a double-stop bend in Box I. The note that's on the seventh fret of the 2nd string isn't part of the A pentatonic minor scale, but it sounds good anyway, and it's easy to play because the third finger barres both notes of the double-stop.

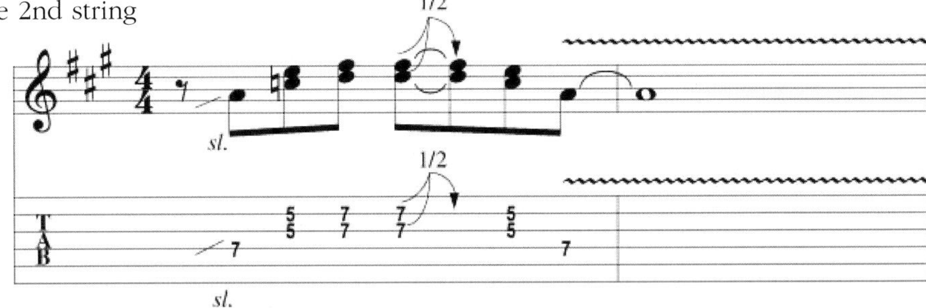

A double-stop bend in Box 1.

Building a solo using Box I

An improvised solo is something that you create, and nobody can show you exactly what to play. But we can show you the tools for soloing so that you can practice and get a feel for it. Beyond that, however, your personality does the talking. For now, start out by getting the feel of playing lead over the 12-bar blues accompaniment pattern that we show you earlier in the article.

Notice that each of the phrases that we show you in the preceding section, "Adding articulations," alternates one active measure (containing lots of notes) with one static measure (containing just one note). This alternation between activity and rest prevents monotony. Play these phrases in the order that we describe in the following instructions, and you have a ready-made 12-bar solo. (If you want, you can play the solo over and over.) To play such a solo, just follow these steps:

1. **For the first four bars of the solo, play the double-stop lick.**

2. **For the next four bars of the solo, play the hammer-on/pull-off lick.**

3. **For the last four bars of the solo, play the "bending the 3rd and 2nd strings" lick.**

We notate the preceding steps in the upcoming notation. Playing this example gives you the feel of playing lead your little solo sounds like a series of phrases — as it should.

Eddie Van Halen

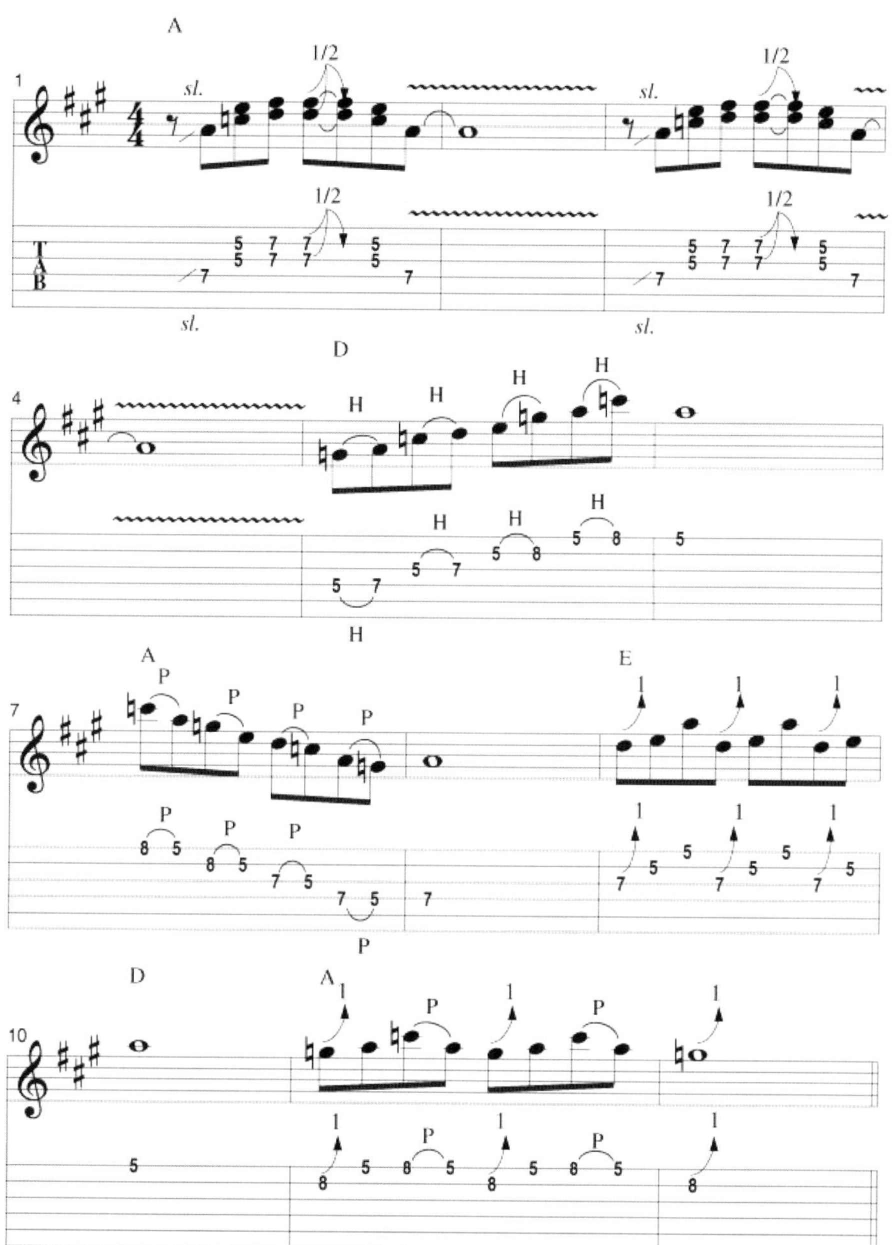

Putting together three Box-1 licks to create one 12-bar solo.

Jimi Hendrix

Boxes II and III

The next two boxes, which we name here Box II and Box III, don't show notes on all six strings as Box I does, because guitarists generally play only the notes on the top two or three strings.

Listen to recordings to get new ideas as you become more confident in your playing. As you hear a recording, you may be able to figure out exactly what the guitarist is playing, because most guitarists use the same boxes, bends, vibratos, and so on that you do.

Box II consists of five notes, as you see below. Notice that the two notes at the top of this box (at the eighth fret) are also part of Box I, but in Box I, you play them with the pinky or third finger. This box shows notes from the A pentatonic minor scale in eighth position. Again, in the figure, we show you the scale degree and fingering for each note, and we show you which note is good for bending.

Notes in Box II.

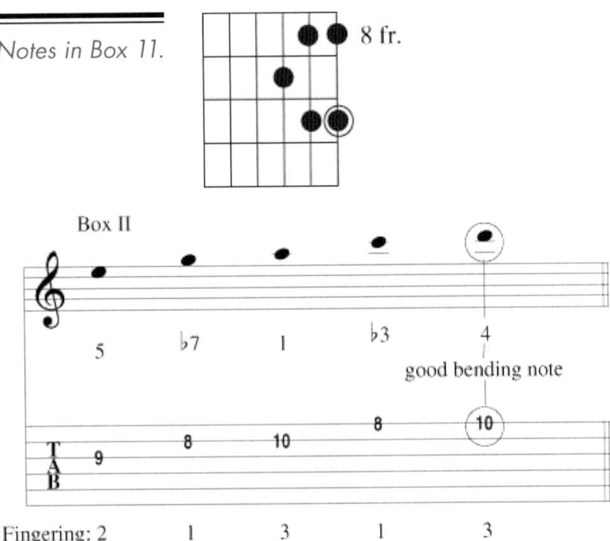

Box II is popular because it features a good note for bending under the third finger, and that note also happens to be the highest note in the box. In playing lead, high is good. You can play the highest note in the box and then make it even higher by bending it up a step. This technique produces quite a dramatic effect. Try it.

Here you see a typical lick using Box II notes that features a bend on the highest note of the box.

A bend on the highest note of Box II.

Box III is a funny one because some of its notes aren't in the A pentatonic minor scale — but guitarists use this box a lot anyway. The following list tells you all the stuff that Box III has going for it:

- Box III is easy to play and memorize — it's exactly like Box II but lies two frets higher on the neck.
- Box III has two notes — F♯ (the sixth degree) and B (the second degree) — that don't fall in the A pentatonic minor scale. And this is a good thing. These two notes are borrowed from the parent major scale (the major scale that starts on the same note — in this case, A), and sometimes guitarists like to add them to the pentatonic minor scale for variety and spice. The predominance of notes from the pentatonic minor scale is what gives classic rock 'n' roll (and blues) its flavour — not the total exclusion of all other notes.
- The good note for bending in Box III falls under the third finger.
- The first degree of the scale, the note on which you often end a phrase, is under the first finger on the 2nd string in this box. You tend to apply vibrato to the ending note of a phrase (especially if you hold it), and this note provides an ideal finger and string on which to vibrato.

Feast your eyes on Box III (in tenth position for the key of A). Again we show you the scale degree and fingering for each note — and the note that's good for bending we circle again.

Notes in Box III.

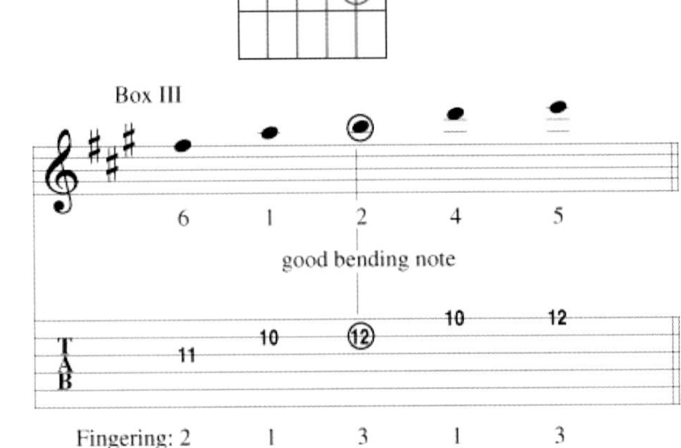

Often, guitarists concentrate on the 2nd and 3rd strings of Box III. The following notation depicts a typical Box III phrase. Don't forget to vibrato that last note!

A typical lick using Box III.

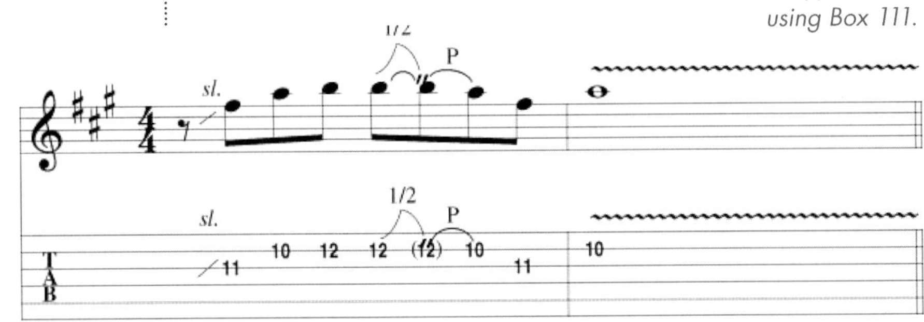

Building a solo by using Boxes I, II, and III

This section simply puts together licks from the three boxes that we describe in the preceding sections. You don't need any new information; you just need to piece together what you know if you read the information we give in those sections. (If you haven't yet, we suggest that you do so now, before you try out the solo we describe here.) In other words, after you make the bricks, you can put them together to make a house.

In the following list, we show you how to build a ready-made 12-bar solo consisting of six two-bar phrases (using three boxes) that we show you in the preceding sections.

Follow these steps:

1. **Play the Box I double-stop lick.**
2. **Play the Box I "bending the 3rd string" lick.**
3. **Play the Box III lick.**
4. **Play the Box I "bending the 2nd string" lick.**
5. **Play the Box II lick.**
6. **Play the Box I double-stop lick again.**

Here's the music to the preceding steps.

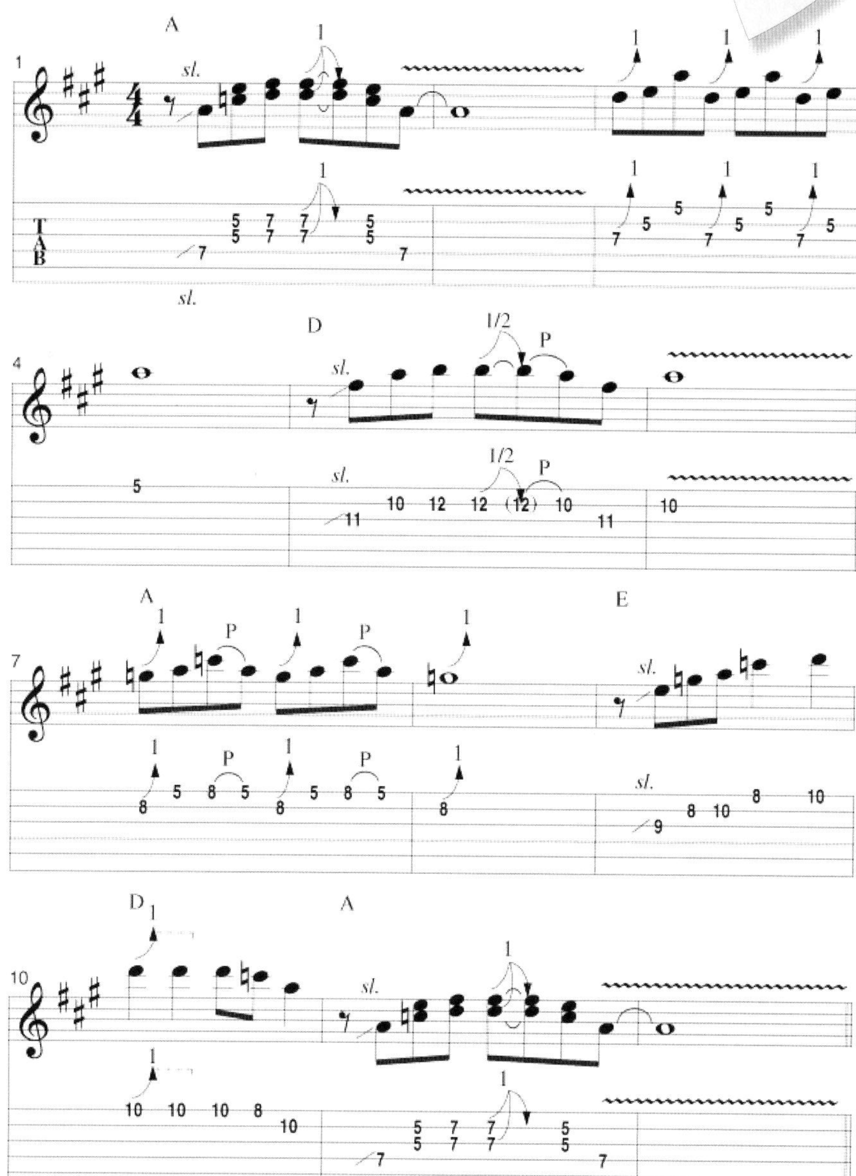

Putting together six two-bar licks from all three boxes to build one 12-bar solo.

As you play this solo over and over, you get a feel for soloing with the three boxes over a 12-bar blues progression. The fun begins after you start making up your own solos. Following are some guidelines for creating your own leads:

- Think in terms of short phrases strung together. You can even play just one short phrase over and over, even though the backing chords change. A good way to make up a phrase is to make it a singable one. Sing a short phrase in your mind but use notes from the box.
- Add some articulation - especially bends, because they sound the coolest. Add vibrato to long notes that end a phrase, sometimes sliding down at the very end.
- Alternate between activity (lots of notes) and rest (a few notes or just one note or even silence for a few beats).
- Move from box to box to give your solo some variety.

Don't be inhibited or worry about making a mistake. In our opinions, you can't really make a mistake, because all the notes in the boxes sound good against all the chords in the backing progression.

The only mistake that you can make is to avoid soloing for fear of sounding lame. Soloing takes practice, but you gradually build confidence.

Playing the Blues

IN THIS ARTICLE

- *Playing electric blues*
- *Playing acoustic blues*
- *Playing songs about heartbreak and sorrow and looking good doing it!*

Playing great blues — following in the musical footsteps of such legends as B.B. King or the late Stevie Ray Vaughan — may be difficult, but playing pretty good blues right away is still fairly easy if you know the form, a couple of scales, and some simple blues moves.

Electric blues is the kind of blues that all the giants of the genre play: Buddy Guy, B.B. King, Albert King, Albert Collins, Johnny Winter, and Duane Allman, among others. We focus here on electric-blues guitar playing, which breaks down fairly neatly into two categories: rhythm and lead.

Blues Rhythm Guitar

Rhythm playing is what you do whenever you're not playing lead — such as accompanying a singer or another featured instrument by playing chords, background figures, and repeated low-note riffs. Rhythm generally requires less technical proficiency than playing lead does and relies more on the guitarist's "feel" than on his technique. To put chord playing into some kind of context, you want to begin with the most popular form, or progression, in the style, the 12-bar blues.

The basic structure of the 12-bar blues form

Blues and rock guitar are similar in that each leans heavily on the 12-bar blues form for song structure (see the previous article). Taking the key of A as an example, the 12-bar blues progression consists of four bars of A, two bars of D, two bars of A, one bar of E, one bar of D, and two bars of A. In music notation, the 12-bar blues progression looks like the following example.

B.B. King is a legend of blues guitar.

13

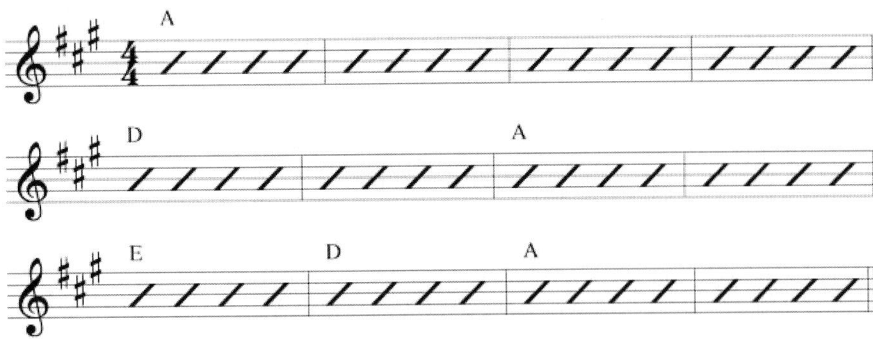

12-bar blues chord progression in A.

Chords in any common progression are often referred to by Roman numerals. These numerals identify the chords generically rather than by key. You always assign Roman numeral I to the chord that names the key you're in. Then, you count up alphabetically, letter by letter, assigning other numbers to chords.

For example, in the key of A (as in the previous example) the A chord is I (Roman numeral one), the D is IV (four), and E is V (five). (You can count letter names on your fingers, starting from A, to confirm that A is I, D is IV, and E is V.) In the key of G, on the other hand, G is I, C is IV, and D is V. By using such a system, if you decide to switch keys, you can always just say, "Start playing at the IV (four) chord in bar 5." If you know which chords are I, IV, and V in that key, you're ready to play. Here's a handy reference that shows the I, IV, and V chords in common keys.

I, IV, V Chords in Common Keys

Key	I	IV	V
A	A	D	E
C	C	F	G
D	D	G	A
E	E	A	B
F	F	B♭	C
G	G	C	D

If you're playing your blues accompaniment by using barre chords, you can remember which chords are which merely by their position on the neck. Say, for example, that you're playing a blues progression in A. If you make an E-based barre chord at the fifth fret (A), you're playing the I chord in A. If you switch to the A-based barre chord form at that same fret, you're now playing the IV chord, or D. Move that same A-based barre two frets higher on the neck - to the seventh fret - and you're playing the V chord, E. See how easy playing the blues can be! Use those same positions anywhere on the neck - an E-based barre chord at any fret, following it with an A-based barre chord at the same fret, and moving that barre up two frets - and you know the I-IV-V progression for whatever key goes with the starting fret.

The following are two important variations of the 12-bar blues form:

- **Quick IV:** Still using the key of A as an example, you substitute a D (IV) chord for A (I) in bar 2. Ordinarily, you must wait until bar 5 to play the IV chord, so switching to it in bar 2 feels pretty quick, hence the name.
- **Turnaround:** A turnaround is a V chord that you play on the last bar (bar 12) instead of a I chord. This change helps draw the music back to the I chord of the first bar, "turning the progression around" to bar 1. Blues guitarists base many lead licks just on the turnaround at the progression's end.

Triplet feel

Blues relies heavily on a rhythmic feel known as a triplet feel (sometimes called a shuffle feel or a swing feel). In a triplet feel, you divide each beat into three parts (instead of the normal two). To get an understanding of the difference between straight feel and triplet feel, recite each of the following phrases out loud, snapping your fingers on each capitalized syllable. (Make sure that you snap your fingers — it's important!)

1. **TWIN**-kle **TWIN**-kle **LIT**-tle **STAR**.

That's a straight feel — each finger snap is a beat, and each beat you divide into two parts.

2. **FOL**-low the **YEL**-low brick **ROAD**.

That's a triplet feel — each finger snap is a beat, and each beat you divide into three parts. Because lots of blues use a triplet feel, you need to know how to play a 12-bar blues accompaniment figure with that feel.

Check out the following notation to see an accompaniment — here with the quick IV (bar 2) and turnaround (bar 12) variation — consisting of nothing more than strummed chords in a triplet rhythm. Typically, the last bar of a blues song uses a progression in which you approach the final chord from one fret above or below it (see measure 13). See the chord diagrams for the fingerings of the 9th chords in the song.

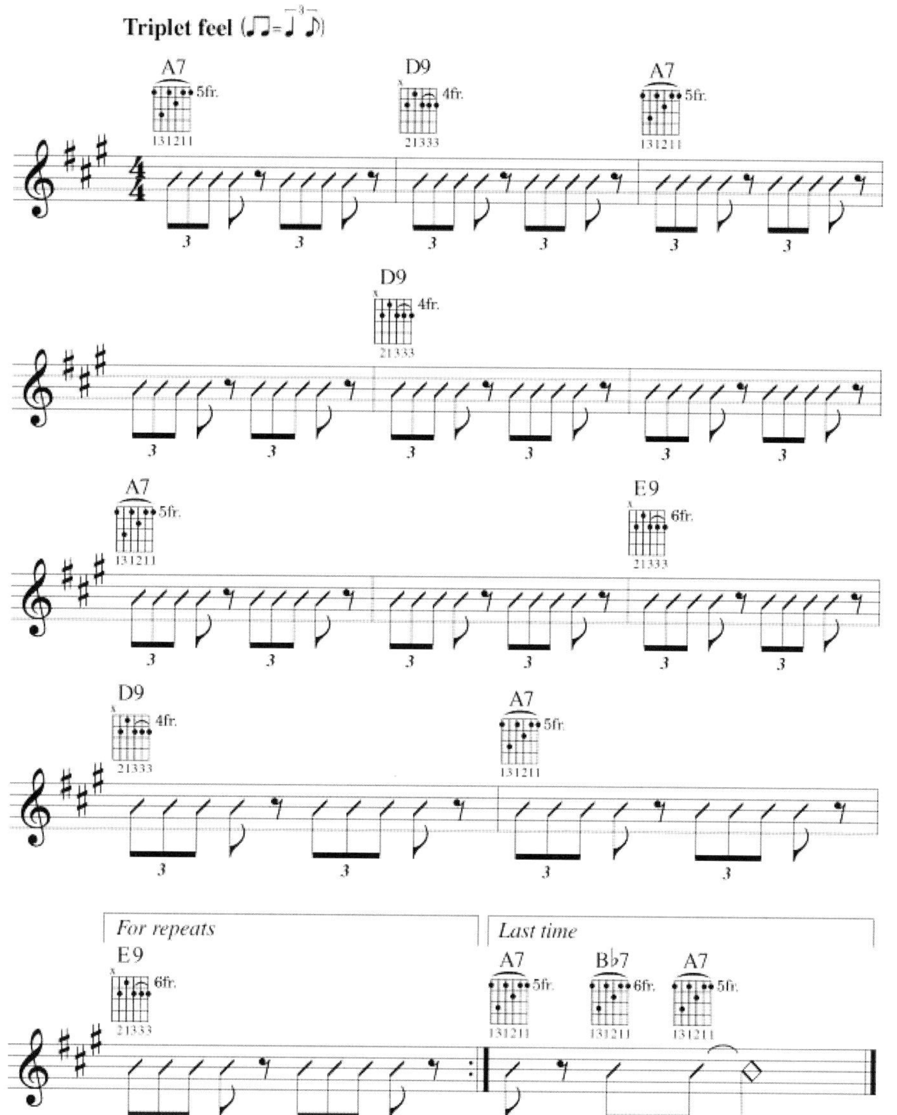

12-bar blues accompaniment with strumming in a triplet feel.

The equivalency (♫ = ♩♪ triplet) that appears next to the words "triplet feel" indicates that you should substitute triplet (or shuffle) eighths for straight eighth notes. In triplet eighths, you hold the first note of each beat a little longer than the second.

Blues Lead Guitar

Blues lead is the single-note melodic line, consisting of a mixture of composed lines and improvised phrases. A great lead solo includes both these elements in one seamless, inspired whole.

The boxes

Blues guitarists improvise mostly by using "boxes" — just as rock guitarists do. A box is a fingerboard pattern — usually outlining a pentatonic minor scale — that vaguely resembles the shape of a box. (The previous article, on rock guitar, gives you more information on pentatonic minor scales and boxes.) By using notes in the box, you can improvise lead lines that automatically sound good as you play them over a 12-bar blues accompaniment.

You may already know how to use boxes to play rock 'n' roll lead guitar, which employs the same scales and chords as blues. If so, you should have no trouble understanding the following example, which shows the three boxes that you can use for soloing in the key of A that we introduce in the previous article; we circle the notes that are good for bending.

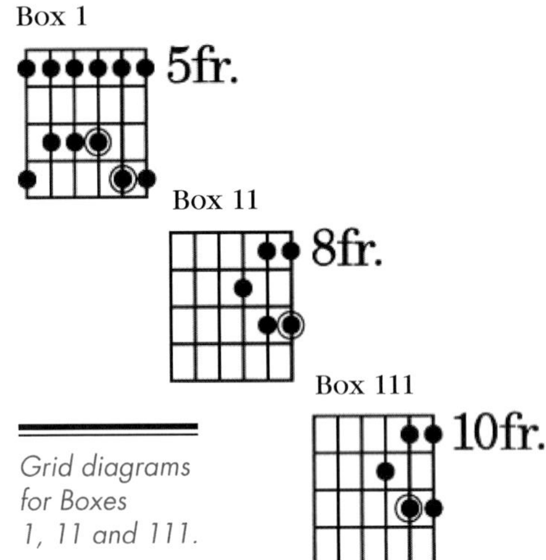

Grid diagrams for Boxes 1, 11 and 111.

A Box V lick with a slide up to Box 1.

Here's a typical lick that uses Box V. A common blues technique is to slide on the 5th string (third finger) back and forth between Box V and Box I. See how nicely all the notes fall under the first and third fingers, even as you move between the boxes.

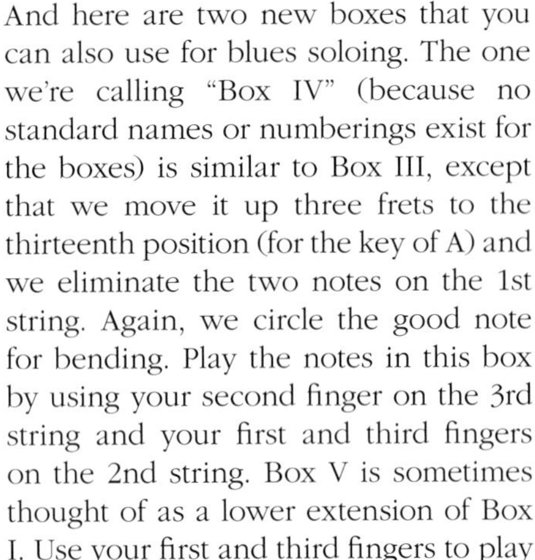

And here are two new boxes that you can also use for blues soloing. The one we're calling "Box IV" (because no standard names or numberings exist for the boxes) is similar to Box III, except that we move it up three frets to the thirteenth position (for the key of A) and we eliminate the two notes on the 1st string. Again, we circle the good note for bending. Play the notes in this box by using your second finger on the 3rd string and your first and third fingers on the 2nd string. Box V is sometimes thought of as a lower extension of Box I. Use your first and third fingers to play the notes on both strings.

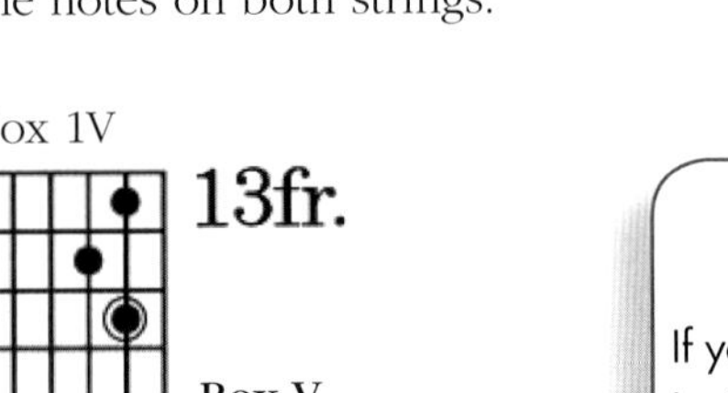

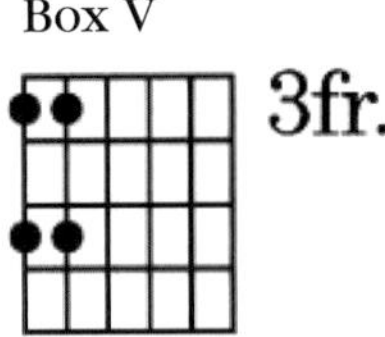

Grid diagrams for Boxes 1V and V.

If you know how to play typical licks by using Boxes I, II, and III (see the previous article), the lick that uses Box IV should give you no trouble. Play with a triplet feel, and make sure that you apply vibrato to the last note for a real blues effect. Notice how the bend falls under the third finger - the best finger for bending.

A Box V lick with a slide up to Box 1.

Adding depth with additional notes

The pentatonic minor scale produces good blues notes, but adding two more notes gives you an even richer sonic palette of note choices. The flatted fifth and the major third help give more definition to a line by introducing a dissonant, or tension-filled, note (the flatted fifth) and another note (the major third) that reinforces the major quality of the I chord.

A flatted fifth is a note that's a half step (or one fret) lower than the regular fifth of a scale. In the A pentatonic minor scale, for example, the E note is the fifth. (Count letter names from A to E on your fingers to confirm that E is five not above A.) The E♭ note is therefore the flatted fifth. A major third is a note that's a half step (or one fret) higher than the regular (minor) third of a pentatonic minor scale. In the A pentatonic minor scale, for example, the C note is the minor third. The C♯ note is the major third.

Creating the blues scale with the flatted fifth

The five-note pentatonic scale works great for basic blues, but for a really funky, crying sound, toss in the flat-five note (E♭ in the key of A) now and then. Adding the flat-five note to the pentatonic scale creates the six-note blues scale. The flat five is particularly dissonant but adds some spice to the more "vanilla-sounding" quality of the straight pentatonic minor scale. But as with any spice, whether salt, fennel, or a flat five, add it sparingly and judiciously.

Boxes I, II and IV, as shown here, consist of notes from the pentatonic minor scale. The notes in circles indicate the added E♭ — the ♭5 (flat five) — this time and not the bending notes. Box I shows the complete (two-octave) A blues scale in fifth position, while Boxes II and IV show partial blues scales that are good to use for improvising.

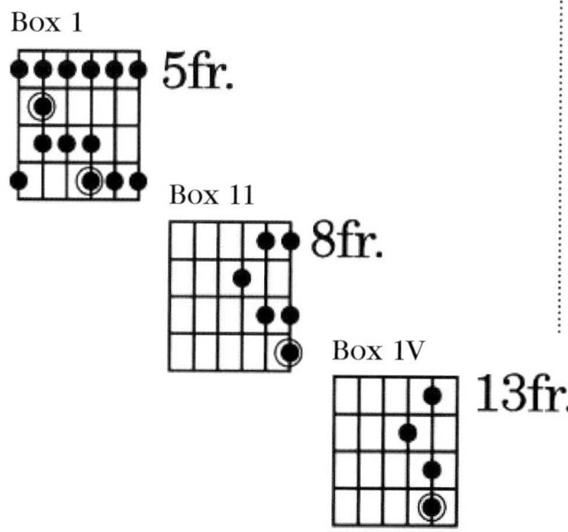

Grid showing the addition of the flat five (♭5) to Boxes 1, 11 and 1V.

Notice in the following typical Box-I blues lick that you can produce the E♭ in two ways — by playing it at the eighth fret of the 3rd string or by bending the seventh-fret note (the typical good note for bending in Box I) up a half step.

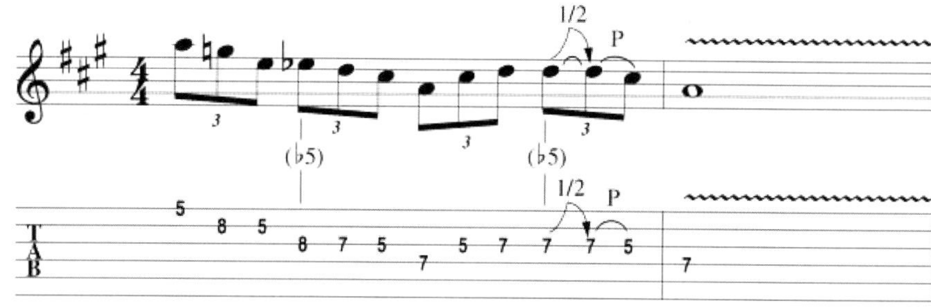

A blues-scale lick using Box 1.

In the following two notations, you see a typical blues-scale lick, first using Box II (in eighth position) and then (the same lick) using Box IV (in thirteenth position). Again, you play the ♭5 both straight and as a bent note (with the third finger) in each position.

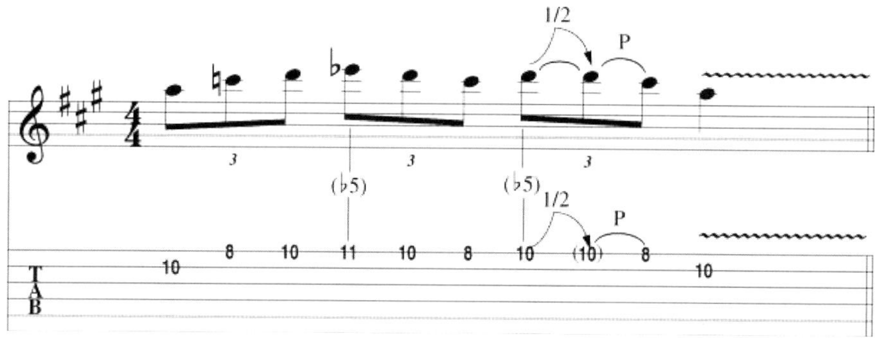

A blues-scale lick using Box 11.

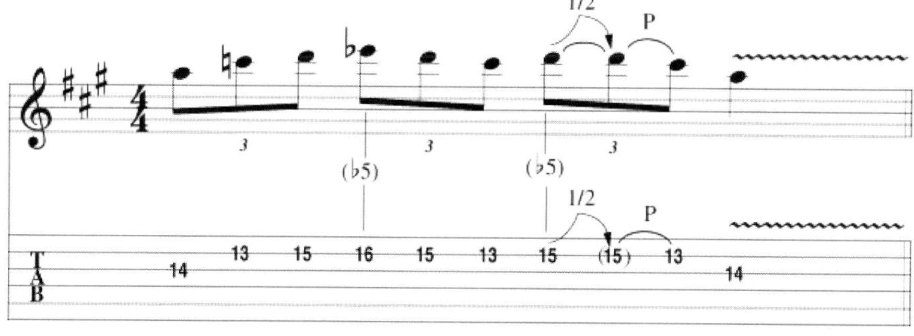

The same blues scale lick using Box 1V.

Borrowing the major third

Another note that blues players commonly add to the pentatonic minor or blues scale is the major third. You can think of this note as one that you "borrow" from the pentatonic major scale or from the full major scale. In the key of A, the added major third is C♯, and the upcoming figure shows where it falls in Box I (the note in the circle). It's the only note that you play with your second finger if you're using Box I (unless you're also using the flat five that we describe in the preceding section).

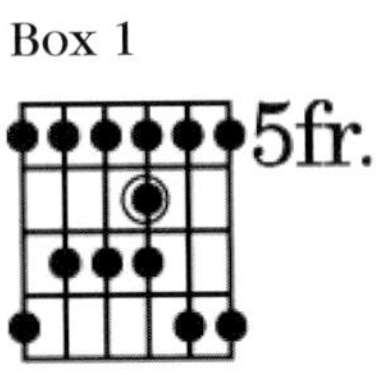

Grid showing the addition of the major third to Box 1.

Very often, you hammer on the major third from the minor third a fret below it, as shown below.

A lick using the major third with Box1.

Even though you use the pentatonic minor scale for soloing, the key of a typical blues song is major (as in A major) because the rhythm guitarist plays major background chords (which contain major thirds). In double-stop licks, often heard in the music of Chuck Berry and the Beach Boys, the end of a descending lead lick usually contains a major third to help establish the key as major rather than minor, as you see below.

A double-stop riff using the major third with Box 1.

Phrasing

Although blues soloing uses many of the same techniques, scales, chords, and boxes as rock soloing does, the two styles are different in the area of phrasing. Lots of steady-flowing eighth notes often characterize rock soloing (think of the solo to "Johnny B. Goode"). But blues soloing (think B.B. King) more often employs phrases that are shorter and sparser (more separated) than those of rock.

In a typical blues melody, you may hear a very short phrase, some empty space, and then a repetition of the same phrase. Usually, these short phrases have a vocal quality to them in that they're expressive, often conveying pain or sorrow. Sometimes, if the guitarist is also the singer, the vocal phrases and the guitar phrases are practically one and the same. The short passage that follows demonstrates the short-phrase concept. Notice how the same figure (the pull-off from the eighth fret to the fifth) sounds good but different if you play it against a different chord (first against A7 and then D7). Repeating a figure after the chord changes is a typical blues technique.

A riff showing typical blues phrasing.

Blues moves

Blues moves are easy to create because they're so short. Make up your own and see how they sound as you play them over the 12-bar blues progressions shown earlier in this article.

REMEMBER

The following notation shows four typical blues moves. A blues move is nothing more than a short, cool-sounding lick (a self-contained musical phrase).

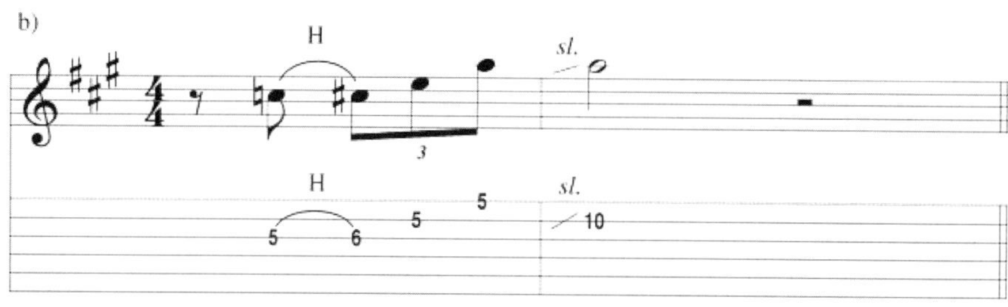

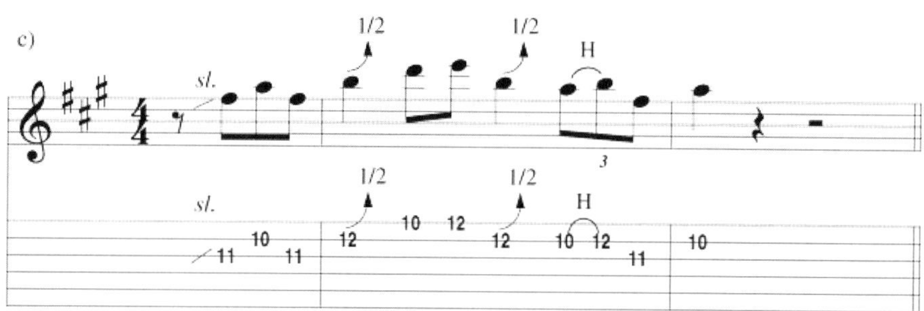

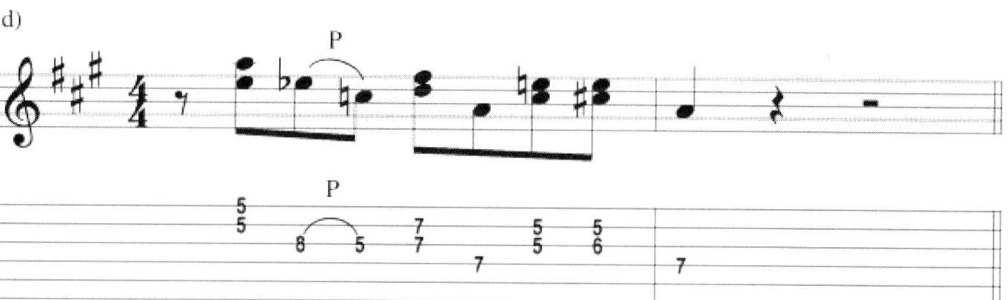

Riffs showing four typical blues moves.

Tackling Techniques of Classical Guitar

IN THIS ARTICLE

- *Sitting correctly* • *Positioning the right and left hand*
- *Cutting and filing your nails* • *Free strokes and rest strokes*
- *Playing arpeggios* • *Playing counterpoint* • *Playing classical pieces*

Classical guitar not only suggests a certain musical style, but also implies an approach to the instrument that's quite different from that of any other style, whether folk, jazz, rock, or blues. Classical guitar encompasses a long tradition of techniques and practices that composers and performers have observed through the ages and to which they still adhere, even with the advent of more modern and avant-garde musical compositions.

Don't get the impression that, because it adheres to certain disciplines, classical music is all rigid rules and regulations. Many guitarists with careers in both the pop and classical fields feel that some aspects of classical guitar playing are liberating, and these rugged individualists have actually tried to infuse classical techniques into pop and rock playing.

Sitting position for classical guitar.

Getting Ready to Play Classical Guitar

You always play classical guitar on a nylon-string guitar (as opposed to the steel-string models used for many other styles), in a sitting position. Beyond that, you must employ certain right-hand strokes (methods of plucking the strings) to get the expected sound. In addition, you must adopt a new approach to left-hand positioning.

How to sit

Real classical guitarists (that is, most real classical guitarists) sit differently from other guitarists in that they hold the guitar on the left leg instead of on the right one. They also elevate the left leg about six inches by using a footstool. If you perform this balancing act, you accomplish the following goals:

- You rest the guitar's treble side (the side closer to the higher-pitched strings) on the left leg, with the back of the instrument resting against your abdomen. The weight of your right arm on the bass side holds the instrument in place (balanced, so to speak). Your hands are thus completely free to play — and only play. You don't need to use your hands to keep the guitar from falling to the floor (unless you jump up suddenly to answer the phone).
- You position the guitar so that the left hand can play any fret at the correct (perpendicular) angle — see the "Left-hand position" section later in the chapter. This allows you to play the higher positions (seventh and up) more easily than you can in the steel-string acoustic sitting position.

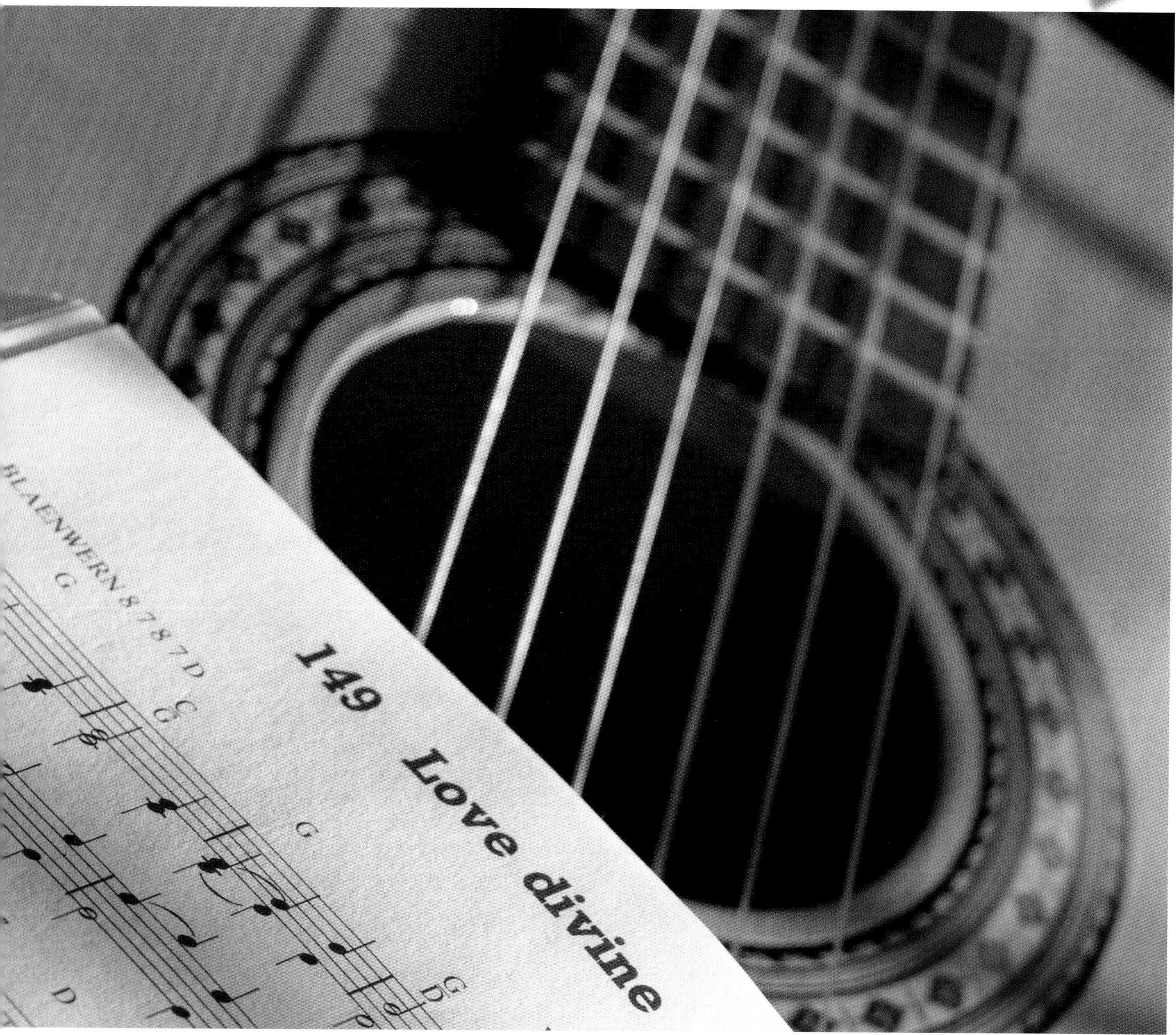

If you just want to try out a few classical-guitar pieces for the fun of it, hold the guitar as you normally do. The music police aren't likely to arrest you, and you can still hear the beautiful arrangement of the notes, even if you're not playing strictly "by the rules."

The right hand

After posture, your right-hand approach is the most critical consideration for achieving a true classical guitar sound. You must play with your right hand in the correct position and execute the correct finger strokes.

Right-hand position

The most important concept about right-hand position is that you hold your fingers — index, middle, and ring — perpendicular to the strings as they strike. (You normally don't use the little finger in classical guitar.)

This positioning is no easy feat. Why? Because your hand, which is an extension of your arm, naturally falls at about a 60-degree angle to the strings. Try it. See? But if you hold your fingers at an angle, you can't get maximum volume from the strings. To get the strongest sound (which you need to do to bring out melodies from the bass and inner voices), you must strike the strings at a 90-degree angle — perpendicular.

Rotate your right hand at the wrist so that the fingers fall perpendicular to the strings and your thumb stays about 1½ inches to the left (from your vantage point) of your index finger, as you see in the photograph. Rest your right-hand thumb and fingers (index, middle, and ring) on the 6th, 3rd, 2nd, and 1st strings, respectively, as shown in the figure. This setup is the basic classical-guitar position for the right hand. Are your fingers perpendicular to the strings?

Correct right-hand position.

If you're serious about perfecting classical right-hand technique, here's a tip to force your fingers into the correct position: Place all four fingers (thumb, index, middle, and ring) on the same string (the 3rd, say), lining them up in a row. By positioning your fingers this way, your thumb can't rest to the right of your index finger. Then, without turning your hand, move each finger to its normal place: thumb to the 6th string, index staying on the 3rd, middle to the 2nd, and ring to the 1st.

The fingernails

Your right-hand fingernails affect the tone of your playing. If your nails are very short, only the flesh of your finger hits the string, and the resulting tone is rather mellow and soft. Conversely, if your nails are very long, only the nail hits the string, and the tone is sharper and more metallic. Most classical guitarists grow their nails somewhat long so that both the flesh and the nail hit the string at the same time, producing a pleasing, well-rounded tone.

Some guitarists own a special fingernail-care kit that contains scissors or clippers, nail files, emery boards, and fine abrasive cloths to enable them to keep their nails at a desired length, shape, and smoothness.

Changing tone colour

You can alter the tone colour of the strings by placing your right hand at different points along the string — closer to the bridge or closer to the fretboard or directly over the sound hole. If you play directly over the sound hole, the tone is full and rich. As you move toward the bridge, the tone becomes brighter and more metallic; and as you move toward the fretboard, the tone becomes more rounded and mellow.

Why do you need to change timbre (tone colour)? Mostly for the sake of variety. If you're playing a piece with a section that repeats, you may play over the sound hole for the first pass and then on the repeat play closer to the bridge. Or maybe you're approaching the climax in a piece and you want to heighten the effect by playing with a brighter, more metallic sound. You can then play closer to the bridge. Printed classical guitar music often indicates these positions, and you can clearly hear the changes in recordings of classical guitar pieces.

If you're serious about playing classical guitar, grow your nails a bit long and cut them so that they're rounded, following the same contour as your fingertips. Then file or buff them with a nail file or emery board. Grow only the right-hand nails. You must keep the left-hand nails short so that they don't hit the fretboard as you press down the strings, preventing the notes from sounding out correctly. But if you're playing classical guitar casually, for fun or just to try it out, don't worry about the length of your right-hand nails. Lots of people play classical guitar with short nails (and with the guitar set on their right leg, too!).

Left-hand position

As you're fingering frets in the classical style, try to think of your left hand as a piece of machinery that you lock into one position — a position that you can characterize by right angles and perpendicularity (to achieve ease of playing and optimal sound). As you move up and down the neck or across the strings, the little machine never changes its appearance. You simply move it along the two directions of a grid — as you would an Etch-a-Sketch. Here's how the machine works:

- **Keep your fingers rounded and arched so that the tips come down to the fingerboard at a 90-degree angle and place them perpendicular to the strings.**
- **Straighten your thumb and keep it pretty much opposite the index finger as you lightly press it against the back of the guitar neck. As you move to higher frets, bring your thumb along, always keeping it opposite the index finger.**

Correct left-hand position.

You can move it across the neck as your fingers do, but don't ever allow it to creep above the fingerboard.

- Move your arm with your hand so that your hand stays perpendicular to the strings. As you play the lower frets, keep your elbow out, away from your body. At the higher frets, bring your elbow in, closer to your body.

Theoretically, no matter what string or fret you play, your left hand position looks the same — like the one in the photograph. Of course, special requirements of the music could force you to abandon the basic left-hand position from time to time. So think of the preceding guidelines as just that: guidelines.

If you've been playing other guitar styles (such as rock or blues) for a while, you probably often see your left thumb tip coming all the way around the neck, sticking out above the 6th string. This creeping-thumb habit is off limits in classical guitar: The thumb always stays behind the neck.

Free Strokes and Rest Strokes

If you had a golf or bowling coach, he'd probably lecture you on the importance of a good follow-through. Well, believe it or not, the same thing's true in plucking a guitar string. Your finger can follow through after plucking a string in one of two ways, giving you two kinds of strokes. One is the free stroke, which you use for arpeggios and fast scale passages. The other, the rest stroke, you use for accentuating melody notes. The thumb, however, virtually always plays free strokes, even when playing melodies. (Free strokes are used in both classical and folk playing; rest strokes are unique to classical guitar.) The following sections describe both strokes.

Playing free strokes

If you pluck a string at a slightly upward angle, your finger comes to rest in the air, above the next adjacent string. (Of course, it doesn't stay there for long, because you must return it to its normal starting position to pluck again.) This type of stroke, where your finger dangles freely in the air, is called a free stroke. Check out the before and after pictures to find out how to play a free stroke.

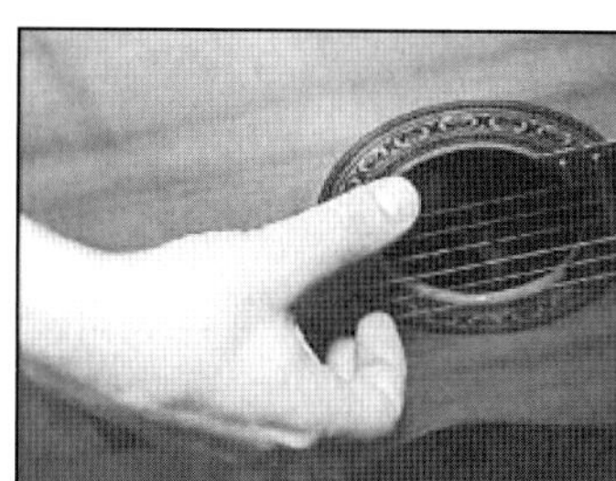

The free stroke. Notice that, after striking a string, the right-hand finger dangles in the air.

In classical guitar, you use free strokes for playing nonmelodic material, such as arpeggios (chords played one note at a time instead of all at once). Try arpeggiating the open strings (thumb on the 6th string, index finger on the 3rd, middle on the 2nd, and ring on the 1st), using all free strokes.

The following notation is an excerpt from a Spanish piece, "Malagueña," that just about every guitar player picks up at some time or other. You play the melody with the thumb while the middle

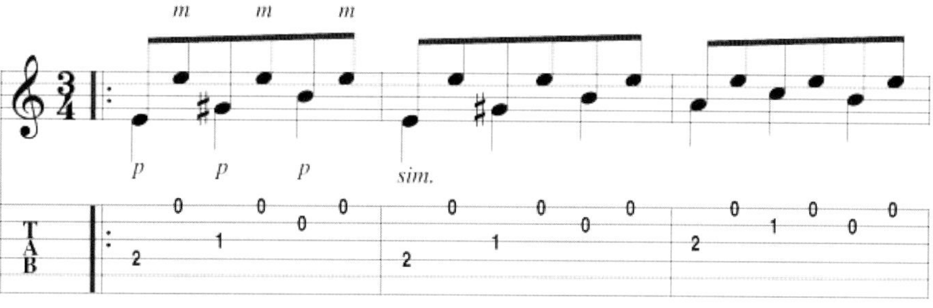

A free-stroke exercise (from the classic piece "Malagueña").

finger plays free strokes on the open high-E string. Classical guitar notation indicates the right-hand fingers by the letters p, i, m, and a, which stand for the first letters of the Spanish names for the fingers: The thumb is p (pulgar), the index is i (indice), the middle is m (media), and the ring is a (anular). You also see these notations used in fingerstyle folk guitar.

Playing rest strokes

The rest stroke uses a different kind of follow-through from the free stroke. Instead of striking the string at a slightly upward angle, pluck straight across (not upward) so that your finger lands, or rests, against the adjacent lower-pitched string. By coming straight across the string (instead of coming across at an upward angle), you get the maximum sound out of the string. That's why rest strokes are good for melody notes; the melody notes are the prominent ones — the ones that you want to accentuate.

The before and after pictures show how to play a rest stroke.

The rest stroke. Notice that after striking a string, the right-hand finger rests against the next string.

Use rest strokes to accentuate melody notes in a classical piece that includes inner voices — filler or background notes on the middle strings (played with free strokes) — and bass notes.

Play the two-octave C major scale shown below slowly, using all rest strokes. Change from second to fifth position at the end of measure 1 by smoothly gliding your first finger along the 3rd string, up to the fifth fret. On the way down, shift back to second position by smoothly gliding your third finger along the 3rd string, down to the fourth fret. Alternate between i (index finger) and m (middle finger) as you go.

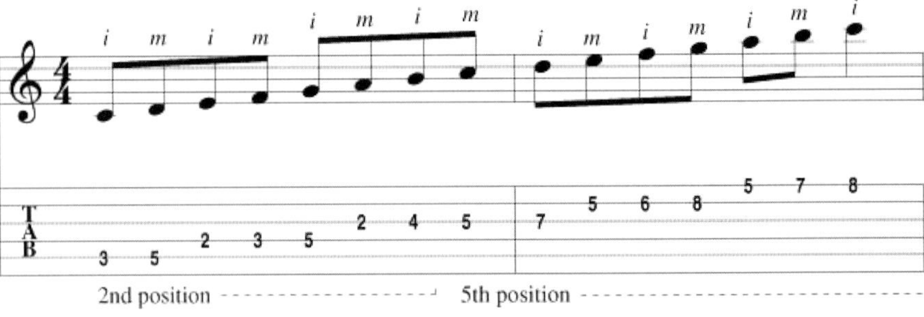

The C-major scale with rest strokes, using alternating fingers.

For the sake of speed and accuracy, alternating between two right-hand fingers (usually i and m) is customary for playing classical-guitar melodies.

Arpeggio Style and Contrapuntal Style

You play most classical guitar pieces in either an arpeggio style or a contrapuntal style. In arpeggio style, you hold chords with the left hand while plucking the strings in succession with your right hand (so that each string rings out and sustains). Usually, you simultaneously play a melody on the top strings (using rest strokes) over the arpeggios.

Contrapuntal classical guitar music usually has two parts — a bass part that you play with the thumb, and a treble part (the melody) that you play (usually by using free strokes) with alternating fingers (for example, i and m). The word contrapuntal refers to the counterpoint style, where you play two or more melodies (usually with different or contrasting rhythms) simultaneously — sort of like what you get if two people with opposing ideas talk at the same time. In music, however, the separate lines support rather than negate each other. Imagine if political debates had that effect.

Combining free strokes and rest strokes in arpeggios

We start you off here with an exercise in arpeggio style. You play the first note of each measure and the notes with stems that point down in the standard notation with the thumb; the other notes you play with the fingers (i on the 3rd string, m on the 2nd, and a on the 1st).

The notes that you play on the 1st string have an accent mark > over them in standard notation. Accent marks tell you to accentuate (or stress) certain notes by playing them

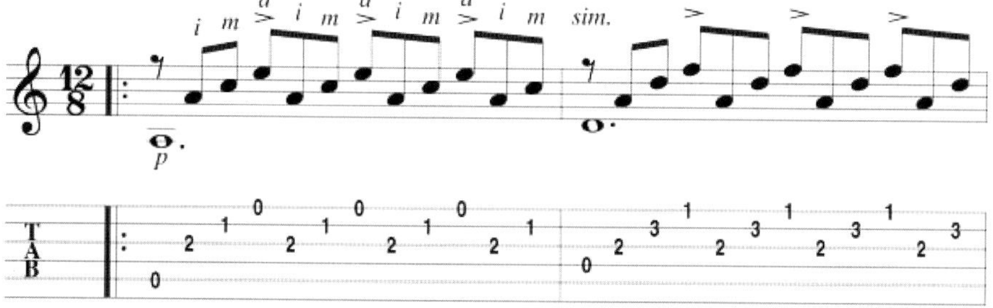

An arpeggio exercise combining free strokes and rest strokes.

The piece doesn't indicate any particular right-hand fingering. As long as you apply the concept of alternating fingers (even loosely) to attain speed and accuracy, you can use whatever fingering feels most comfortable to you. No single way is really right or wrong. We do indicate the left-hand fingering, however, because this particular fingering is the only one that's feasible for this piece. The slanted line in front of the 2 on the second beat of measure 3 and the third beat of measure 5 indicates that you're using the same finger you used to play the previous note.

Practice by playing only the top part with the (alternating) fingers a few times. Then play the bass line alone with the thumb a few times. Then play both parts simultaneously.

louder to bring them to the fore. In other words, use the more powerful rest stroke for accented notes and free strokes for all other notes. The sim. means to keep playing the same fingering pattern throughout the exercise.

Remember to hold down all the notes of each measure simultaneously with the left hand, for the duration of the measure.

Before combining rest strokes and free strokes, play the piece using all free strokes to get the feel of it. After you're comfortable with it, add the rest strokes to the notes on the 1st string.

Point/counterpoint

This last piece is an excerpt from a composition by an unknown composer of the Baroque era — an era during which contrapuntal music was very popular. Play the downstem notes (in the standard notation) by using the thumb. Use alternating fingers (free strokes) to play the melody.

A contrapuntal exercise.

Improving Your Musicianship

There's no substitute for earnest, dedicated practice if you want to become a guitar god. Figuring out a few important things about the way music works can help guide the way you work and play on the guitar and make you a better musician.

Get with the Rhythm

Rhythm is the most basic force in music, and almost everyone can tap their foot or clap their hands to the beat. But you can go further in your pursuit of rhythm by identifying note duration values (quarter notes, eighth notes, triplets, sixteenth notes, and so on), understanding meters and time signatures, and sight-reading rhythmic notation in context and up to tempo. Doing these things gives you a much deeper appreciation for the beat than just "that thing you tap to." Recognizing rhythms helps you visualize what you hear and better memorize rhythmic figures and repeated rhythm patterns.

Familiarize Yourself with Pitch

The musical alphabet only goes from A to G, but it's the basis for your entire musical vocabulary. In fact, it's the basis for all things melodic and harmonic. Being able to name the pitches on the musical staff, guitar fingerboard, and piano keyboard increases your knowledge of the fingerboard and can help in scale construction, chord building, and sight-reading on the guitar.

Train Your Ear to Hear

The concept of ear training involves aspects of the first three tips of this chapter (improving your rhythm, pitch, and harmony skills), but it applies to a broader strategy of getting your ears enrolled in a program of focused study. Ear training, under various names, is offered in all college-level music schools, regardless of your instrument. But you also can follow your own curriculum with individual study or with the help of a teacher or friend.

Perform Live for a Crowd

When you play live in front of people — either with other musicians or for an audience — you develop valuable skills that you just can't accomplish when practicing in private. Mustering your energy and marshaling your nerves in the right balance contributes to creating a potentially more powerful performance than you could achieve at home alone. Performing is just like any other skill: The more you do it, the better you become at it.

Compose Your Own Melody and Improvise a Bit

You may not (yet) be the next Paul Simon or Lennon and McCartney, but you should still try your hand at writing a song, composing a melody, and improvising over an accompaniment. Doing so taps different skills than simply memorizing music. You may not always produce something brilliant, but when you do spontaneously create something that works, it's a great feeling.

Discover Harmony

Musicianship goes beyond rhythm and melody, and the next logical concept to tackle — especially for the guitarist who can play chords as easily as single notes — is harmony. Understanding how chords are built and recognizing the differences in their qualities (major versus minor, minor seventh versus dominant seventh, and so on) will help you recognize their sound and function in the music.

Polish Your Playing with Expression

Music isn't just about playing the correct note names precisely in the rhythms indicated. Music is ultimately an expressive act, so composers and performers also deal with articulation (how notes are struck or sounded) and expression (how music is performed). A good first step is being able to identify terms used to indicate expression (which are usually written in Italian) and symbols used to indicate articulation.

Listen to Lots of Music

Listening to music is what many people do for fun, but for guitarists, it's part of the job! (Aren't we lucky?) Listen to as much music as you can, especially in the style you're interested in learning. Be sure to listen critically, too. Try to identify the chords in the piece, the intervals in the melody, the instruments being played, and the techniques a performer uses to achieve a certain sound. Listening with a critical ear helps you develop your own sense of taste and solidifies your memory of the music and of that particular performance.

Watch a Performer's Body Language

Whether viewed on TV or from the fifth row in a concert hall (which is preferable, if you can afford it!), watch how performers play their instruments, hold their hands, move their bodies, and place their heads. Performing music is a whole-body experience, and you can often pick up good moves from watching great performers.

Test Yourself by Teaching

Teaching is often a great way to gain perspective on what you think you already know. Having to show something to someone else often reveals gaps in your own knowledge, even if only for a moment. For example, you may know how to play a certain passage, but when your friend asks you to slow it down, you may find that you can't! It's a common phenomenon, but it forces you to rethink (and sometimes relearn) your approach to playing something. Taking what you know and presenting it to someone who's unfamiliar with that idea is a great way to cement your own knowledge.

Guitar Accessories

IN THIS ARTICLE

- *Cranking up the wattage with amps*
- *Completing your arsenal*
- *Understanding the importance of the little things*

Some of the products that we describe in this article are essential — for example, cases and strings (and amps if you're playing electric) — but you can think of others merely as accessories. We do think that all these items are useful and have some musical or practical application. You find no plugs for bumper stickers and mugs that read "Guitarists are strum-thing special" in these pages — just the short list of stuff that can really help you out.

Amps

Strictly speaking, you can play an electric guitar without any amplification, but playing that way's not much fun. Without an amp, you hear the notes buzzing like little musical mosquitoes, but you don't achieve any expression or tone. And you can't possibly rattle the windows and shake the floorboards with your newly learned "Smoke on the Water" riff unless you're wired up and have decibels to burn.

Amps come in two general flavors — practice and performance varieties. The biggest differences between practice amps and performance amps boil down to size, wattage, and cost. The photo shows a practice amp and a performance amp.

Getting started with a practice amp

If you have limited funds, start out with what's known as a practice amp — one that has a decent feature set (tone controls, reverb, and two or more volume controls so that you can sculpt your distorted sound) and that delivers a good sound but at low volumes (6 to 12 watts is typical on practice amps).

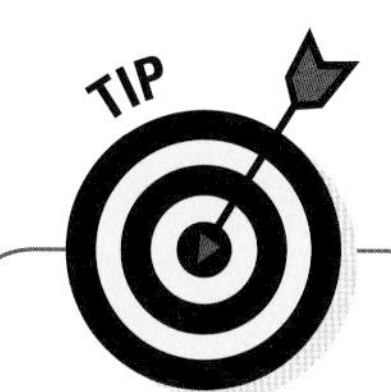

You can't start to develop a fully mature and individual tone until you have both a quality guitar and a decent amp to run it through. But if you must skimp somewhere, we suggest that you skimp on the amp side - at first.

Practice amps can run as little as £150 and boast features that appear on their higher-priced performance counterparts. In amplifiers, power — not features — is what drives up the price. Power is expensive to build, requiring heavy-duty transformers, speakers, and cabinetry. For home and casual use — such as jamming with a couple of friends in a garage or basement — 15 or 20 watts is often plenty loud enough, and 6 to 12 watts is sufficient for solo practicing and playing along with your stereo.

Features, on the other hand, such as tone controls and effects (reverb, tremolo), are easier to implement because the manufacturers can stamp them onto a chip and install it on a circuit board. Following are some useful things to look for in a practice amp:

- **Multiple-gain stages**: Gain is the technical word for "loudness power," and having two or more of separate volume controls on an amp gives you more flexibility in shaping the distorted sound.

- **Three-band EQ**: EQ, or equalization, is tone controls for bass, mid, and high. An EQ device is a fancy tone control that gives you increased flexibility over the bass, mid-range, and treble makeup of your sound.

- **Built-in reverb**: Reverb is an echo effect that makes the guitar sound like it's playing within a given environment — rooms of varying sizes, a concert hall, cathedral, canyon, and so on.

- **Channel switching via footswitch**: Channel switching enables you to access different sets of volume and tone control. Some practice amps include it; others don't. Decide whether that feature is important enough to pay for in a practice amp. You can always get your distorted sound through an external effect, such as a stomp box, but that's a little bit more of a hassle.

- **Headphone jack**: A headphone jack is a very handy thing in a practice amp as it enables you to get a fully amp-treated sound without going through the speaker. Great for late-night practice sessions!

Performance amps, such as the one on the one (right), are bigger and more powerful than the practice amp (above).

Powering up to a performance amp

The greater power of a performance amp doesn't just mean that the amp is louder. Increased power also delivers a cleaner, purer signal at higher volumes. In other words, if two amps of different power are producing the same overall loudness, the more powerful amp yields the cleaner signal.

A 50-watt amp is usually more than sufficient for home and normal performing circumstances, such as playing in a five-piece band at a local pub. If you play larger venues or play in a genre that requires unusually loud levels — such as heavy metal — go with 100 watts. Some players who desire a squeaky-clean sound and who run in stereo (requiring double the power) may opt for 100 watts regardless, because they can stay cleaner at louder levels.

Many amps can operate at either 100 or 50 watts by enabling you to select the power via a switch. Why would you want to operate at 50 watts if you paid for a 100-watt amp? Because a 50-watt amp "breaks up," or distorts, sooner (at a lower level) than a 100-watt one does, and for many types of music (blues, rock, metal), this distortion is desirable.

Except in guitar amps, the vacuum tubes that formerly powered all electronics have been replaced by solid-state electronics (which consists of transistors and, later, microchips).

The latest generation of amps feature digital technology to emulate a variety of guitar tones and effects. Many argue, however, that tube technology still produces the best tone for guitars because, although they're not as efficient or even as accurate in faithfully reproducing the original signal, tube amps actually deliver the most musical tone. All your favourite guitarists record and play exclusively with tube amps, from the 100-watt Marshall to the Fender Twin, to the Vox AC30 and the MESA/Boogie Dual Rectifier.

As a beginner, you may not appreciate (or care about) the differences between tube and solid-state tone. You can get good-sounding distortion out of a solid-state amp anyway, and these are usually cheaper, so you should probably go with a solid-state amp and ignore the whole tone debate. Besides, you may prefer to get your distortion sound from a pedal, and then the whole issue is moot. Look instead for features such as built-in effects (reverb, chorus, and so on) and a headphone jack. Above all, listen to the sound and turn the knobs. If you like what you hear and you feel comfortable dialing in the different sounds, the amp is for you.

A Case for Cases

A guitar case is so important to your guitar that many manufacturers include the case in the price of the guitar. These companies make cases specially designed for particular models and ship the guitars inside these cases to the retailer. This practice makes buying the guitar without the case difficult — and rightly so.

To buy a serious instrument and then try to carry it away from the store without the appropriate, quality protection is a foolish way to save a few bucks. The most important gesture of respect that you can show your instrument is to give it a safe place to sleep.

Cases come in three basic types. Each has its advantages, and the protection factor is proportional to cost: The more expensive the case, the better the protection that it offers your instrument. Here's a rundown:

- The hard case is the most expensive option (£50 to £80 and more) but offers the best insurance against damage to your guitar. It's composed of leather- or nylon-covered wood and can even survive the rigors of airline baggage

People who live in big cities and take public transportation favour gig bags. With the gig bag over their shoulder and a luggage cart toting an amp in one hand, they still have a hand free to feed a token into a subway turnstile and hold the poles on a train. But a gig bag isn't nearly as protective as a soft case, and you can't stack anything on top of a bagged guitar.

handlers, providing crush-proof protection to your instrument. They can drop heavy objects on the case and stack it safely under other luggage items without any damage accruing to the precious guitar inside.

The safest thing to do is to go with a hard case, unless you have some really compelling reason not to.

- The soft case isn't completely soft, being in fact more stiff than truly soft. It usually consists of some pressed-particle material, such as cardboard, and can provide some protection for your instrument — for example, if someone drops a coffee mug on it (an empty coffee mug, that is). But that's about it. You can pick up these cases for about £20.

- The gig bag provides almost no protection against shock because it's a form-fitting nylon, leather, or other fabric enclosure — you know, a bag. Gig bags zip shut and are about the consistency of any other soft luggage carrier. They cost anywhere from £15 to £100. The advantage of gig bags is that they're light, they fit on your shoulder, and they take up no more room than the guitar itself — making them the ideal case if you're trying to fit your electric guitar into the overhead bin of an airplane.

Capos

A capo (pronounced KAY-po) is a spring-loaded, adjustable-tension (or elastic) clamp that wraps around the neck of a guitar and covers all the strings, forcing them all down to the fretboard at a given fret. This device effectively raises the pitch of all the strings by a given number of frets (or half steps). In some cases, you may want to tune your guitar with the capo on, but most of the time, you tune up without it and then place it on the desired fret.

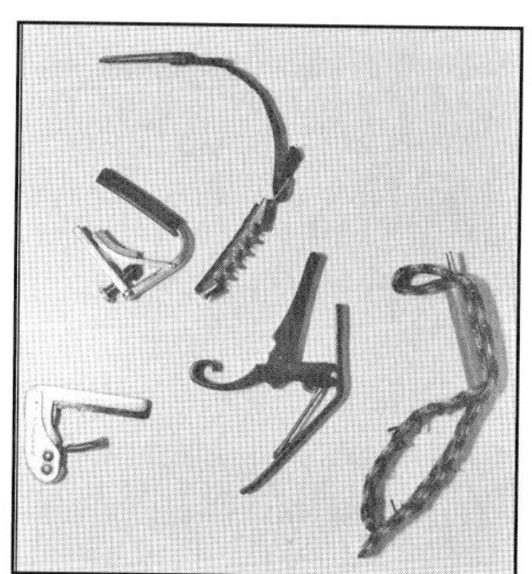

A variety of capos. Capos raise the pitch of the open strings.

Capos enable you to transpose the music you play on your guitar to another key, while you still play the chord fingerings in the original key. The photograph shows a few different capo types you can find at most music shops.

Capos cost between £3 and £20, with the elastic-band type being the cheapest. The higher-priced clamp and screw-on types are more popular with serious capo users because you can put them on with one hand, and these types of capos generally hold the strings down better than the elastic kinds do.

Effect Pedals and Devices

Electric guitarists seldom just plug into an amp and start playing. Well, they may start out that way, but if you listen to the radio — or any recorded guitar music, for that matter — you quickly notice a lot more going on than just a "straight" guitar sound. At the very least, you hear some ambient treatment in the form of artificially created echo, or reverb, as the effect is known in guitar lingo. You may hear some (intended) distortion, especially in rock and blues music, and you may hear additional effects, such as wah-wah, vibrato, and other electronic manipulations.

Welcome to the wonderful, wacky world of effects. Effects are devices that plug in between your guitar and amplifier and enable you to alter your signal in all sorts of creative and unusual ways. Scores and scores of these little devices are available from all different manufacturers and in all price ranges. You can buy them as individual units or as an all-in-one box, called a multi-effects processor. But whether you go for the package deal or à la carte, effects can spice up the basic sound of your guitar in all sorts of exciting ways.

Most effects come in the form of foot-accessed pedals, also known as stomp boxes because they reside on the floor and you activate them by stepping on a footswitch. This setup enables you to selectively turn effects on and off while playing the guitar without interruption. The picture shows a typical effects setup with a reasonable number of pedals in the signal chain (that is, the path from guitar to amp).

Dozens of different types of effects are available — more than you could possibly own, not to mention use all at once. The price of these individual units varies, too, with distortion boxes as cheap as £30 and digital reverbs and delays as much as £120 (or more). To help you sort through the myriad of flavours and types, following is a list of some of the most popular effects:

- **Distortion:** This effect simulates the sound of a guitar signal driven too hard for the amplifier; the device overdrives the signal to the point that it breaks up — but in a musically pleasing way. Distortion, to a guitarist, can mean anything from a slightly fat, warm quality to a fuzzy sustain, to screaming chain-saw fuzz, as used by metal and grunge bands.
- **Chorus:** This effect simulates the sound of many guitars playing at once, making the overall sound fatter. Increasing the speed yields a warbling or tremolo-like effect. The Police's "Every Breath You Take" exemplifies the chorus sound.
- **Flanger/Phase shifter:** These two devices produce similar effects that create a whooshy, swirly, underwater sound, heard on early Van Halen albums and in the rhythm guitar sound of many funk songs of the 1970s.
- **Pitch shifter:** This device (also known as a harmonizer) enables you to play in harmony with yourself by splitting your signal into two paths, the original and a user-defined musical interval, such as a major third (four half steps away); it also provides choruslike effects. A popular fixed-interval pitch shifter is the octave pedal, used to great effect by Jimi Hendrix, which produces a pitch one or two (or both) octaves (12 half steps) lower than the original.
- **Digital delay:** This device produces a discrete repetition of your sound, good for echoes, spacious effects, and creating rhythmically timed repeats of your notes. The analogue version was a tape-echo device that actually recorded the sound on magnetic tape and played it back moments later. Tape echoes still enjoy some popularity because of their unique, vintage-sounding, tonal quality (which is inferior to the digital version in terms of exact replication of the original signal). Listen to the opening of Guns N' Roses "Welcome to the Jungle" to hear the sound of digital delay.
- **Wah-wah pedal:** This effects pedal is a type of frequency filter (which varies the bass and treble content of a signal) that imbues the guitar with expressive, voicelike characteristics (it actually sounds as if it's saying "wah"). You control the sound by raising and lowering a foot pedal. This device was made popular by Jimi Hendrix and was a staple of the disco-guitar sound. Eric Clapton also gave the wah a workout on "White Room" during his Cream days.
- **Reverb:** This effect reproduces the natural echo sound produced in environments such as a large room, gymnasium, cathedral, and so on. It's usually included on amps in a limited version (often having only one control), but having it as a separate effect gives you a lot more variety and control.
- **Tremolo:** Like reverb, tremolo was included on many amps from the '50s and '60s (such as the Fender Twin Reverb) and is now available in a pedal. Tremolo is the rapid wavering of the volume (not pitch, like vibrato) that makes your guitar sound as if you're playing it through a slowly moving electric fan. Tommy James and the Shondells' "Crimson and Clover" features a prominent tremolo effect.

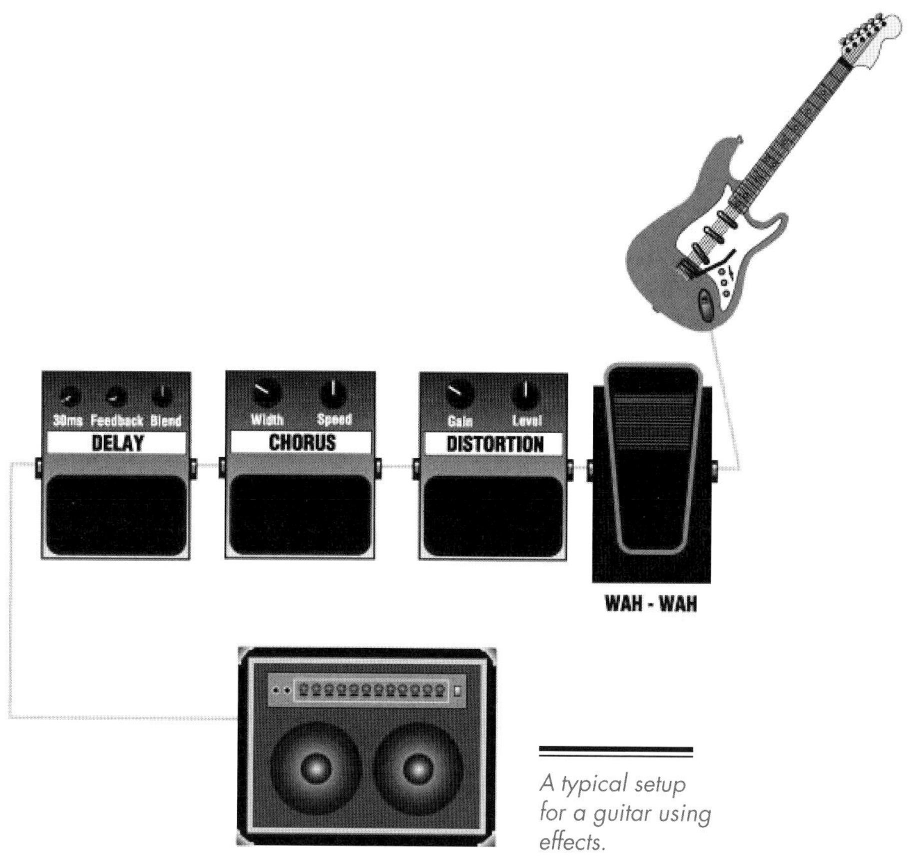

A typical setup for a guitar using effects.

More Must-Haves

Less glamorous than an amp or a wah-wah pedal, sure, the following accessories are nonetheless indispensable:

- **Picks**: You're sure, in your musical career, to lose, break, toss to adoring fans as souvenirs, and otherwise part company with hundreds of picks, so don't get attached (in a sentimental sense) to them. Treat them as the inexpensive, expendable commodity they are. Stock up with your favourite colour and gauge (thickness) and always carry spares in your wallet, the car, the flaps of your shoes, and any other . . . er, convenient place.

- **Straps**: Straps come in all kinds of styles and materials, from nylon to woven fabric to leather. The first rule in choosing a strap is that you get the most comfortable one that you can afford. Wearing a guitar on your shoulder for long periods of time can cause discomfort, and the better the strap is, the more it protects your muscles against strain and fatigue. Appearance is a close second to comfort as a factor in deciding what strap to buy. You must like the look of your strap, as its function isn't just utilitarian but aesthetic as well.

  If you own more than one guitar, you're best off with a strap for each type of guitar, electric and acoustic. That way, you don't need to keep adjusting it as you switch from electric to acoustic and back again.

- **Strings**: You always need to keep extra strings on hand for the simple reason that, if you break one, you need to replace it immediately. To do so requires that you carry at least an extra full set — any one of your six strings could break. Unlike car tires, where one spare fits all, guitars use six individually gauged strings. Woe to the guitarists who keep breaking the same string over and over — they're going to have an awful lot of partial sets around! Fortunately, string sets are cheap — about £5 if you buy them in single sets and cheaper still if you buy in boxes of 12 sets. Or, you can buy single strings for about £1 apiece.

Getting Strung Along: Changing Strings

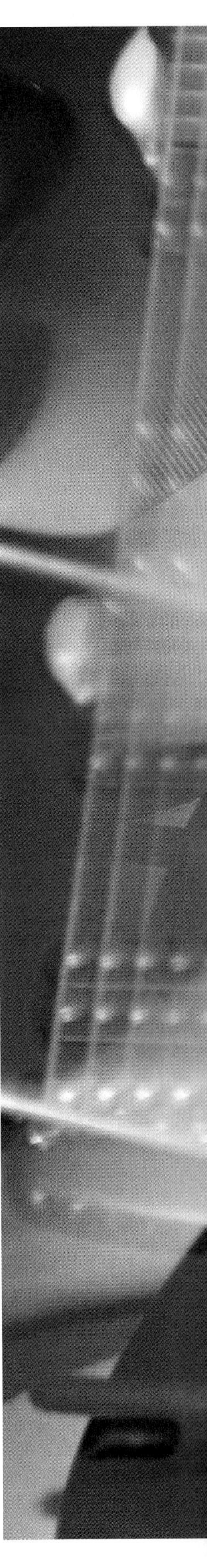

IN THIS ARTICLE

- *Restringing a steel-string acoustic guitar*
- *Restringing a nylon-string guitar*
- *Restringing an electric guitar*

Many people consider their guitars to be delicate, precious, and fragile instruments: They seem reluctant to tune their strings, let alone change them. But changing strings isn't something you should be shy about. Jump into it with both feet, and you improve the sound of your guitar, help to prevent broken strings at inopportune moments, and perhaps even identify other maintenance problems. During periodic string changing, for example, you may discover a gouged bridge slot or a loose or rattling tuning post.

You should probably replace your strings when

- They exhibit visible signs of corrosion or caked-on dirt or grime.
- They don't play in tune, usually fretting sharp, especially in the upper register.
- You can't remember the last time you changed them and you have an important gig (and don't want to chance any breakage).

Removing Old Strings

Obviously, to put on a new string, you have to remove the old one. Unless you're really in a hurry (such as in the middle of the first verse, trying to get your new string on and tuned up by the guitar solo), you can take off any string by turning the tuning peg to loosen the string so much that you can grab the string from the center and pull it off the post. You don't need to wind it completely off the post by using the peg.

A quicker method is to simply snip off the old string with wire cutters. It seems weird and brutal to snip off a string, but neither the sudden release of tension nor the cutting itself hurts the guitar.

The only reason not to cut a string is to save it as a spare, in case the new one breaks while you put it on (rare, but it happens). An old B string is better than no B string.

A common misconception is that you should maintain constant string tension on the guitar neck at all times. Therefore, you may hear that you should replace the strings one at a time because removing all the strings is bad for the guitar, but this simply isn't true.

Replacing strings one at a time is convenient for tuning but is no healthier for the guitar. Guitars are made of tougher stuff than that.

Stringing a Steel-String Acoustic Guitar

Generally, steel-string acoustic guitars are probably easier to string than classicals or electrics (which we cover in later sections in this article).

Changing strings step-by-step

Following are step-by-step instructions on restringing your guitar. You have two places to attach your new string: the bridge and the headstock. Start by attaching the string to the bridge, which is a pretty straightforward task.

Step 1: Attaching the string to the bridge

Acoustic guitars have a bridge with six holes leading to the inside of the guitar. To attach a new string to the bridge, follow these steps:

1. **Remove the old string and pop out the bridge pin.**

Bridge pins sometimes stick, so you may need to use a table knife to pry it out, but be careful not to ding the wood. A better alternative is the notched edge in a peg winder or needle-nose pliers.

2. **Place the end of the new string that has a little brass ring (called a ball) inside the hole that held the bridge pin.**

   Just stuff it down the hole a couple of centimetres. (How far isn't critical, because you're going to pull it up soon.)

3. **Wedge the bridge pin firmly back in the hole with the slot facing forward (toward the nut).**

   The slot provides a channel for the string to get out.

4. **Pull gently on the string until the ball rests against the bottom of the pin. Keep your thumb or finger on the pin so that it doesn't pop out and disappear into the abyss.**

Be careful not to kink the string as you pull it.

5. **Test the string by gently tugging on it.**

   If you don't feel the string shift, the ball is snug against the bridge pin, and you're ready to secure the string to the tuning post, which is the focus of the following section.

Step 2: Securing the string to the tuning post

After securely attaching the string to the bridge pin, you can focus your attention on the headstock. The steps are slightly different for the treble strings (G, B, E) and the bass strings (E, A, D). You wind treble strings clockwise and bass strings anticlockwise.

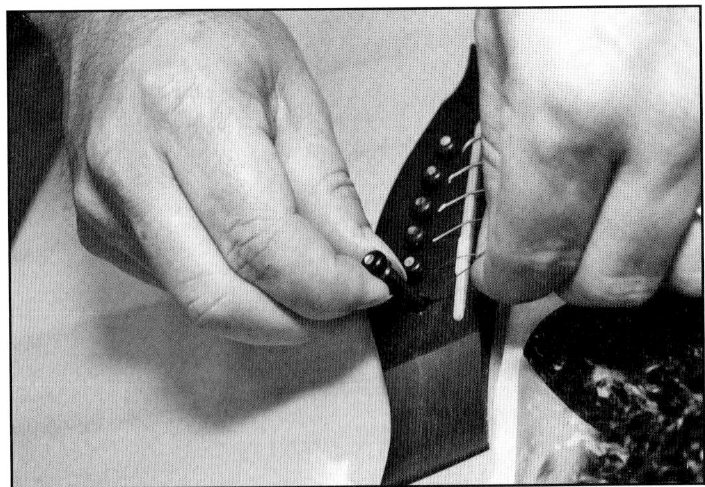

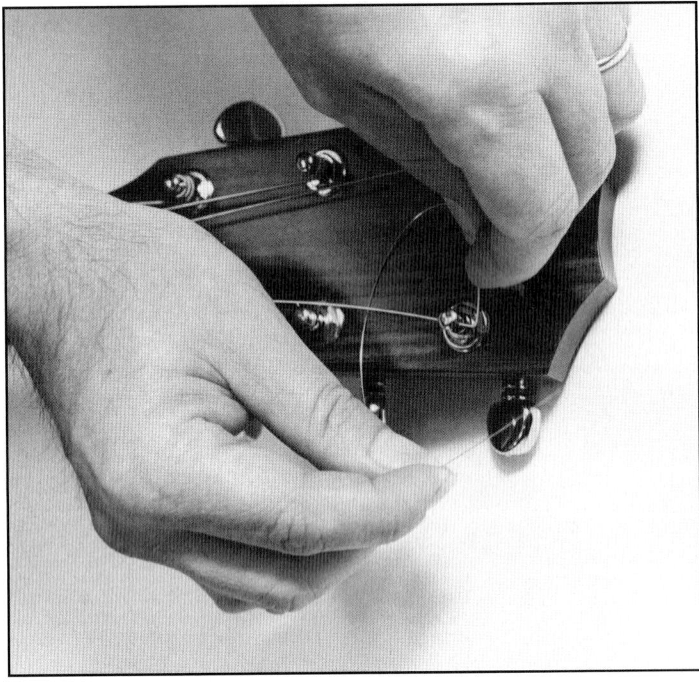

To attach a treble string to the tuning post, follow these steps:

1. **Pass the string through the hole in the post.**

   Leave enough slack between the bridge pin and the tuning post to enable you to wind the string around the post several times.

2. **Kink (or crease) the metal wire toward the inside of the guitar.**

   The photo shows how to kink the string to prepare it for winding.

(Above left) How to place the new string in the bridge and position the bridge pin.

(Below left) String kinked to the inside of the headstock with slack for winding.

(Above) The treble string wraps around the post in a clockwise direction, bass strings wrap around the post in an anticlockwise direction.

3. **While keeping the string tight against the post with one hand, wind the tuning peg clockwise with the other hand.**

   This step is a bit tricky and requires some manual dexterity (but so does playing the guitar). Keep your eye on the post to ensure that as the string wraps around the post, it winds down, toward the headstock surface. Check out the photo to see how the strings wrap around the posts. Be sure that the strings go into the correct slot in the nut.

   Winding the string downward on the post increases the breaking angle - the angle between the post and the nut. A sharper angle brings more tension down onto the nut and creates better sustain, the length of time the note continues. To get the maximum angle, wind the string so that it sits as low as possible on the post. (This fact is true for all guitars, not just acoustics.)

To attach a bass string, you follow the above steps except that you wind the strings anticlockwise in Step 3 so that the string goes up the middle and goes over the post to the left (as you face the headstock).

If you find that you've left too much slack, unwind the string and start again, kinking the string farther down. If you don't leave enough slack, your winding doesn't go all the way down the post, which may result in slipping if the string doesn't have enough length to grab firmly around the post. Neither situation is tragic. You simply undo what you've done and try again.

Tuning up

After you secure the string around the post, you can begin to hear the string come up to pitch. As the string draws tight, place it in its correct nut slot. If you're changing strings one at a time, you can just tune the new one to the old ones, which, presumably, are relatively in tune.

After you get the string to the correct pitch, pull on it in various places up and down its length to stretch it out a bit. Doing so can cause the string to go flat — sometimes drastically if you left any loose windings on the post — so tune it back up to pitch by winding the peg. Repeat the tune-stretch process two or three times to help the new strings hold their pitch.

Using a peg winder to quickly turn the tuning pegs reduces your string-winding time considerably. A peg winder also features a notch in one side of the sleeve that can help you pop a stuck bridge pin. Just make sure that you don't lose the pin when it comes flying out!

After the string is up to pitch and stretched out, you're ready to remove the excess string that sticks out from the post. You can snip this excess off with wire cutters or bend the string back and forth over the same crease until it breaks off.

Whatever you do, don't leave the straight string length protruding. It could poke you or someone standing next to you (such as the bass player) in the eye or give you a sharp jab in your fingertip.

Stringing Nylon-String Guitars

Stringing a nylon-string guitar is different from stringing a steel-string acoustic because both the bridge and the posts are different. Nylon string guitars don't use bridge pins (strings are tied off instead) and their headstocks are slotted and have rollers, as opposed to posts.

Changing strings step-by-step

In one sense, nylon strings are easier to deal with than steel strings are, because nylon isn't as springy as steel. Attaching the string to the tuning post, however, can be a bit trickier. As you do with the steel-string acoustic, begin by securing the bridge end of the string first and then turn your attention to the headstock.

Step 1: Securing the string to the bridge

Whereas steel-string acoustic strings have a ball at one end, nylon strings have no such ball: Both ends are loose. (Well, you can buy ball-ended nylon-string sets, but they're not what you normally use.) You can, therefore, attach either end of the string to the bridge. If the ends look different, however, use the one that looks like the middle of the string, not the one that has the loosely coiled appearance. Just follow these steps:

1. **Remove the old string, as we describe in the section "Removing Old Strings," earlier in this article.**
2. **Pass one end of the new string through the hole in the top of the bridge, in the direction away from the soundhole, leaving about 1½ inches sticking out the rear of the hole.**
3. **Secure the string by bringing the short end over the bridge and passing it under the long part of the string, as the picture on the right shows. Then pass the short end under, over, and then under itself, on the top of the bridge, as you see in the right-hand picture.**
4. **Pull on the long end of the string with one hand and move the knot with the other to remove excess slack and cause the knot to lie flat against the bridge.**

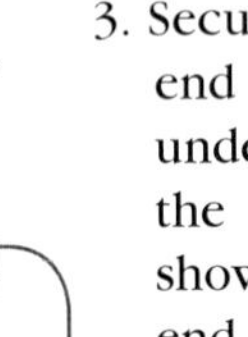

You may need a couple tries to get the end at just the right length, where not too much excess is dangling off the top of the bridge. (You can always cut the excess away, too.)

Make your loop come from the outside (that is, approaching from the left on the lower three bass strings, and from the right on the upper three treble strings).

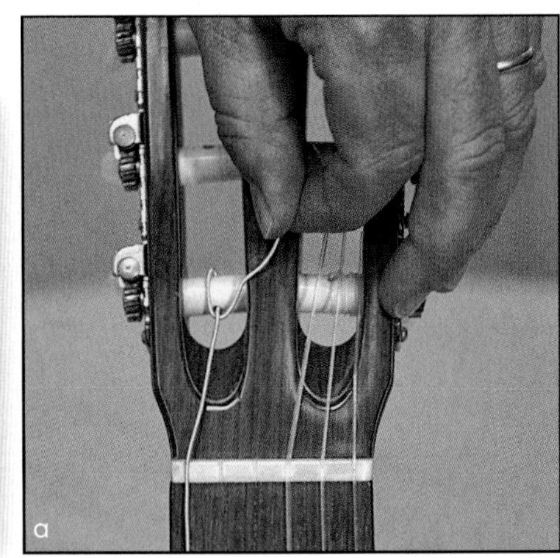

Step 2: Securing the string to the tuning post

On a nylon-string guitar, the tuning posts (called rollers) pass through the headstock sideways instead of going through perpendicularly as on a steel-string acoustic or electric guitar. This configuration is known as a slotted headstock.

To attach the string to the tuning post in a slotted headstock, follow these steps:

1. **Pass the string through the hole in the tuning post. Bring the end of the string back over the roller toward you; then pass the string under itself in front of the hole. Pull up on the string end so that the long part of the string (the part attached to the bridge) sits in the U-shaped loop you just formed, as shown in the picture above.**
2. **Pass the short end under and over itself, creating two or three wraps.**

   Doing so holds the loose end firmly in place, as the photo shows, and prevents the string from slipping out of the hole.
3. **Wind the peg so that the string wraps on top of the loop you just formed, forcing it down against the post.**
4. **Pull the string length taut with one hand and turn the tuning peg with the other hand.**

   Wrap the windings to the outside of the hole, away from the centre of the guitar.

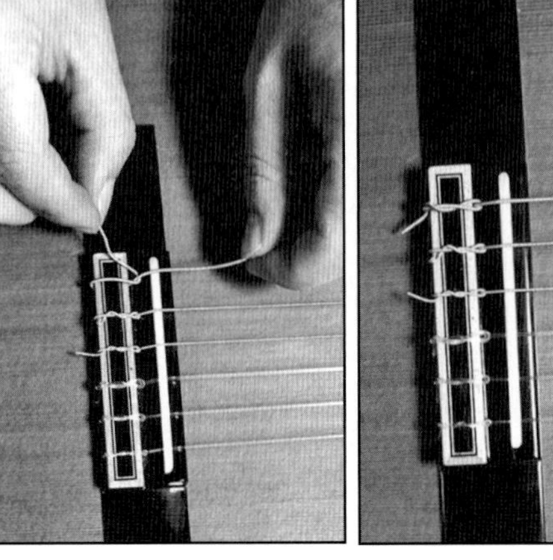

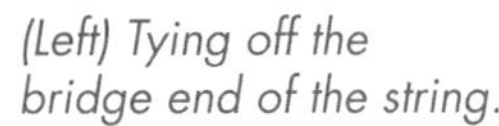

(Left) Tying off the bridge end of the string.

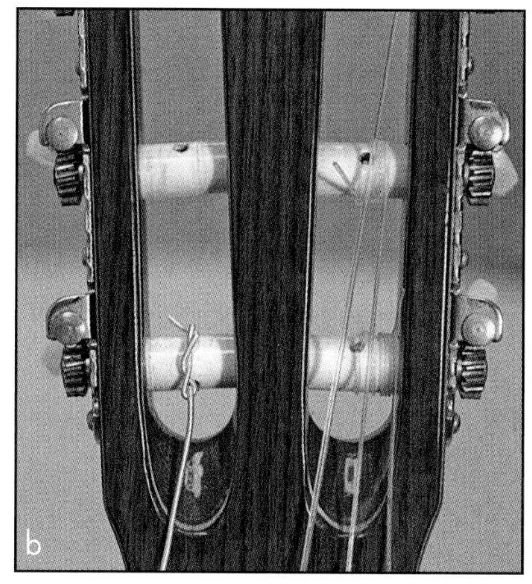

(Left) Creating a U-shaped loop with the short end of the string (a). Creating wraps to hold the short end of the string in place (b).

Tuning up

As you continue turning the tuning peg, the string slowly comes nearer to pitch. Nylon strings, like steel strings, require quite a bit of stretching out, so after you get the string initially up to pitch, grab it at various places around its length, pull on it, and then tune it up again. Repeat this process two or three times to keep the guitar in tune longer.

Snip away the excess after you're done with all six strings. Nylon strings aren't as dangerous as steel strings if any excess protrudes, but the extra string hanging out is unsightly, and besides, classical guitarists are a little fussier about how their instruments look than acoustic guitarists are.

Stringing an Electric Guitar

Generally, electric guitarists need to change their strings more often than do steel-string acoustic or classical guitarists. Because changing strings is so common on electric guitars, builders take a more progressive approach to the hardware, often making changing strings very quick and easy. Of the three types of guitars — steel-string acoustic, classical, and electric — you can change the strings on electric guitars most easily by far.

Changing strings step-by-step

As you would on steel-string acoustic and nylon-string guitars, begin stringing an electric guitar by first securing the string to the bridge and then attaching the string to the headstock. Electric strings are similar to steel-string acoustic strings in that they have ball ends and are made of metal, but electric strings are usually composed of a lighter-gauge wire than steel-string acoustic strings, and the 3rd string is unwound, or plain, whereas a steel-string acoustic guitar's is wound. (A nylon-string's 3rd string also is unwound but is a thicker nylon string.)

Step 1: Securing the string to the bridge

Most electric guitars use a simple method for securing the string to the bridge. You pass the string through a hole in the bridge (sometimes reinforced with a collar, or grommet) that's smaller than the ball at the end of the string - so the ball holds the string just as the knot at the end of a piece of thread holds a stitch in fabric. On some guitars (such as the Fender Telecaster), the collars anchor right into the body, and the strings pass through the back of the instrument, through a hole in the bridge assembly, and out the top.

You might attach a string to an electric from a top-mounted bridge or through the back. The following steps show how to secure the strings to the bridge.

1. **Remove the old string, as we describe in the section "Removing Old Strings," earlier in this article.**

2. **Anchor the string at the bridge by passing the string through the hole (from the back or bottom of the guitar) until the ball stops the movement.**

   Then you're ready to focus on the tuning post. You do this on all but a few guitars.

Step 2: Securing the string to the tuning post

In most cases, the posts on an electric resemble those of a steel-string acoustic. A post protrudes through the headstock, and you pass your string through the post's hole, kink the string to the inside (toward the center of the headstock), and begin winding while holding the long part of the string with one hand for control.

Some electric guitars, notably Fender Stratocasters and Telecasters, feature string retainers, which are little rollers or channels screwed into the top of the headstock that pull the top two or four strings down low onto the headstock, sort of like a tent stake. If your guitar has string retainers, make sure that you pass the strings under them.

Some tuners feature a locking mechanism, so that you don't need to worry about winding, slack, and all that bother. Inside the post hole is a vicelike device that clamps down on the string as it passes through. A knurled (ridge-covered) dial underneath the headstock loosens and tightens the vice.

Some guitars have tuners with slotted posts instead of a hole. These devices also enable quick string changes, because you simply lay the string in the slot at the top of the post, kink it, and begin winding. You don't even need to leave any slack for winding.

The Care and Keeping of Guitars

IN THIS ARTICLE

- *Cleaning your guitar*
- *Protecting your guitar*
- *Maintaining the proper environment*

Guitars are surprisingly hardy creatures. You can subject them to a rigourous performing schedule, keep them up all night, bang on them relentlessly, and they don't mind a bit.

If you don't abuse it or subject it to extreme conditions, a guitar not only stays structurally sound for decades, but it also plays in tune and remains comfortable in your hands. In fact, guitars actually improve with age and use. We should all be so lucky!

Cleaning Your Guitar

If a guitar gets dirty, it doesn't exactly come home with mud on its shirt and grass stains on its trousers, but it does collect a laundry list of its own washday terrors.

Removing dirt and grime

Unless you live in a bubble, dust and dirt are part of your environment. Certain objects just seem to attract dust (for example, the top of a TV set), and guitars definitely attract their fair share. If dust collects under the strings on your headstock and bridge, you can dust them off by using a cloth or a feather duster. Feather dusters may seem silly things that only uniformed maids in old films use, but they serve a purpose: They knock the dust off an object without applying pressure (which can scratch a delicate finish). So even if you don't use a feather duster — or if your maid's outfit is at the cleaners — be sure to dust lightly.

As dust mixes with the natural moisture content of your hands and fingers (and forearm, if you play in short sleeves, shirtless, or in the raw), that dust becomes grime. Grime can stick to all surfaces, but it's especially noticeable on your strings.

The strings

The natural oils from your fingertips coat the strings every time you play. You can't see this oily coating, but it's there, and over time, these oils corrode the string material and create a grimy buildup (which is not only icky, but also impedes play and can actually injure the wood over time). String grime makes the strings go dead sooner and wear out faster than they normally do; if you let the condition go too long, the string grime can even seep into the pores of the fingerboard. Yuck!

The best way to combat the grimy-buildup menace is to wipe down the strings after every playing session, just before you put the guitar back in the case. (Notice that we're assuming that you put the guitar back in the case — another "case" of good preventative maintenance.) Chamois (pronounced "shammy") is a great material to use to wipe the strings because it doubles as a polishing cloth; a (clean) cotton nappy, however, works well, too (but no disposable nappies, please). Bandannas may give you that Willie Nelson/Janis Joplin appeal, but they're not made of good absorbent material, so keep your bandanna around your neck or on your head, and don't wipe your guitar with it.

Give the strings a general wipe down and then pinch each string between your thumb and index finger, with the cloth in between, and run your hand up and down the string length.

This dries the string all the way around its circumference and shucks off any grunge. That's all you need to do to maintain clean strings and increase their useful life many times over. (And while you're at it, wipe the back of the guitar neck, too.)

The wood

A guitar is mostly wood, and wood likes a good rubdown. (Hey, who doesn't?) If you have a really dusty guitar — for example, one that's been sitting open in a musty attic for a while — blow the excess dust off before you start dusting with a cloth (or feather duster). This simple act may prevent a scratch or abrasion in the finish.

Gently rub the various places on the guitar until it's dust-free. You may need to frequently shake out your dust cloth, so do so outside, or you're going to be wiping sneezes off your guitar as well as the dust. Unless your guitar is really dirty - maybe displaying some caked-on gunk that you don't even want to know the origin of - dusting is all you need to do to the wood.

If dullness persists or a grimy film is clearly present over the finish, you can rub your guitar down with furniture polish or, better yet, guitar polish. Guitar polish is made specifically for the finishes that the manufacturers use on guitars, whereas some furniture polish may contain abrasives. If you're at all in doubt, use the guitar goop that music stores sell. And follow the directions on the bottle.

Although the guitar-goop companies write this information on the label, it bears repeating here: Never put any liquid or spray polish directly onto the guitar surface. Doing so could soak and stain the wood permanently. Pour or spray the substance onto your dustcloth and work it in a bit before putting the cloth to wood.

To dust between the strings in hard-to-reach places such as the headstock, bridge, and pickup areas, use a small camel's hair paintbrush. Keep the brush in your case.

The hardware

Grimy buildup doesn't really hurt hardware (tuners, bridges, and so on) the way that it can more porous wood, but it certainly looks bad — and you don't want to appear on MTV with hardware that's duller than your drummer. (Just kidding, fellow percussionists!)

Rubbing with a dustcloth is all you really need to do for your guitar's hardware, but you can certainly use a mild jewellery or chrome polish if you want — as long as it's not abrasive. Polish not only removes really greasy residue (which a simple wipe won't do), but also brings the hardware to a lustre — very important for TV lights.

Many inexpensive hardware components are dipped, meaning that they have a thin coating of shiny metal over an otherwise ugly and mottled-looking surface. So you don't want to rub through the coating (which could happen with repeated polishing). And you certainly don't want to get any liquid polish in the moving parts of a tuning machine.

Don't ever touch the pickups of an electric guitar with anything other than a dry cloth or your dusting brush. Pickups are magnetic and abhor liquid as much as the Wicked Witch of the West did. You don't want to risk upsetting a pickup's sensitive magnetic fields with liquid.

Caring for the finish

Acoustic guitars have a finish of lacquer or another synthetic coating to protect the wood's surface and give it a shiny appearance. Whether your instrument has a high-gloss finish or the satin variety (more subdued and natural-looking), the plan is the same:

If your finish ever cracks because of a ding (a small inadvertent gouge, such as occurs if you bang your guitar into the corner of the table), take it to a repairperson quickly to prevent the crack from spreading like a spider pattern on a windshield.

- **Keep the finish dust-free so that it stays shiny and transparent for years.**
- **Don't subject your guitar to direct sunlight for long periods of time.**
- **Avoid drastic humidity and temperature changes.**

Following these simple guidelines helps keep the finish from checking (cracking) as it swells and shrinks along with the wood.

Protecting Your Guitar

If you play guitar, you certainly don't want to keep it a secret. Well, in the beginning maybe, but after you can play a little bit, you want to bring your music to the people. Taking your guitar out into the world requires protection. Never leave the house without putting the guitar in some kind of protective case.

On the road

If you're traveling in a car, keep the guitar in the passenger compartment where you can exercise control over the environment. A guitar in a boot or untreated luggage compartment gets either too hot or too cold in comparison to what the humans experience up front. (Guitars like to listen to the radio, too, as long as it's not playing disco or Milli Vanilli.)

If you must put the guitar in with the spare tire, push it all the way forward so that it can benefit from some "environmental osmosis" (meaning that it's not going to get quite as cold or hot next to the climate-controlled passenger cabin as it is at the rear of the car). This practice also helps if, heaven forbid, you're ever rear-ended. You can pay a couple of quid to get your car repaired, but all the king's horses and all the king's men can't restore the splinters of your priceless acoustic should it absorb the brunt of a bumptious BMW.

A hardshell case is a better form of protection for a guitar than either a nylon gig bag or a cardboardlike soft case. With a hardshell case, you can stack things on top, whereas other cases require the guitar to be at the top of the heap, which may or may not please an obsessive car-packer.

Nylon gig bags are lightweight and offer almost no protection from a blow, but they do fend off dings. If you know the guitar is never going to leave your shoulder, you can use a gig bag. Gig bags also enable an electric guitar to fit in the overhead compartments of most aircraft.

TIP

If you store the guitar, you can lay it flat or on edge. The exact position makes no difference to the guitar. You don't need to loosen the strings significantly, but dropping them down a half step or so ensures against excess tension on the neck, should it swell or shrink slightly.

In storage

Whether you're going on a long holiday, or doing three-to-five in the slammer, you may, at some point, need to store your guitar for a long period of time. Keep the guitar in its case and put the case in a cupboard or under a bed. Try to keep the guitar in a climate controlled environment rather than a damp basement or uninsulated attic.

Providing a Healthy Environment

Guitars are made under specific temperature and humidity conditions. To keep the guitar playing and sounding as the builder intended, you must maintain an environment within the same approximate range of the original.

Keep the environment near room temperature (about 22 degrees Celsius) and the relative humidity at about 50 percent, and you're never going to hear your guitar complain (even if you have a talking guitar).

Temperature settings

A guitar can exist comfortably in a range of temperatures between about 18 to 27 degrees Celsius. For a guitar, heat is worse than cold, so keep the guitar out of the sun and avoid leaving a guitar to sit in a hot car all day.

If your guitar's been cold for several hours because it was riding in the back of the van that you drove from north Scotland to Cornwall in December, give the guitar time to warm up gradually after you bring it indoors. A good practice is to leave the guitar in its case until the case warms up to room temperature. Avoid exposing the guitar to radical temperature shifts if at all possible to prevent finish checking — the cracking of your finish that results because it can't expand and contract well enough with the wood beneath it.

Humidity

Guitars, whether they're made in Hawaii or Harlow are all built under humidity-controlled conditions, which stay at about 50 percent. To enable your guitar to maintain the lifestyle that its maker intended for it, you must also maintain that humidity at about 45 to 55 percent. Guitars that get too dry crack; guitars that absorb too much moisture swell and buckle.

If you can't afford either a humidifier or dehumidifier, you can achieve good results with the following inexpensive solutions:

- **Guitar humidifier:** This item is simply a rubber-enclosed sponge that you saturate with water, squeeze the excess out of, and then clip onto the inside of the soundhole or keep inside the case to raise the humidity level.
- **Desiccant:** A desiccant is a powder or crystal substance that usually comes in small packets and draws humidity out of the air, lowering the local relative humidity level. Silicagel is a common brand, and packets often come in the cases of new guitars.
- **Hygrometer:** You can buy this inexpensive device at any hardware shop; it tells you the relative humidity of a room with a good degree of accuracy (close enough to maintain a healthy guitar anyway). Get the portable kind (as opposed to the wall-hanging variety) so that you can transport it if you need to or even keep it inside the guitar case.

Handling Do-It-Yourself Repairs

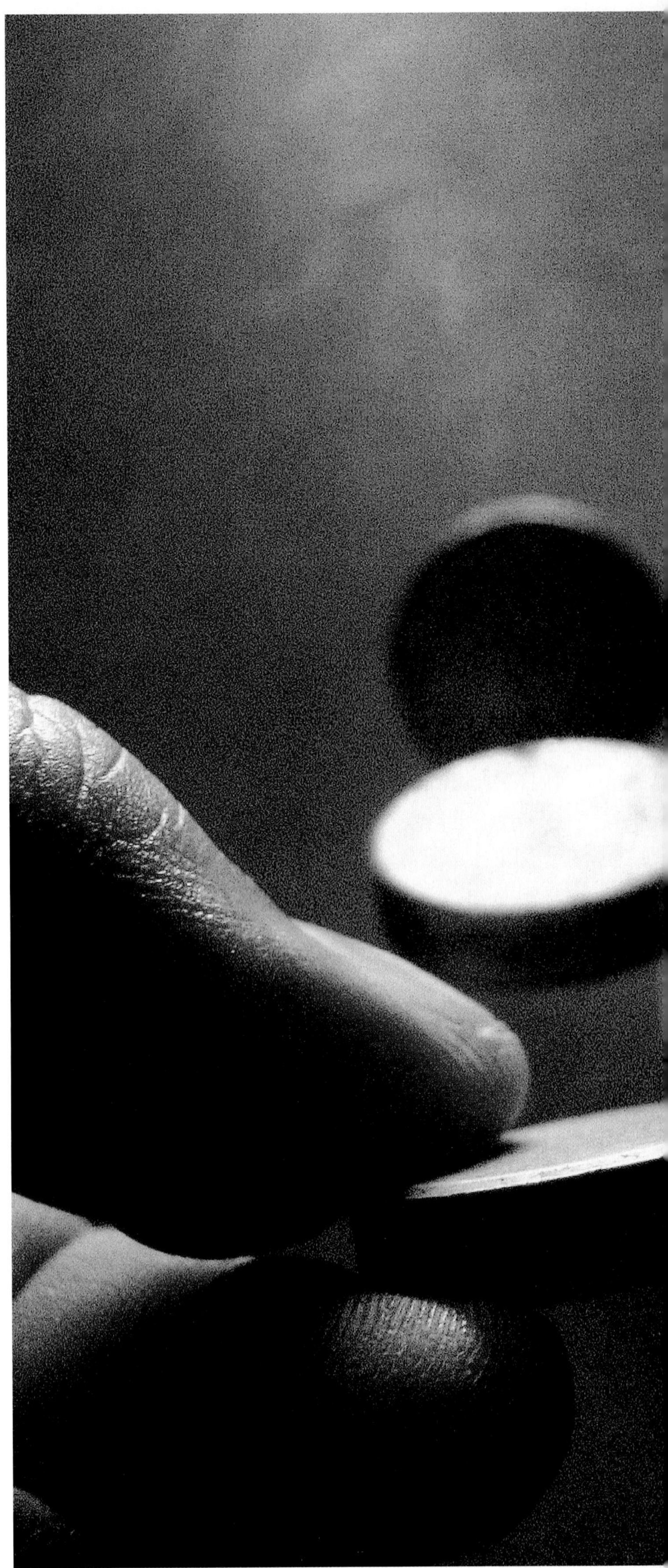

IN THIS ARTICLE

- *Tightening connections*
- *Adjusting the neck and bridge*
- *Replacing worn-out parts*
- *Knowing when to call in a professional*

If you turn on the light in your house and the bulb blows, do you call a handyman? Of course not. You look at the dead bulb to note its wattage, go to the cupboard, get the right replacement bulb, and in a jiffy, you're bathed in 60-watt luminescence. You suffer no anxiety about performing that "repair," right? If you can develop this same intuitive approach toward your guitar, you can perform simple adjustments, tweaks, and repairs.

Tightening Loose Connections

A guitar is a system of moving parts, many of which are mechanical, and as anyone who's ever owned a car can attest, moving things come loose. In guitars, the hardware connections are what typically work themselves loose, such as the nuts on the bridge post or the screws that hold down the pickup covers.

If you hear a rattle, try strumming with one hand to re-create the rattle while touching the various suspects with your other hand. As you touch the offending culprit, the rattle usually stops. Then you can take appropriate measures to tighten up whatever's come loose. (Screws in tuning machines, pickup covers, or jack plates are the most common.) Usually that involves using ordinary tools — screwdrivers, wrenches, chain saws (just kidding) — but designed for the appropriated-sized screws, nuts, and so on. Take an inventory of the sizes and shapes of the screws, nuts, and bolts on your guitar and create a miniature tool kit just for fixing your instrument.

Adjusting the Neck and Bridge

Guitars do change over time, especially if your environment experiences temperature and humidity swings. If the temperature and humidity change frequently, the guitar naturally absorbs or loses moisture, which causes the wood to swell or shrink. This condition is normal and doesn't hurt the guitar.

The problem with this expansion and contraction lies in the fact that the playing and setup tolerances are fairly critical, so a slight bow in the neck results in a guitar that plays buzzy or is suddenly much harder to fret. If this situation occurs, you can often correct the problem through a simple adjustment of the neck and/or bridge.

Tightening and loosening the truss rod

The neck of most guitars has what's known as a truss rod, which is a one- or two-piece adjustable metal rod that goes down the inside of the centre of the neck. You can adjust the truss rod with a nut located at one end.

Different manufacturers put them in different places, but they're usually at the headstock, under a cap just behind the nut, or where the neck joins the body, just under the fingerboard. Some older models don't have truss rods or, in the case of old Martin guitars, have truss rods that you can't adjust without taking off the fingerboard. All newer guitars have accessible truss rods.

The necessary truss-rod adjustment depends on which way the neck bows:

- If your neck bows outward between the seventh and twelfth frets, creating a large gap that makes pressing down the strings difficult, tighten the truss rod by turning the nut clockwise (as you face the nut straight on). Tighten the nut a quarter turn at a time, giving the neck a few minutes to adjust after each turn. (You can play during the adjustment time.)
- If your neck bows inward between the seventh and twelfth frets, causing the strings to buzz and fret out (that is, come in contact with frets they're not supposed to as you press down the strings), loosen the truss rod with the truss-rod wrench. Turn the nut a quarter turn at a time, enabling the neck to adjust after each turn.

If you can't correct the problem in a few full turns, stop. You may need a qualified repairperson to investigate. Overtightening or overloosening a truss rod can damage the neck and/or body.

All guitars come with their particular truss-rod wrench, so if you don't have a truss rod wrench for your guitar, try to find a replacement immediately. (Try your local guitar store first and, failing that, get in touch with the manufacturer itself.)

Action

Action is how a guitar plays, specifically the distance of the strings to the fingerboard. If the strings sit too high, they're hard to fret; if they're too low, buzzing occurs. In either case, you have to adjust the action.

You usually do this by raising or lowering components of the bridge known as saddles (the parts just in front of the bridge where the strings sit). You raise or lower the saddle by turning the hex screws with a tine hex wrench. Turn the screw clockwise to raise the saddle; turn it counter-clockwise to lower the saddle. If the saddle has two hex screws, be sure to turn them the same amount so that the saddle stays level. (The photograph shows the saddles' hex screws.)

Turn the saddles' hex screw to raise or lower the action.

Intonation

Intonation refers to the accuracy of the pitches produced by fretting. For example, if you play the twelfth fret, the resulting

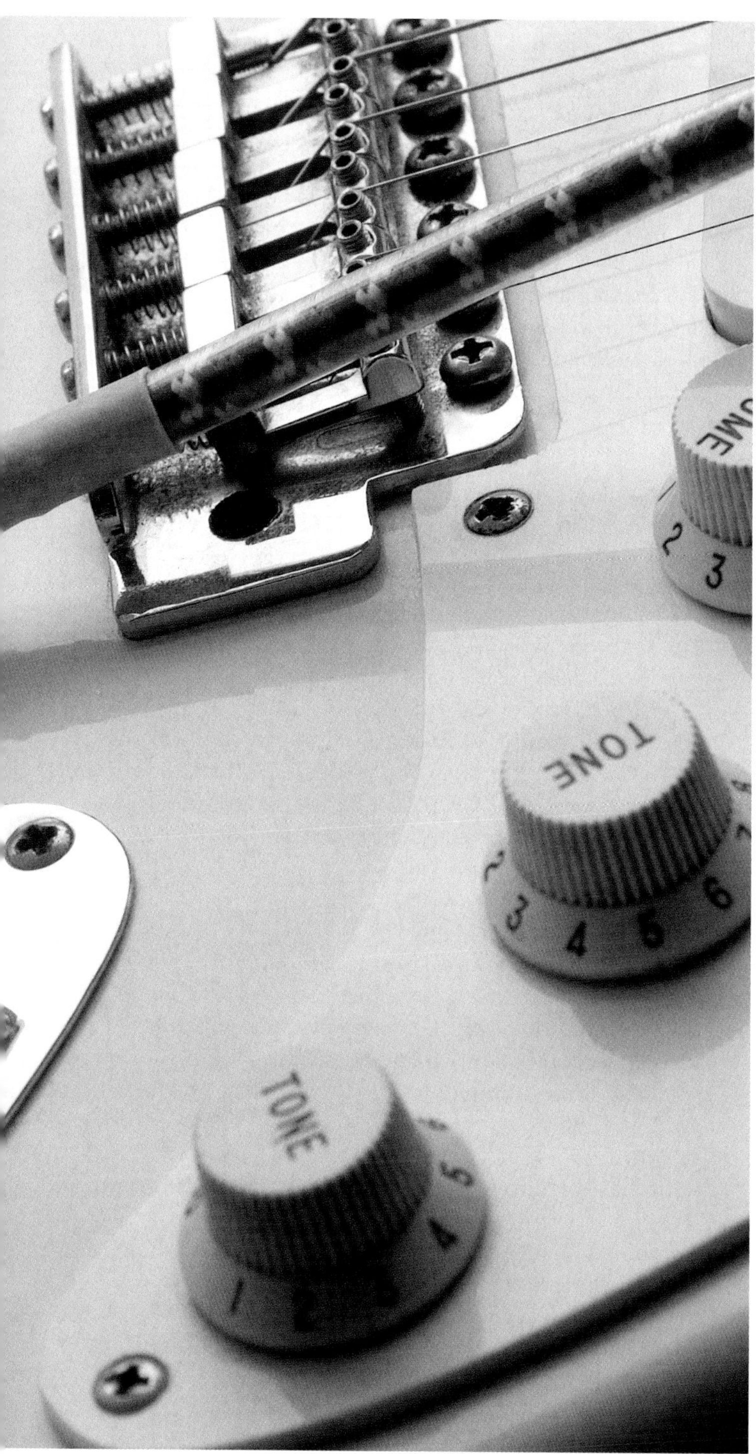

note should be exactly an octave higher than the open string. If the twelfth fret note is slightly higher than an octave, your string is fretting sharp; if the twelfth fret note is slightly lower than an octave, the string is fretting flat. You can correct a string's intonation by moving the saddle away from the nut if the string frets sharp, and toward the nut if the string frets flat. Different bridges have different methods for this, but the right method is pretty obvious after you look at the bridge assembly carefully.

In one common mechanism (used on Fender Stratocasters and Telecasters), screws at the back of the bridge determine the saddle front-to-back position. Here's how they work:

- Turning the screw clockwise (with a simple Phillips or flat-head screwdriver-being careful not to ding the top with the handle as you turn the screw) pulls the saddle back toward the bridge, which corrects a string that frets sharp.
- Turning the screw counter-clockwise moves the saddle toward the nut, which corrects a string that frets flat.

Keep in mind that adjusting the saddle for a string corrects only that string. You must perform intonation adjustments for each string. So don't invite us to that 38-string guitar's intonation adjustment!

Put on brand-new strings before you adjust the intonation. Old strings often fret sharp and don't give you a true reading of your intonation.

Replacing Worn or Old Parts

The following sections list all the parts on your guitar that are most likely to wear out or break and need replacing. You can perform any of these fixes yourself without doing damage to the guitar — even if you screw up.

Tuning machines

Tuning machines consist of a system of gears and shafts, and as the clutch on your car usually does eventually, tuners can wear out. Tuning machines deal with a lot of stress and tension, and we don't mean the kind that you endure at your job.

Tuning machines simply screw into the guitar's headstock with wood screws (after you push the post through the hole and fasten the hex nut on top); so, if you have a worn or stripped gear, consider replacing the entire machine. If more than one tuner is giving you trouble, consider replacing the entire set.

Check that the replacement machine has its screws in the same positions as the original, because you don't want to drill new holes in your headstock. If you're having trouble matching the holes of your new machines with the existing ones already drilled in your headstock, take the guitar to a repairperson.

Strap pins

Strap pins are the little "buttons" that you put through your strap holes to attach the strap to your instrument. The strap pins usually attach to the guitar with ordinary wood screws, and they can sometimes work themselves loose. If simply tightening the wood screw with a screwdriver doesn't do the trick, try applying a little white glue on the screw threads and put it back in. If it's still loose, take the guitar to a repairperson.

Bridge springs

If an electric guitar doesn't have a whammy bar, its bridge affixes directly to the guitar's body. This setup is known as a fixed bridge. If the guitar does have a whammy bar, however, it has a floating bridge. A floating bridge is one that is held in place by the string tension (which pulls it one way), and a set of metal springs — known as bridge springs — which pull in the opposite direction, holding the bridge in balance. You can find the springs (which are about 5 centimetres long and 1 centimetre wide) in the back cavity of the body. The picture shows you an example.

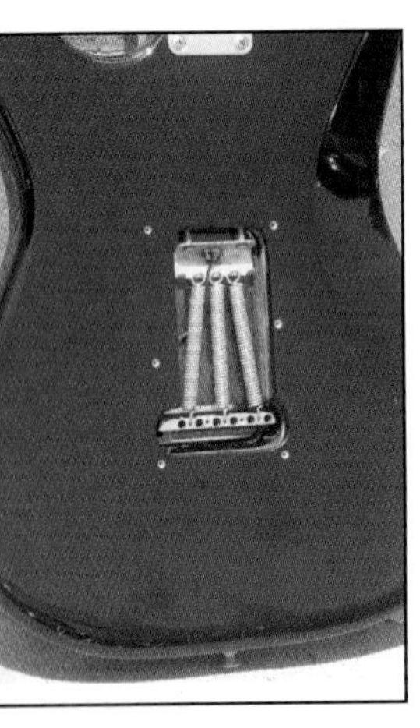

The bridge springs, shown through the guitar's back cavity.

If one of the springs loses tension through age and wear, your guitar goes out of tune when you use the whammy bar. When this happens, replace the springs; change them all at once so that they wear evenly. The springs just slip onto little hooks, and with a little tugging and the aid of pliers, you can pop them off and on in no time. You can even tighten the screws on the plate (called the claw) where the hooks attach, increasing the spring tension. Don't worry — these springs don't go sproingggg and hit you in the eye or go flying off across the room.

Crackling controls

Dust and rust (oxidation) pose a potential threat to any electronic connection, and your guitar is no exception. If your volume and tone knobs start to make crackling or popping noises through your speaker whenever you're plugged in, or if the signal is weak, inconsistent, or cuts out altogether in certain positions on your controls, some foreign matter (however minute) has probably lodged itself in your controls.

Vigorously turn the knobs back and forth around the trouble spot to work out the dust or rub off the little bit of corrosion that may be causing the problem. You may need to perform this action several times on each knob, in different places in the knob's travel. If turning the knobs doesn't do the trick, you may need a repairperson to give your pots (short for potentiometer, the variable resistors on your volume and tone controls) a thorough cleaning.

Loose jacks

On electric guitars, you do a lot of plugging and unplugging of your cable, and these actions can eventually loosen the output jack, causing a crackling sound through the speaker. This crackling indicates a disconnected ground wire. Here's the fix: Take off the jack plate or pick guard and locate the detached wire causing the problem.

If you're handy with a soldering iron, attach the broken wire back to its original lug, and you're done. You may even feel like a real electrician. If you're not handy, have a friend who is do the job or take the instrument in to the shop.

Replacement pickups

Replacing your pickups can seem like a daunting task, but it's really a very simple one. Often, the best way to change your sound (assuming that you like the way your guitar plays and looks) is to substitute replacement pickups for the originals — especially if the originals weren't too good to begin with. Here's how:

1. **Purchase pickups of the same size and type as the originals.**

   Doing so ensures that they fit into the existing holes and hook up the same way electrically.

2. **Connect and solder two or three wires.**

   Clear directions come with the new pickups.

3. **Seat the pickups in the cavities.**

   You're not dealing with high-voltage electricity either, so you can't hurt yourself or the electronics if you wire something backward.

Changing your pickups is like changing your car's oil. You can do the job yourself and save money, but you may choose not to because of the hassle.

Again, however, if you don't feel comfortable doing the job yourself, enlist the aid of a handy friend or take your guitar to a repairperson.

Keeping the Right Tools At the Ready

Assemble a permanent tool kit containing all the tools that you need for your guitar. Don't "cannibalize" this set if you're doing other household fixes. Buy two sets of tools — one for general use and one that never leaves your guitar case or gig bag. Look at your guitar to determine what kind of tools you may need should something come loose. Determine (through trial-and-error) whether your guitar's screws, bolts, and nuts are metric or not. Here's a list of what you need:

- **A set of miniature screwdrivers:** A quick inspection of the kinds of screws on an electric guitar reveals different-sized Phillips-head and slotted varieties in several places: the strap pins, the pickup cover, the pickguard, the tuning-machine mounts, the set screws (the screws that hold the tuning button to the shaft), the string retainers (the metal devices on the headstock — between the tuning posts and the nut — that hold down the strings on Strats and Teles), the volume and tone controls, and the on-the-neck back plates.
- **A miniature ratchet set:** You can also find several places for bolts: the output jack and the tuning-post collars (hex-shaped nuts on top of the headstock that keep the posts from wobbling). A miniature ratchet set gives you better leverage and a better angle than does a small crescent wrench.
- **A hex wrench and an Allen wrench:** The truss rod takes its own tool, usually a hex wrench, which usually comes with the guitar if you buy it new. If your guitar doesn't have one (because you bought it used or you've lost it since buying it new), get the right one for your guitar and keep it in the case at all times.

  Floating bridge systems, including those by Floyd Rose, require hex or Allen wrenches to adjust the saddles and other elements of the assembly. Keep these wrenches on hand in case you break a string.

Ten Things That You Can't Do Yourself

Some repairs always require a qualified repairperson to fix (assuming that anyone can repair them at all). Among such repairs are the following:

- Fixing finish cracks.
- Repairing dings and scratches (if they're severe and go through the finish to the wood).
- Filing worn frets. (If frets start to develop grooves or crevices, they need a pro to file or replace them.)
- Fixing pickup failure or weakening. (One pickup is seriously out of balance with another, you have possible magnetic damage to the pickup itself, or one of the electronic components in a pickup fails.)
- Fixing dirty volume and tone knobs (if vigorous turning back and forth no longer eliminates the crackle such dirt causes).
- Solving grounding problems. (You check the cavity and no wires are loose, but you still have inordinate noise problems.)
- Fixing severe neck distortion (twisting or severe bowing).
- Healing certain injuries and breakage (such as the nut, fingerboard, or headstock).
- Refinishing or restoring your guitar's wood. (Don't even get near your guitar's finish with a sander or wood chemicals.)
- Rewiring your electronics. (You decide, say, to replace your five-way with on/off switches, install a coil-tap and phase-reversal switch if any two adjacent pickups are active, plus insert a presence-boost knob in place of the second volume control . . . .)

If you have any anxiety about performing any repair or maintenance routine, take the guitar to a repairperson. A repairperson can tell you whether the problem is something you can fix yourself and maybe even show you how to do it correctly the next time the problem occurs. You're much better off being safe (and out a couple of quid) than taking a chance of damaging your guitar.

Figuring Out What Ails Your Axe

Generally speaking, guitars never wear out, although you may need to replace some parts and perform some tweaks along the way: Unlike your car or body, you don't need to do anything much to a guitar to keep it in excellent health. Consult this quick guide to diagnose a guitar-related problem that you may already have.

Guitar Problems and Solutions

Symptom	Solution
Strings have lost lustre, are difficult to play, or fret sharp	Replace strings and wipe down new strings after every use to prolong their life
Dull or dirty wood	Wipe with cotton or chamois cloth, apply guitar polish
Dull or greasy-looking	Wipe with cloth, apply jewellers' polish
Guitar swells and cracks due to moisture absorption; or guitar dries and cracks due to insufficient moisture	Place in a humidity-controlled environment of 45–55 percent at room temperature (18–24° C)
Rattling or buzzing from hardware as you play	Tighten loose hardware connection with screwdriver or wrench
Difficulty in fretting because strings are sitting too high; or buzzing because strings sit too low	Lower or raise the string saddles at the bridge
Neck bows outward (away from strings) between seventh and twelfth frets, causing strings to be too high and difficult to fret	Tighten truss rod to make neck arch upward slightly
Neck bows inward (into strings) between seventh and twelfth frets, causing strings to be too low and making strings buzz	Loosen truss rod to make neck sag slightly
Strings fret sharp; or strings fret flat	Adjust intonation by moving saddles toward bridge; or adjust intonation by moving saddles toward nut
Tuning machine breaks or gears strip	Purchase and install replacement, making sure that mounting holes align exactly with holes already in headstock
Strap pin screw comes loose and doesn't hold tight in hole	Apply plastic wood or white glue and replace, allowing substance to dry completely
Movable bridge has too much play or feels too loose; or bridge feels stiff and doesn't respond well to whammy bar manipulations	Replace, tighten, or add springs to the tailpiece in the rear cavity; or remove springs or loosen plate
Crackling volume or tone knob or pickup selector switch	Vigorously turn the knob or switch back and forth to work out the dirt or corrosion
Crackling pickup jack	Solder loose or broken wire back to appropriate lug
Pickups break, wear out, or no longer give you desired sound	Purchase compatible replacement set, follow included directions, neatly solder all connections

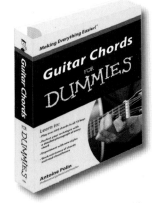

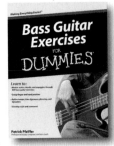

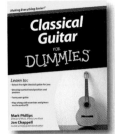

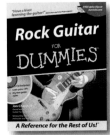

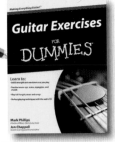